FINANCIAL
Adulting

ASHLEY FEINSTEIN GERSTLEY

FINANCIAL
Adulting

EVERYTHING YOU NEED TO
BE A FINANCIALLY CONFIDENT
AND CONSCIOUS ADULT

WILEY

Published by John Wiley & Sons, Inc., Hoboken, New Jersey.
Published simultaneously in Canada.

For general information on our other products and services or for technical support, please contact our Customer Care Department within the United States at (800) 762-2974, outside the United States at (317) 572-3993 or fax (317) 572-4002.

Wiley publishes in a variety of print and electronic formats and by print-on-demand. Some material included with standard print versions of this book may not be included in e-books or in print-on-demand. If this book refers to media such as a CD or DVD that is not included in the version you purchased, you may download this material at http://booksupport.wiley.com. For more information about Wiley products, visit www.wiley.com.

Library of Congress Cataloging-in-Publication Data:

Names: Feinstein Gerstley, Ashley, author.
Title: Financial adulting : everything you need to know and do to be a
   financially confident and conscious adult / Ashley Feinstein Gerstley.
Description: Hoboken, New Jersey : Wiley, [2022] | Includes index.
Identifiers: LCCN 2021054276 (print) | LCCN 2021054277 (ebook) | ISBN
   9781119817307 (cloth) | ISBN 9781119817321 (adobe pdf) | ISBN
   9781119817314 (epub)
Subjects: LCSH: Finance, Personal. | Adulthood.
Classification: LCC HG179 .F3925 2022 (print) | LCC HG179 (ebook) | DDC
   332.024—dc23/eng/20211208
LC record available at https://lccn.loc.gov/2021054276
LC ebook record available at https://lccn.loc.gov/2021054277

Cover images: © choness/Getty Images
Cover design: Wiley

SKY10032381_011422

For anyone who has ever felt that the financial world was not for them.

This is for you.

Contents

Preface

If anyone were to know about personal finance, you'd expect it to be me. I majored in finance in college (at Wharton) and then worked in finance. I learned a ton and I know that a lot of what I learned translates to what I do now. Yet, never once in college or in my time working in corporate finance did anyone talk about my own money – my personal finances.

As I went through my twenties and thirties, and was trying to "adult," I continued to come across new financial systems I had to understand and navigate. First it was understanding how to put together a budget and afford life, then retirement and investing, then insurance and credit, then navigating finances with a partner and buying a home, and then planning financially to start a family. Each new milestone came with a system that was just as complex and opaque and daunting as the one before, even for someone who has a background in finance and helps people with their personal finances all day, every day.

Taking all this in took a lot of time, learning from mistakes (big and small) and seeing that each of these systems does not serve people equally. As a woman, and later a mother, I experienced differences from say, what my husband (a white man) experienced, but I also know that as far as women* and mothers go, I'm probably as lucky as they come.

Let's Talk About My Privilege

I am a white, nondisabled, cisgender, heterosexual, upper-middle-class woman, mother, and business owner, and I benefit greatly from intergenerational wealth.

Intergenerational wealth is any type of financial support provided by the generation(s) before you.

This is a tremendous privilege. It means that not only have I received financial support from family, but also that I have not had

---

*When I use the term *woman* or *women*, I am referring to anyone who identifies as a woman.

to support them. Having to support parents and grandparents is a financial reality for many.

Coming from an upper-middle-class family, there's a security in knowing that if something were to happen financially, I'd be okay. It's not necessarily a spoken-about safety net, but I know it exists. I know that if all else fails (or even kind of fails), I'll have a place to go (and it's probably a really nice place).

I graduated without student loan debt. My parents paid for my college education and my living expenses for those four years – and all the years leading up to it.

My parents gave me a monthly stipend the first year I moved out on my own in New York City as I adjusted to managing my own money. My husband, Justin, and I had our wedding paid for by our parents, and our parents have given us gifts to support us in everything from our first home purchase to helping pay for our children's school to taking us on vacations.

Why Do I Share All This?

First and foremost, most don't share my privilege. Intergenerational wealth, or even the opportunity to build intergenerational wealth, has not been available to much of the population, especially BIPOC[†] families. I cover this in detail in Chapter 2.

At the same time, I have so much gratitude for our parents – for their generosity and what they've been able to build and share with us. I hope to be able to support my children in similar ways.

Despite all my privilege and finance background, being a financial adult was really challenging. As I experienced predatory insurance sales (more on this in Chapter 10), came across credit repair scams (Chapter 12), or try to navigate childcare as a working mom (Chapter 4), what comes up, over and over again, is that if it's this challenging for me, I can only imagine how challenging it is for others who don't share that privilege.

Privilege has to be part of the personal finance conversation. We can't pretend we're all starting from the same place – we're not.

[†]When I use the term BIPOC, I am referring to Black, Indigenous, and People of Color.

We have to call out our privilege or this is never going to change. It's not okay to attribute our financial success to our individual actions alone.

JEWS AND MONEY

As a proud Jewish woman writing a book about money, I want to address one of the most common forms of antisemitism: economic libel. This is the accusation and conspiracy theory that Jews are obsessed with money, are all rich, and control the world's finances. These very damaging stereotypes and tropes are used to demonize and dehumanize the Jewish people and delegitimize their human experience.

Although economic libel started much earlier, it was intensified during the Middle Ages when the Church outlawed "usury," the act of lending money for interest. Jews, who were restricted from most other professions, were essentially funneled into professions that dealt with finances (because they were outlawed to Christians). This was out of necessity, not choice.

I've seen a rise in antisemitism across the political spectrum. Given conspiracy theories about "Jewish privilege" (a concept championed by former KKK leader David Duke), I was even hesitant to use the word *privilege* in this book. As financial adults we need to beware of misinformation no matter where it's coming from. We need to challenge our own beliefs about money but also our beliefs about other people and money. I've included more resources in the Financial Adulting toolkit (financialadultingbook.com).

While being Jewish in and of itself is not a privilege, Jewish people who pass as white benefit from white-dominant culture. Jewish people who are not white-passing experience the discrimination and racism that comes with being a person of color. I talk about intersectionality in Chapter 2.

I'm Hopeful

Despite all the problems, I'm hopeful. If I weren't hopeful, I wouldn't be writing this book.

I see the personal finance conversation changing. I see more and more people uncovering and talking about what's wrong with our financial systems. I see personal finance educators and creators of all different races/ethnicities, economic backgrounds, and perspectives having these conversations.

I see more and more new companies popping up that aim to solve financial inequalities and serve people with transparency and integrity. I see companies that already exist shifting and learning.

I'm hopeful.

I'm Learning

I've been a money coach for over 10 years, but in the past couple of years I've realized that I've been providing financial education tainted by my privilege and experience. I was a white feminist working for the equality of white women and because of my privilege and ignorance, I didn't even realize it.

I've been doing the work ever since. Feminism is for *all* women and while it gets a radical rap, it is just the belief that women and men are equal and should be treated that way. Shocking, I know. We all should be feminists. Despite how obvious it sounds, we have a long way to go until women, and especially women of color, experience our financial systems equally or fairly. I have had the opportunity to learn from the example and wisdom of many incredible intersectional feminists and personal finance experts and you'll see that I feature many of their voices in this book.

So this book will be different. This book is a personal finance how-to (on lots of topics) with a look at some of the inequalities in our system and a sprinkle of exposé – because as financial adults we have to learn to navigate the systems we've got but also want to understand where they are unfair so we can use the privilege we have to change them. We can continue to do the work together.

I'm excited for you to join me on this journey.

CHAPTER 1

What Is a Financial Adult?

W hen I graduated college and started working in my first (and my second) job, I was far from being what I would consider a financial adult. One might expect that we would start acting like financial adults as soon as we get our first paycheck or move out on our own, but for most of us, it doesn't come until later (sometimes much, much later).

What I've noticed from my own experience, and hearing from thousands of others about their money lives, is that there is usually some type of impetus for becoming a financial adult. Something happens that causes us to care about our finances. It might be wanting to switch careers, getting into a new exciting relationship, or watching a close family member suffer through a traumatic financial experience, but something happens that inspires us to take action.

Now, it's important to acknowledge that the opportunity to *not* be a financial adult comes with tremendous privilege. Many people, much younger than legal adult age, have had to become financial adults due to stressful economic circumstances, systemic inequities, and poverty. In those cases, waiting for inspiration to become a financial adult was not an option. We talk more about this later.

Why Aren't We Financial Adulting?

When I give talks, I often poll the room of people and say, "Raise your hand if you think you *should* know more about money and personal finance." It doesn't matter who is in the crowd, almost every hand goes up – *every* time. This even happens when I'm speaking at a bank. And I get it. I was one of those people who worked at a bank and didn't know anything about my own finances.

When it comes to money and personal finance, most of us feel ashamed that we don't know more and haven't made as much progress as we'd like toward our goals.

Missed Out on Early Basics

But the truth is, we are not set up for success. Most of us didn't learn about personal finance in school and unless a parent or mentor went out of their way to teach us about money, we probably didn't even learn about it growing up.

Talking to parents, I discovered that this was far from a malicious choice. Many found dealing with money so stressful that they didn't want to burden their children with that stress before they needed to. Others thought that they had made so many mistakes, who were they to teach their kids about money?

Regardless of our backgrounds and upbringings, we get to a certain place in our lives where we have to deal with money almost every single day. Yet most of us have learned very little about it and it can feel too taboo to bring up our questions, even to our closest friends and family.

Not to mention, many come from families where they are the financial first, like first generation. The financial first to go to college and navigate paying the tuition bills that come with. The financial first to have a W-2 salary and a 401(k) as part of their compensation package.

You might even have an early memory where you asked someone like a parent or teacher a question about money and they shut you down: "Oh, we don't talk about that," "You can't ask questions like that," or "I don't know, I don't handle that."

From these experiences, you end up internalizing the idea that money is an inaccessible or shameful thing, and not to be talked about and discussed. You probably make some major assumptions about money – that it's bad, not for you, or something only greedy people care about. When it's time to engage with your own money, you bring these beliefs with you and they have a great impact on your relationship with money.

It might sound weird, but we have a relationship with money just like we have a relationship with a friend or colleague, in how we interact and relate to it. When we believe money is shameful and greedy, we might avoid dealing with it. Imagine if you treated your best friend the way you treat your money. I'm sure she wouldn't appreciate being ghosted!

Unsure of Where to Get Help

When it's time to figure out something in our financial lives, we probably start by googling (I know I did). I found pages and pages of results and resources with contradicting evidence and advice, often shaming me for my choices. I decided it might be easier to ask a financial professional or expert, but it was hard to know how to find someone and whom to trust.

The financial services industry is the least trusted of any other industry. Only 2% of people really trust financial professionals[1] – and for good reason! We hear horror stories from friends and see media coverage of the terrible things that happen. Between 2005 and 2015, 87,000 financial advisors (7% of them)[2] were disciplined for misconduct or fraud. And that's just the ones who were caught.

Then there's the natural conflict of interest we feel in our own interactions with financial professionals. The people who are supposed to be educating us are the same people who are selling us things, and they earn big commissions from those sales. This can lead to a lot of misinformation and recommendations that are not in our best interest.

Don't even get me started on the jargon and unnecessary complexity that's been perpetuated to keep the majority of the population out of the conversation.

Money Is Tied to Emotion

Money is also really emotional and in a lot of ways is very similar to food. I believe food and money are so similar that I wrote a book called *The 30-Day Money Cleanse*, which applies the principles of a juice cleanse to budgeting and developing our money mindset.

Sometimes we know exactly what we *should* be doing to reach our goals but really struggle to follow through on those actions. Nutritionists say, "Only eat until you're full" or "Weight loss is just about calories in minus calories out." This all sounds simple but if it were actually that straightforward, there wouldn't be a multibillion-dollar dieting industry.

One of the reasons money is so emotionally charged is that it comes with a lot of promise. If I could just pay off my credit card debt, I would finally get ahead of my expenses. If I could afford that vacation to Tahiti, I'd feel so much more fulfilled and refreshed. If I could purchase a home, I'd feel much more financially stable.

Money means different things to different people, but having it (versus not having it) makes a tremendous difference in our lives. Don't let anyone tell you otherwise.

Companies use this emotional pull to sell us things. Ads promise that if we just buy this one thing, we'll finally feel smart enough, beautiful enough, like we belong, or [insert desire here]. Brands play off our emotions to get into our wallets. They spend millions of dollars to do it, know way too much about us, and are absolutely brilliant at selling us things.

Because of everything we have working against us, financial experts who spout shame and fear drive me nuts. The system is rigged; so many other industries (financial services, credit cards, retail) benefit when we make financial missteps or choices that don't align with our best interest. To ignore that is ignorant and unhelpful.

It's Easy Not to Think About Money

Technology has also played a part in keeping us from financial adulthood. Back in the day, people had to use cash or write a check (and then balance their checkbooks). While technology has made our lives much more convenient, it's also made it a lot easier to lose track of where our money is going.

We hop in and out of Lyfts without actually having to pay, we click one button and the next day packages show up at our door, and we swipe our credit cards, which feels very different than handing over a wad of $20 bills.

Then There's Oppression

Not to mention the systemic racial and gender gaps that affect every aspect of our financial lives. Women, and much more so, women of color and moms, earn far less for the same work than white men. They have to pay more for the same things (it's called the pink tax), pay higher rates for credit despite having the same or better profiles, and face discrimination in the workplace.

The Black and Indigenous communities have been stripped of wealth over and over again through policy and theft since the United States was built on the free labor of the enslaved. This, along with policy and discrimination, has created the vast racial wealth gap in the United States.

If you are BIPOC, you carry generations of oppression into your financial life.

But There Is Good News . . .

All this is to say, it's no wonder we're not feeling like financial adults! We have so much working against us when it comes to our finances. We need to show ourselves some grace and understanding as we navigate a financial world that's not built for us.

Did my rant resonate? What are some reasons you might not feel like a financial adult *yet*?

_____

_____

_____

_____

Read over your list from this exercise. This is really important.

If you are still punishing yourself for your past financial mistakes after reading all this, go back and read it again!

Despite all of that (and I know it's a lot), I'm still a financial optimist. Understanding what we have working against us is actually the best strategy to know how to move forward. There are specific actions we can take and shifts we can make as individuals to improve our financial lives and overcome many of these roadblocks.

We can understand and champion the changes we need to see at the top, all the while taking action in our own lives.

We can go from financial hot mess to financial adult and I'm here to show you exactly how to do it. I've seen thousands of people transform their financial well-being and bring others with them, one step at a time.

So, What Exactly Is a Financial Adult?

Being a financial adult is a lot less daunting than it sounds. It doesn't mean you know everything about money or never make any mistakes. I still make mistakes all the time. We're each on our own money journeys and will continue to grow, learn, and make mistakes. It's all part of the "fun."

Being a financial adult can actually be easy and straightforward. That doesn't mean you won't have to dedicate some time and put in some work, but it doesn't have to be a struggle. And it certainly doesn't mean that you have to give up your current lifestyle in exchange for your financial future. Personal finance is, as the name suggests, personal.

This is also a completely judgment-free zone. Yes, I'm talking no judgment from our experts and educators but also, as much as possible, from ourselves, too. I know, easier said than done. But we'll work on that.

After going through this book you will be a confident and conscious financial adult. Here's what that means.

A Financial Adult Takes Small, Consistent Steps That Add Up to Big Results

When it comes to improving our financial lives, action is everything. We can learn and read about money all day, every day, but until we take action, it won't meaningfully impact our lives.

What I find has the biggest impact is taking small consistent steps over time. Not only does that make change a lot more manageable (and easy), we start to see results and that builds our motivation. This inspires us to take more steps and our results become exponential.

So it's a win–win. Small steps make it easy but also lead to big results. This financial adulting program will provide you with the small steps needed to get there.

A Financial Adult Understands What's Happening with Their Money

This one might sound simple but it's actually tremendously powerful and profound. Understanding what's happening with your money means you know what's coming in and where your money is going, whether that's where you're spending it or how you are allocating it toward your goals.

As a financial adult, you have a clear picture of what you have and where you have it, and understand what's happening with your investments (including your retirement).

We have a tendency not to want to know what's happening with our money. We might be afraid of what we'll find, thinking it will be less stressful to not know and remain unaware. But until we know what's happening, we can't do anything about it. And there's no power in that.

Once we know what's happening with our money, we can make conscious and intentional choices. We can make sure our finances align with our goals and what's most important to us. We can choose to support organizations and causes we believe in and vote for our values with each dollar we spend and invest.

Clarity and awareness give us choices. And that's exactly what we need before we can make a plan. I feel a sigh of relief already!

A Financial Adult Feels Confident in Their Financial Plans, Knowing They Will Get to Have and Experience What They Want in Life (Which Is the Whole Point of Having Money Anyway!)

This one is a biggie! Financial plans often get a bad rap. We think of financial plans, especially budgets, as being overly restricting or limiting our fun. That's why we understandably avoid making them. But that comes at a really high cost.

Having a financial plan actually does the opposite of restricting us. It gives us peace of mind. Can you imagine knowing exactly how and by when you will reach your financial goals? Now imagine that you can also build in the things that make you really happy. You can spend on the nonessential things you really want without feeling guilty because it's all part of the plan.

Now we're talking.

A Financial Adult Understands the Critical Context of Equity and Personal Finance, Recognizes That Privilege Can and Should Be Used to Help Close Racial and Gender Wealth Gaps, or Realizes That They May Be Starting at a Disadvantage Due to Historic and Systemic Obstacles

We can't talk about personal finance without talking about equity. While much of the work you'll be doing in this book is about transforming your own financial well-being, that doesn't mean there aren't systemic inequities at work.

We don't start on an equal playing field. BIPOC communities face significant disadvantages compared to white communities, LGBTQ+* communities face discrimination and costs that straight communities don't, women are not on an equal playing field to men, and BIPOC women, specifically Black women, Latinas, Native women, and mothers, face both systemic racism and sexism. There are racial and gender gaps in earning, debt, investing, homeownership, and the list goes on and on.

Financial adults understand this critical context and recognize that their privilege can and should be used to help close racial and gender wealth gaps. Financial adults also understand they may be coming from a place of disadvantage due to historic and systemic obstacles.

---

*When I use the term *LGBTQ+*, I am referring to anyone who identifies as Lesbian, Gay, Bisexual, Transgender, Queer, Questioning, and any other sexual identities.

I am by no means an expert and still have a lot of learning to do, which is why I'm excited to turn to the experts in the coming chapters in this book. What I do know is that the more BIPOC, feminist, and anti-racist people who build individual wealth, the more we'll see the institutional changes, changes in leadership, and changes in policy we want to see.

Time to Get Started

That's it. That's what it means to be a financial adult. Doesn't it sound powerful?

I do this work because I know that when more feminists are financial adulting and can build meaningful wealth (yes, I want you to be wealthy!), we'll solve many (if not most!) of the problems we face in the world.

The following pages take you through how to get there step by step, exercise by exercise. There is space to work through the exercises in the book but you can also fill them out in a separate notebook if you don't like writing in books or are going through a second (or third) time. I'm a big believer in action so you'll also find a checklist of action steps at the end of each chapter. I reference additional resources and goodies throughout the book that you can get at financialadultingbook.com. There are also special callouts with specific tips and ideas for those navigating financial adulting with a partner.

I definitely recommend reading the book from start to finish but I hope it also serves as a resource you can come back to again and again.

When it's time to revisit your 401(k), you can turn to Chapter 7 for everything you need to know. When you are ready to start negotiating your next promotion (hint: start ASAP), you can revisit the exercises in Chapter 4.

And when your bestie asks you how you got so confident about your money, you can send her a copy of this book so you can be financial adults together (see the power of accountability in Chapter 14). Isn't that why you have a gift budget in your financial plan (Chapter 5)?

Okay, here we go! Happy financial adulting!

CHAPTER 2

Equity and Personal Finance

You might be wondering why a chapter on equity comes before any of the financial how-to in a personal finance book. After reading this, I hope you'll wonder why it's not the first thing covered in every single personal finance book.

Because, when the minimum wage has been $7.25 since 2009 while prices of goods have gone up 27% since then,[1] it doesn't matter how well you budget.

When you have an overall racial wealth disparity of 8 to 1,[2] and a gender wealth disparity of 3 to 1 for women, 50 to 1 for Black women, and 100 to 1 for Latinas,[3] explained by the enslavement of Black people and systemic oppression, that's not going to be resolved by investing alone.

When mothers are paid 30% less,[4] just for being mothers, are offered no paid leave, and childcare prices are astronomical, women continue to struggle and those who can drop out of the workforce by the millions.

The Idea That You Can Pull Yourself Up by Your Bootstraps Is a Scam

Black people are paid less, the things they own are worth less, but then you tell me to pull myself up by my bootstraps.

—Tiffany Aliche, The Budgetnista

Oof. This quote stuck with me during our interview. Tiffany Aliche (a.k.a. The Budgetnista) is a financial educator, bestselling author of *Get Good With Money*, and a Black woman. You'll be hearing a lot more from her (you're welcome). I was very intentional about featuring different voices, ethnicities, economic backgrounds, perspectives, and expertise throughout this book. Know that these are people I respect immensely. These are people I was giddy to interview. These are people I consider my financial adulting leaders and friends. You can find a list of where to follow and connect with each of them in the Financial Adulting toolkit (financialadulting book.com).

Okay, back to scams. I repeat, telling people to pull themselves up by their bootstraps is a scam.

Financial education is important and we'll get into why and what that needs to look like, but until we see real significant changes from the top – I'm talking changes in government and corporate policy – financial literacy can't and won't solve our problems.

Mehrsa Baradaran, author of *The Color of Money* and professor at UC Irvine, shares, "I wrote my book to debunk the myth that you can leave the systems of credit, banking, and federal policy intact and you alone or your community can accumulate wealth, work hard, save your money, and close the wealth gap. Of course it works in individual cases but we take these individual cases and exceptions and make rules of them."

In our interview, Dasha Kennedy, financial activist and founder of The Broke Black Girl, shared about the link between politics and personal finance:

When people say leave politics out of money, there's no way to do that. When how I pay taxes is decided through policy, how much I'm going to pay in childcare is decided through policy, how my kids' schools are funded is decided through policy, and how much I'm going to be paid is decided through policy, we can't leave that out. And to even think that that's possible comes from a place of privilege. If you have an overflow of money and access to capital, policy

probably really doesn't matter to you because you have your
saving grace. But for me, I have to care about those things
because it impacts my money.

That's why when people say they educate about personal finance
but "stay out of politics," it's complete BS.* Policy is critical and completely intertwined with our financial lives.

Financial adults understand the smart money moves they can
make, but they also understand and advocate for the changes that need
to be made at the top.

I am a white, upper-middle-class, cisgender, heterosexual, nondisabled woman. And as a financial adult, I'm going to use that privilege
to bring all other women up with me. I can't call myself a feminist or
anti-racist if I don't believe and care about equality for all women.

Not to mention (and this is just icing on the cake), it's what's best for
all people: our wallets, our planet, everything. As Sallie Krawcheck, the
co-founder and CEO of Ellevest, says, "Nothing bad happens when women
have more money." And I bet she wouldn't disagree with me taking it a
step further and saying, the world changes for the better. Much better.

The Racial Wealth Gap

Farnoosh Torabi, financial expert and host of the *So Money* podcast,
calls the racial wealth gap a "wealth chasm," because that's more
reflective of the size of the gap.

So what is this wealth chasm? Mehrsa explains that "across every
income and education level, there's a massive racial wealth gap." The
average white family has a median net worth of $188,200 compared
with $24,100 for Black families, $36,100 for Hispanic families, and
$74,500 for groups of all other races/ethnicities.[5] Dasha shares that the
richest 400 Americans have more wealth than all the Black households
in the United States combined. That's the chasm.

Let's break it down in numbers.

---

*When I say BS, I mean *bullshit.*

	Net Worth
White	$188,200
Black	$24,100
Hispanic	$36,100
Other*	$74,500

Disparities in Wealth Gap by Race and Ethnicity

Other families – a diverse group that includes those identifying as Asian, American Indian, Alaska Native, Native Hawaiian, Pacific Islander, other race, and all respondents reporting more than one racial identification – have lower wealth than white families but higher wealth than Black and Hispanic families.

Source: Federal Reserve Board, 2019 Survey of Consumer Finances.

Because the "Other" category includes such a diverse group, it's important to note that there are large wealth disparities within the Asian American Pacific Islander (AAPI) community. A 2016 study of Los Angeles showed that while Japanese, Asian Indian, and Chinese households had a higher median wealth than white households, Koreans, Vietnamese, and Filipinos had 15×, 6×, and 1.5× less wealth, respectively.[6] As of 2000, American Indian households had a wealth gap to white households of 11×.[7]

These numbers were taken before the onset of the COVID-19 pandemic, which disproportionately impacted communities of color financially, so these numbers are most likely worse than the study indicates. Reports say that with current policies in place, it will take 228 years to close the gap.[8]

A *Very* Quick History Lesson (That We Missed in School)

The racial wealth gap in our country dates back to enslavement, when white America built its economy (and wealth) with the free labor of people who had been kidnapped and enslaved and when Indigenous

People were forced and displaced from their land, which was a tremendous loss of community wealth.

I didn't learn about most of this important history in school and I can only include a small glimpse in this book. To better understand the true scope of how policy after policy excluded and exploited BIPOC communities, I've included more resources in the Financial Adulting toolkit.

The 1862 Homestead Act

Through the Homestead Act, more than 270 million acres[9] of land (10% of the United States),[10] previously inhabited by Indigenous People, was sold (but really gifted for an extremely discounted price) to citizens and intended citizens for $1.25[11] per acre (equivalent to about $34[12] today!) in 1.6 million 160-acre plots. While there isn't much data on the race/ethnicity of homesteaders, it's believed that the overwhelming majority of plots went to white people. In the year 2000, the wealth of more than 46 million adults (25% of the United States) could be traced back to this policy.[13]

Freedman's Savings Bank

After the Civil War, in 1865, Freedman's Savings Bank was created by the U.S. government for those previously enslaved to deposit money and receive financial education. It's important to remember that previously enslaved Black people were starting with nothing, while white Americans had been building wealth for hundreds of years.

Henry Cooke, a white financier on the board of directors of the bank, used the bank's money to make speculative investments in railroads (Mehrsa calls it the "subprime market of that time") and the bank eventually went under. More than 61,000 Black Americans lost $72 million[14] in today's money (over half the Black community's accumulated wealth) that was never recovered, despite the bank being protected by the federal government. This incident starts a distrust of the financial system that gets reinforced and lingers for hundreds of years.

Tulsa Race Massacre of 1921

In 1921, a very segregated Tulsa had a thriving business district that was often called Black Wall Street. Kevin Matthews II, founder of BuildingBread and a Tulsa native, shares: "A white mob burned and bombed the nation's wealthiest Black neighborhood, killing an estimated 300 Black people, leaving 9,000 people homeless, destroying 1,200 businesses and causing between $50 and $100 million in property damage, all in 24 hours. The city then passed laws preventing people from building on land that was burned as a result of the massacre. Insurance companies labeled it a 'riot' to deny payments to Black people despite the fact that there were at least six airplanes used in the attack."

The Federal Housing Administration (FHA)

The FHA was created as part of President Franklin D. Roosevelt's New Deal, and insured and guaranteed all federal approved mortgage loans, which Mehrsa explains made them "easy, risk free, and abundant."[15] Mehrsa shares in her book, "If you could save a few thousand dollars, you could buy a house, build wealth, and become middle class." And your new mortgage payment in the suburbs would probably be lower than your rent in the city. This opportunity was only available to those who met the "gold standard" – people who were white, middle class, and male. "Between 1934 and 1968 98% of FHA loans went to white Americans," creating white suburbs and leaving Black Americans renting in redlined neighborhoods.

Redlining

Redlining was the Home Owners Loan Corporation (HOLC) system of maps that rated neighborhoods on their perceived risk and stability. On the maps, green areas, rated A, were "homogeneous and white" while red neighborhoods, rated D, were predominantly Black. Neighborhoods with African Americans or Latinos were automatically rated D (red) and were ineligible for mortgages. The FHA used these maps for their own lending process.

Mehrsa acknowledges that the HOLC and FHA "were not creating these preferences, but reflecting the reality that white Americans preferred to live in segregated communities."[16] That said, "The FHA was unwilling to use the strength of the government and its leverage in the credit market to challenge racism."

Redlining was just one of the many Jim Crow laws[17] (a collection of state and local statutes that legalized racial segregation). Despite this history, Mehrsa believes that change is possible and that there is a lot of room for optimism around closing the gap. At the same time, many of the events mentioned were in response to progress, so she says we need to be "a little wary of celebrating before we're done."

The Gender Wealth Gap

Then there's the gender wealth gap. Women own $0.32 for every $1.00 a white man owns. This gap is far greater for women of color. Black women and Latinas own $0.02 and $0.01, respectively, for the white man's dollar. $0.01!

Median Wealth	
All single men	$10,150
All single women	$3,210
Single white men	$28,900
Single white women	$15,640
Single Black women	$200
Single Hispanic women	$100
Single Black mothers	$0
Single Hispanic mothers	$50

The Gender and Racial Wealth Gap
Source: Data from Women and Wealth—Insights for Grantmakers. *Asset Funders Network, 2015.*

Where does this come from? Our personal finances are all interconnected. Each area of our money lives impacts each of the other areas. The wage gap combined with the pink tax (see Chapter 5) requires women to take out more debt. Even when women have the same credit profile as men, they pay higher interest rates (discrimination). This all leads to women investing less and buying less real estate (and the mortgages cost more for women when they do).

Then there's *intersectionality*, a term coined by lawyer and civil rights activist Kimberlé Crenshaw. Women of color, LGBTQ+, people with disabilities, and mothers experience these gaps in a compounding way. Kimberlé describes intersectionality as "a prism, for seeing the way in which various forms of inequality often operate together and exacerbate each other."[18] Yes, there is inequality based on gender identity, race/ethnicity, class, and sexual orientation, but many people are subject to some or all of these inequalities, not just one, and there's a cumulative effect.

Wait, you might be wondering why I included motherhood. A large part of the pay gap is due to motherhood. *What?* Mothers earn less for the same work than fathers do, experience workplace discrimination, and are pushed out of the workforce due to the lack of childcare and corporate support of parents, and this not only impacts their lifetime income but also their ability to invest, their access to retirement accounts, and their need to take on debt.

Not to mention, women live longer, which means they need more money in order to retire. It's enough to make you scream.

Another Gap That Has a History

In addition to all the current factors that play into the gender wealth gap, the world of money has historically been less accessible to women. The personal finance sector was created for and by men, leaving women out until very recently. These systemic barriers have set the stage for the gender wealth gap.

The Equal Credit Opportunity Act (ECOA) of 1974

Until 1974 when the ECOA passed, a woman couldn't take out a credit card in her own name without a male co-signer, like her husband or father. That's recent history. The act also granted women the ability to take out their own mortgage. Before then, many women seeking their own loans were laughed out of banks.

Women's wages were discounted by as much as 50% during the loan process when lenders decided how much they could borrow. You can imagine how that impacted what homes they could afford. Here's a hint – homes worth much less than those of their male counterparts.

The Equal Pay Act of 1963 and the Pregnancy Discrimination Act of 1978

At work things were similarly bleak. There was no requirement for equal pay until 1963 (still a big problem) and women could be *legally* fired for being pregnant until 1978 (it still happens illegally).

In addition, investing culture was dominated by white men. There wasn't one woman on the New York Stock Exchange until Muriel "Mickey" Siebert purchased a seat in 1967. Years earlier, women tried to make a stock exchange of their own in order to get a piece of the action.

The Double X Economy

Inequality has a real cost. Linda Scott, a professor emeritus at the University of Oxford and author of *The Double X Economy*, coined the phrase "Double X Economy" to address the systemic exclusion of women from the financial order (all over the world). Linda says "gender inequality causes poverty" – so it's not only the missed economic opportunity; "there's hunger that's attributable to this, there's war, there's disease. There's all types of terrible things."[19]

I had the incredible opportunity to interview Linda for this book and she talked about the cost of not focusing on women, and gave the specific recent example of the pandemic Shecession of 2020.

> **DEFINITION:** The **Shecession (from the Skimm)** is the economic downturn that disproportionately affected women. Especially women of color. Not only are women more likely to work in hard-hit industries like hospitality and leisure, but many left their jobs due to lack of childcare.

From Linda:

From an economic perspective, those who run the world's economies are chasing growth (they want the economies to grow). Right now governments are trying to recover from the economic impact of the pandemic and for the most part they've ignored the special needs of women. It has been manifestly evident throughout the pandemic that women are suffering to a different degree and for different reasons than men, and obviously will need different solutions. And rather than deal with those needs, they are being pooh-poohed and set aside.

It's pretty ridiculous because on average, in the global economy, women contribute just under 40% of GDP and in the United States they contribute at least 40% of the GDP[20] and make up more than half the workforce. In 41% of families, women are the primary breadwinner. And if women decided to form their own country, they'd immediately be big enough to join the G7 (the world's seven largest developed economies). When you're trying to kickstart an economy it doesn't make sense to ignore women!

Women are the world's most valuable wasted resource.

Linda's book starts with the Gloria Steinem quote, "The truth will set you free, but first it will piss you off." Yep. Feeling that. But Linda shares some concrete actions we can take. We'll get to those shortly!

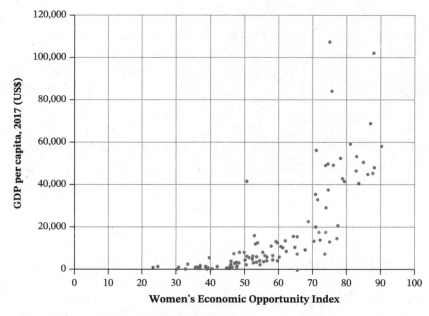

Women's Economic Opportunity and GDP

Each dot on the graph shown here represents a country's Women's Economic Opportunity Index score as related to GDP. There are approximately 100 nations shown in the graph; all those for which the data was available were included. In the graph, the upward-right direction of the dots indicates that more economic freedom for women corresponds positively to GDP per capita. Other data has converged to reach the same conclusion.

Sources: World Bank Database for GDP at purchasing power parity; Economist Intelligence Unit for the Women's Economic Opportunity Index; World Economic Forum for the National Competitiveness Index.

> **DEFINITION: Gross domestic product (or GDP)** is the most common method to track an economy's health. GDP represents the value of all the goods and services produced over a specific period of time within a country. A **recession** is measured as two quarters of negative GDP growth.

We Need Women to Be Wealthy

You know I believe this to my core. This is why I do the work that I do. I believe that getting more money into women's hands will solve many of the problems we see in the world today. A lot of brilliant experts (including Linda) agree with me.

Farnoosh weighs in: "When women are wealthy they have more financial agency. They can make decisions for themselves and get out of bad situations. We have to remember that we are still living in a sexist patriarchal world so we need money to help us combat those external headwinds."

Women invest 90%[21] of their income back into their families, compared with 35% for men. When women have more wealth it's better for children, it's better for families, it's better for companies, and it's better for the economy as a whole.

What Needs to Happen to Close These Gaps

The following are some of the proposed policy reforms that came up over and over again in my conversations with experts, but this list is by no means exhaustive. For more resources, head to the Financial Adulting toolkit.

Raise the Minimum Wage

80% of minimum wage workers[22] are adults, two-thirds are women, and almost 25% are women of color (who make up 17% of the population). Raising the minimum wage to $15 would more than double the earnings of over 700,000[23] women and give substantial raises to millions more. Now that's wage gap progress. In raising the minimum wage, it's critical to include people with disabilities. In most states, corporations are legally allowed to pay people with disabilities well below the minimum wage. Many politicians are working on eliminating this law.

Cancel Student Loan Debt

Student loans are a women's issue. Women have two-thirds of all student loan debt[24] and the student loan debt burden disproportionately affects women of color. Linda says, "Women have to take out more debt in order to get the same jobs as men. And then they have to pay back the loans at a lower salary than men." Alleviating some or all student debt is a way to remove the burden and level the playing field.

Tax the Super-Wealthy

I use the term *super-wealthy* because people are often worried that an increase in taxes will affect them. Most experts I spoke with were focused on taxing the richest people, people who bring home millions and millions or have net worths in the billions. This would allow for more programs to invest in underserved communities.

Farnoosh says, "I do find it problematic when the 50 richest Americans have as much wealth as half the U.S. I believe in the redistribution of the dollars in this country with the goal of supporting equity. I believe in taxing the rich more than others. I don't believe in trickle-down economics. I think the rich ought to pay a higher percentage in taxes and the government needs to give the working class a realistic opportunity to achieve wealth by reducing their taxes, and giving them more free access to things like healthcare, food, and housing."[25]

Pay Reparations

In Mehrsa's book she writes about reparations: "An essential first step in dealing with the wealth gap is to acknowledge that it was created through racist public policy. Full justice demands a recognition of the historic breach of the social contract between America's constitutional democracy and Black Americans. And contract breach requires a remedy." She doesn't recommend any remedy specifically but says we should encourage our policymakers to come up with "creative proposals that garner full and meaningful financial inclusion that reverse the effects of historic exclusions from wealth creation."

Mandate Paid Leave

Caregiving responsibilities disproportionately fall to women and due to these responsibilities, combined with a lack of paid leave (almost one in four mothers have returned to work within two weeks of giving birth[26]), women are often forced to spend time out of the workforce.

Research shows that workers can expect to lose up to three or four times their annual salary for each year out of the workforce due to the loss in future income and raises.[27]

Women who have paid leave are more likely to stay in the workforce the year following birth and are 54% more likely to report wage increases.[28] Paid leave for fathers also plays an important role. For every month a father takes paternity leave, his partner's income increases by 6.7%.[29,30]

Build a System of Universal, Affordable, High-Quality Childcare

Linda argues that building a childcare system would actually be the most important and impactful intervention worldwide. She says it should be treated as "economic infrastructure" (meaning it's available to everyone) and because "it's the biggest barrier to women participating in the economy it would *easily* pay for itself." She adds that "there's really no excuse for not doing it except for the stupid old fashioned idea that in some moral world women should be at home. And I try to make it clear in the book that that idea comes from a history of keeping women captive." Burning rage!

Reform Our Healthcare System

Medical expenses are the number-one cause of personal bankruptcy in the United States and debt rates are much higher for those who are uninsured or underinsured, which are disproportionately people of color. As you can imagine, high medical expenses and resulting medical debt impact a family's ability to plan, save, and build wealth.

Build a Bigger Coalition

Linda says "we've allowed feminism to be cast as a left-wing issue. The left wing claims it and the right wing disdains it, but among the American public, treating women and men equally is just what decent people do. It's a core centrist value and we should start treating it that way." She argues that "these issues, issues around capital and the economy, are things that in my experience, speak very strongly to republican, financially conservative women." She believes we can build a bigger coalition from all political parties.

Equality versus Equity

The distinction between equality and equity is extremely important in personal finance. Dasha describes *equality* as giving everyone the exact same personal finance resources and saying "I provided you with tools, now it's up to you to use them," whereas *equity* is giving people the resources that apply specifically to their experiences and needs, especially those in communities that are impacted by systemic gaps and discrimination.

Dasha explained:

Black women live at the intersection of race and gender so we're always fighting two battles. 81% of Black mothers are the primary breadwinners of their homes.[31] That means four out of five Black families depend on the paycheck of a Black woman to survive. The conversation around personal finance will be different for us.

When I first started as a financial educator, I'd hear other educators swear off credit and say "Credit is bad. If you can't afford it now, don't get it." But this is a very privileged and judgmental perspective. For Black women, and Black people as a whole, credit can be a saving grace because it fills the gap when we're not paid fairly and our families haven't had the opportunity to build wealth. Instead of swearing it off, equity is teaching people how to understand it and leverage it if it's needed.

Because personal finance systems look different for each of us depending on our privilege, race, gender, and sexuality, we need more nuance and perspective in financial education.

Your Education Matters

In talking to so many people, especially women, about their financial lives, I've found a common thread in many of our stories. So many of our financial successes come from someone who gave us a nudge. This might be a colleague who urged us to set up our 401(k), a friend who sat down with us to show us how she budgets, or the colleague who bravely shared what she's getting paid so we could compare.

When we get educated around our money, not only do we lift ourselves and our families up, we can be an example of what's possible and we can give others the nudge they need. We bring others up with us and that has a tremendous impact.

Your Financial Adulting Action Items

☐ Understand that politics and money are inseparable.

☐ Understand the racial and gender wealth gaps – where they come from, how they are perpetuated, and how they currently affect your own personal finances.

☐ Help close the gap. In addition to the resources here, you can learn more in the Financial Adulting toolkit. Build your knowledge, use your voice, and vote for leaders who believe in the changes you do.

☐ Support financial educators (and businesses) who share your values and are women and BIPOC-owned.

☐ Become a financial adult. As you learn and achieve more, you'll bring yourself and others up with you.

As you go through each of the following chapters covering different financial topics, you'll see that equity, privilege, and policy are integral parts of the big picture – no more financial advice in a silo. That's the first step to being a financial adult. First up, your money goals!

CHAPTER 3

Your Money Goals

The whole point of having money is to have and experience what you want, and that looks different for each of us. To you it might mean financial freedom and peace of mind, giving to organizations you believe in, being able to take care of your parents, buying new sneakers each month, or traveling a few times per year.

I call these your goals. They can look like more traditional money goals – build up a rainy-day fund, pay down your debt, and save for retirement. But they also can include lifestyle upgrades and using your money for good.

Why Have Financial Goals?

> You know all those things you've always wanted to do, have, and experience? You should do, have, and experience them!

Getting clear on your goals is one of the most important parts of being a financial adult. When you have goals, and realistic plans to achieve them, you can feel confident that they will happen.

Goals are also motivating and can drive you to take the actions you need to make them happen.

The key is not only understanding your goals but building them into your financial plans. Otherwise, you can have the goal of saving $200 per month toward your rainy-day fund, but will have no idea if that's feasible or can actually happen given your income and expenses.

Remember, while we can always make smarter money moves, try not to compare yourself with others. You may have things in common, but gender and race/ethnicity add differentiating factors of privilege. You have no idea what another's journey has been like or where they started financially.

Start by Listing Out Your Goals

Set a timer for 10 minutes and let yourself dream about what you want. These can be smart money moves, fun things that bring you joy, and both short-term and long-term aspirations.

Even think about the feelings you want to experience. What would you need to achieve financially to feel financial freedom, peace of mind, or stability? Write down anything that comes to mind. We'll narrow the list down later.

List out your goals.

_____ _____

_____ _____

_____ _____

_____ _____

_____ _____

Important Goals to Consider

Here are some important money goals to consider adding to your list:

- Rainy-day fund (a.k.a. an emergency fund)
- Retirement (a.k.a. work-optional)
- Paying down high-interest debt (a.k.a. paying off credit cards)
- Investing (a.k.a. making your money grow)

Time to Prioritize

Prioritizing means deciding which goals come first. Rank each of the goals you listed in the previous exercise in order of priority, with number one being your highest-priority goal. Consider which goals are most important to you, what's most urgent financially, as well as your timeline.

Do you want to pay off *all* of your student loans before saving for your future home? Do you want to aggressively save for retirement (and retire early!) or take an extra vacation each year? This is an extremely personal choice that each of us needs to make for ourselves. Some want to retire early and are willing to forgo some spending to do it. Others would rather spend more now and retire at a more typical age.

That being said, there are some commonly accepted financial guidelines to help you with prioritizing your money goals.

Priority #1: Some Rainy-Day Funds

Having some savings for emergencies is of top priority. If we don't have any money in savings and an emergency expense comes up, we'd have to either put expenses on a high-interest credit card or borrow. And in some cases, we wouldn't be able to pay because with certain expenses, like rent, paying with a credit card is not always an option.

Now, that doesn't mean you have to fully fund your rainy-day fund before anything else, but you definitely want a few months of emergency expenses saved up (more on how much you need later). In my conversation with Lauren Anastasio, a CFP and director of financial advice at Stash, she made the distinction between a crisis fund and a rainy-day fund. You want to have your crisis fund saved first and foremost, which might be a month's worth of expenses or $1,000. I call this your minimum rainy-day fund. Then once you max out your 401(k) match (priority #2) and pay off high-interest credit card debt (priority #3), you can focus on fully funding your rainy-day fund (or your ideal rainy-day fund).

Priority #2: 401(k) Match

401(k) matching, when available, is free money your employer gives you when you contribute up to a certain amount to your 401(k). But really it's part of your total compensation. If your company matches 3%, then for any amount you contribute toward your 401(k), up to 3%, they match it dollar for dollar. That's a 100% return. I talk about this more in Chapter 7.

Priority #3: High-Interest Credit Card Debt

Credit cards come with interest rates that are often as high as 15–30%. Holding a balance on your credit cards costs you money in interest. If you make $100 monthly payments on a credit card with a $5,000 balance and an interest rate of 20%, you'd pay the card off in nine years and pay $5,840 in interest. Yikes! This is not to depress you or make you feel guilty, just to show that this is why paying off high-interest credit cards should be high on your priority list.

Priority #4: Retirement (a.k.a. work becoming optional)

We'll be talking a lot about retirement (in Chapter 7) but this means saving up enough money so you don't have to work. It's really important because other than credit cards (which are way too expensive), saving (but really investing) is the only real way to fund your retirement. Also, retirement accounts are tax-advantaged so it's a win–win.

Everything Else

By everything else I mean deciding between paying off student loans, investing outside of retirement accounts, saving for a home, and everything in between. Here it's a matter of balancing what makes the most sense financially with what's important to you.

What makes the most sense financially typically depends on interest rates, both the interest rates you're paying for debt and the interest rates you would earn by investing the money. Interest rates on student loans vary widely but it's typically recommended that if the interest rate on your student loans is 7% or more, it makes sense to prioritize paying those down before investing outside of retirement accounts (which have added tax benefits).

While these are great guidelines, you can't ever be sure what your investments in real estate or the stock market will earn during the years you decide to invest and not pay down your debt. It's always important to keep your motivation in mind. If your student loans don't bother you, and you're really excited to get started investing, you might decide to allocate funds 50/50. It doesn't have to be all or nothing.

Add a priority ranking to each goal, starting with #1 (top priority) and working your way down.

Goals	Priority
Example: Build minimum rainy-day fund	#1

Make Sure Your Goals Are SMART Goals

Smart goals are:

Specific: Describe the goal.

Measurable: With money goals, this is the amount.

Attainable: Is it possible? Is the outcome in your control?

Relevant: Is it worthwhile? Are you willing and motivated to put in the work to achieve it?

Time-Bound: By when you will achieve it.

"Save more money" turns into "I'll save $3,000 toward my rainy-day fund this year by saving $250 per month."

Go ahead and rewrite all of your goals as SMART goals here. Write them in order of priority, starting with priority #1.

1. _____

2. _____

3. _____

4. _____

5. _____

How Much Is Enough?

As you get specific with your goals, you might not be sure how much is enough. Here's how to figure out how much is enough for some common money goals.

How Much Do I Need in My Rainy-Day Fund?

The typical recommendation is to have three to six months of expenses saved for an emergency. The idea is that if you lose your job, you have some time to find a new one or if someone in your family gets sick, you can take time off to take care of them.

Think through a couple of emergency situations – fun, I know. How many months of living expenses would you like to have covered? Depending on your specific job and industry, it might take more or less time for you to find a new role if you lost your job. It's also important to take your health insurance coverage into account. If something happened, what is the maximum you'd have to pay out of pocket? If you aren't sure, don't fret. We talk about this in detail in Chapter 10.

Instead of using your typical spending to calculate your rainy-day fund, you might decide to only cover your necessities like bills and some food. Multiply the number of months by your estimated monthly spending. You might decide that at a minimum you'd like three months saved but ideally you'd like to have six months saved. You can break that into two separate goals.

How much do you want in your rainy-day fund?

# of Months		Monthly Spend		Rainy-Day Fund
Example: 3 months	×	$3,000	=	$9,000
	×		=	

HOW DO I USE MY RAINY-DAY FUND?

We talk a lot about building up our rainy-day funds, but we don't talk enough about actually using them when we need them. Once you've built the habit of saving every paycheck, it can feel painful and even unnatural to use the money set aside. People who've retired report a similar feeling when depleting rather than building their retirement money. But that's what it's there for!

To make this easier on ourselves, we should be very clear from the start about when we'll use the money in our rainy-day fund (probably the scenarios that you walked through in the previous exercise). What constitutes an emergency?

If a situation arises where it makes sense to use your rainy-day fund, make the conscious choice to use it. Transfer a month's worth of expenses to your checking account instead of transferring money over every time you need it (like a slow painful drip). This feels a lot more powerful and less agonizing. Once your situation changes, you can work to build it back up.

How Much Do I Need in My Walkaway Fund?
Wait . . . What's a Walkaway Fund?

Dasha Kennedy urges all people, especially women, going into a relationship to have a walkaway fund saved in a bank account that only they have access to. For her, that means. "If I needed to pick up tomorrow and walk away, I have what I need for housing, basic necessities, and day-to-day expenses. That's a fund I will always keep."

Dasha recommends having six months of expenses set aside for anything you'd spend if you were to walk away. And it makes sense if you think about how long it can take for things to get sorted out in a divorce, including assets to be distributed or alimony to be paid. You don't want to be waiting and putting things on credit cards or, worse, staying in a situation that's unhealthy or even harmful because of money. 99% of cases involving domestic violence include some form of financial abuse.[1] The walkaway fund could be your biggest form of financial activism yet.

Note: This can overlap with your rainy-day fund, as long as only you have access to it.

How much money would you like in your walkaway fund?

# of Months	×	Monthly Spend	=	Walkaway Fund
Example: 6 months	×	$3,000	=	$18,000
	×		=	

How Much Do I Need to Buy a Home?

When we're saving up to buy a home we often focus mostly (if not only) on the down payment, which is typically 20% of the cost of the home. This is usually the largest cost, but if it's the only thing we're prepared to pay for, things are going to get financially stressful. We cover this in detail in Chapter 9 – get excited.

How Much Money Do I Need to Retire?

As you can imagine, when it comes to retirement, there are a lot of variables that we won't know while planning. We talk a lot more about this in Chapter 7, including some important calculations, but for now,

Lauren recommends using 15% of your income as a retirement savings target. So if you are earning $50,000, you'll want to be saving $7,500 per year toward retirement.

How Much Do I Need to Move Out on My Own?

In order to rent a place, you'll often be required to pay the first and last month's rent, as well as a security deposit (usually the size of one rent payment) – so that's three months' rent. Depending on how you find the apartment, there may or may not be a fee you pay the broker. Don't forget to incorporate the cost of the move itself and any furniture you plan to buy. Make sure you add in the changes to your new utilities to your monthly spending as well.

With any of these goals, you'll want to plan to have the money (or at least enough of the money) available when it's time to pay. So if you plan to move August 1st but have to pay the first, last, and security a month earlier, you'll want to have it saved by July 1st.

How Much Do I Need to Start a Family?

The costs to start a family can vary widely, depending both on circumstance and preference. Fertility treatments like IVF may or may not be covered by your company's insurance and, if not covered, can create out-of-pocket costs of, on average, $23,000 per round.[2,3]

Once pregnant, the largest costs in the first few years are the health bills associated with giving birth (more on this in Chapter 10), getting set up with the baby gear (nursery, stroller, car seat, etc.), and then childcare. Childcare costs depend on where you are located, what childcare choices are available, and whether you have family available to help.

Add up the total one-time costs and the total ongoing costs. Once you have an estimate for the upfront cost, divide it by the number of years (or months) you estimate until you will need the money. This gets you to your goal contribution amount. For the ongoing costs Lauren recommends creating a budget based on your new child expenses and current income (I'll show you how soon). The total cost of the first year of a child's life generally can range from $16,000 to $50,000. That doesn't mean you need to have that amount saved in cash, but to be prepared with a combination of savings and lifestyle adjustments.

With goals like this that seem more ambiguous it can sometimes feel silly to plan, but it's so much better to have something set aside than to wait until you have more information. You can and should adjust these goals as you learn more or things change, but don't wait to start!

How Much Do I Need to Take Care of Family or Elder Dependents?

For many, caring for parents or other chosen family is part of the financial plan. It might be a current reality or a reality in the future. This can influence where you choose to live (because you'll need more rooms), savings plans, retirement plans, and, really, all the plans.

One of the hardest parts of making a plan is having a conversation with the individual(s) you may want to take care of. Understanding their wishes as well as what resources they have available, if any, will help tremendously in your planning.

Much like other financial goals (like retirement), there are many things you won't know. Do your best to make an educated estimate and adjust as you have more information.

How Much Do I Need to Start a Business?

This depends so much on the business but doesn't have to be expensive. Are there any one-time costs to get set up? What costs are ongoing? For example, you might pay $200 to get your website set up initially but then the cost of maintenance is $10 per month. You'll want to incorporate both types of costs into your plan.

How Much Do I Need to Take Time Off to Travel?

Cinneah El-Amin, a personal finance travel creator and the founder of Flynanced, walked me through her four-step process for mapping out the cost of travel.

1. **Start with flights.** Cinneah searches Google flights and sets up an alert as soon as she has the idea for a trip.

2. **Think about accommodations.** For group travel, Cinneah prefers Airbnb and loves Booking.com for smaller, more intimate trips because there is no prepayment and cancellation is free.

3. **Plan for trip "extras."** Cinneah then gets a quote for travel insurance (look to see what you already have covered if you're using credit cards) and checks whether there are any visa requirements, that her passport is up to date (if it's an international trip), and if there are any COVID test requirements and fees.

4. **Give yourself spending money.** Cinneah recommends budgeting for daily spending money so you're not relying on credit cards or savings to fund your daily expenses.

5. **Add it all up.** This is what you want to have saved in your travel fund (more on this in Chapter 5).

Now that you know "how much," adjust your SMART goals accordingly.

For the Love of Money: Money Goals with a Partner

If you are partnered up, it's great to do this exercise on your own, but then you'll also want to include your partner in your goal planning. You might have some shared goals and some goals that are just your own. You might agree on the priority ranking for some and disagree for others. This is all okay! What's most important is that you have a conversation and come up with a plan together.

Maybe you contribute jointly to certain goals and then you each contribute to your respective individual goals. If you disagree on the ranking of a goal, you might compromise and contribute to two at the same time and/or encourage one another to contribute to individual goals. There are a million and one ways to figure it out, and know that the plan you come up with isn't set in stone. Try some things out and see how they go. Adjust from there.

Decide How Many Goals to Work Toward

If we focus on one goal, we achieve it more quickly. That being said, choosing one goal can be really difficult when we have lots of things we are excited to accomplish. Also, a goal like retirement is something we may be working toward until we get there, and we probably want to make other things happen in the meantime.

On the other hand, if we focus on too many goals at once, we won't see any real meaningful progress because the money is spread across too many areas. That's not motivating. Choosing two to five goals is usually a good sweet spot.

Write down the goals you plan to work toward. If you choose to work toward three goals, write the top three goals from your list. If seeing it this way has you wanting to reprioritize, go for it!

1. _____

2. _____

3. _____

4. _____

5. _____

Make a Preliminary Plan

Break each goal you plan to work toward down into monthly contributions. You can do this by dividing the amount you need for the goal by its timeline. If I want to save $3,000 for my rainy-day fund this year, that's $250 per month ($3,000/12). If I want $50,000 for a down payment in three years, that's $1,389 per month ($50,000/3 years = $16,667 per year/12 months = $1,389). If you prefer to contribute biweekly or weekly, do that instead.

It might be unrealistic to save $250 or $1,389 per month. That's just a starting point to give you an idea. You can start small and go up from there. If you receive one-time or less frequent sources of income like a bonus, commission, inheritance, or payout, that can also go toward your goals.

Important Reminder: Not everything has to go toward your goals. You might decide on a celebration gift for part of the money as well.

When making your preliminary plan you'll also want to decide where the money goes. If you're paying down debt, the money will go directly to your debt payments, but if you are building your rainy-day fund, you'll want to have a savings account for that.

Goal	How Much	How Often	Where
Example: Minimum Rainy-Day Fund	$250	Monthly	HYSA (high-yield savings account)

Use Your Goals to Focus

There is so much personal finance information and advice out there. This information overload can be overwhelming and lead to analysis paralysis, and becomes a big part of why many of us (myself included) don't get started financial adulting. Part of being a financial adult is knowing what you need to know and what you do *not* need to know. Saying "see ya" to all the info we don't need to know makes this manageable.

I sat down with Elyse Steinhaus, who leads finance content at theSkimm, because theSkimm is all about "skimming down" big topics to what we need to know to live our smartest lives. Money is an important part of that. Elyse recommends paying attention to personal finance information that affects your specific goals and not stressing about the rest.

"If you're buying a home, you'll want to be watching average mortgage rates and what the housing market is doing" she says (more on this in Chapter 9). This information will help you make a decision that will pay off in the long-run and directly impact your goals, "like deciding how much you want to save and what you need to do to get your credit score up, so you can qualify for the best rate possible." You don't need to read about it all over. You can stick with some sources and experts you trust. This book and the Financial Adulting toolkit are a great place to start.

Your Financial Adulting Action Items

- ☐ List your financial goals and rank them by priority, starting with #1. Remember – try not to compare yourself with others!
- ☐ Turn each of your goals into a SMART goal so you know exactly how much you need and by when you want to achieve each goal (it's okay to guesstimate until you have more info!).
- ☐ Decide how many goals to work toward at once.
- ☐ Make a preliminary plan to achieve your goals (we'll make sure these plans are workable in the next few chapters).

Big congrats on mapping out your goals! This is a big step and a great starting point. But we can't know if these plans for our goals are workable without looking at our income and expenses. We'll come back to these goals later. Budgeting, here we come . . .

CHAPTER 4

All About Income

Once you have mapped out your money goals, it's time to put together your financial plan.

What Is a Financial Plan?

A financial plan is a realistic and optimistic plan of your financial situation and goals for the next 12 months (and beyond). It includes everything from spending to saving, paying off debt, giving, saving for retirement, and investing. It also includes a current snapshot of where your money is and what you owe.

If you're familiar with my work, you might know that I also call a financial plan, a happiness allocation. It's a plan to allocate our money in the ways that will make us the happiest in the short term and long term. How we talk about money matters. When we use terms that bring us joy or help align our actions with our motivation, it reframes how we think about and interact with our money. Depending on our privilege and lived experience, money may have some very negative connotations for us.

A financial plan is a living document. It can and will adjust over the course of the year.

Financial plans give our money a purpose. When we map out our finances (mainly our income, expenses, and what we want to go toward our goals), we can plan for the bigger things we want to accomplish.

In Chapter 3 I show you how to map out your goals. Your financial plan can make those goals a reality. When you look at your income and expenses in partnership with your goals, you can see exactly how to make them happen or what needs to adjust.

This plan will also reduce spending-induced guilt and provide peace of mind. When you buy something, you won't have to wonder if you can afford it or if the purchase is being made at the expense of other goals. You can feel confident that you're on track to achieve your long-term goals while simultaneously enjoying your money.

What Does a Financial Plan Actually Look Like?

A financial plan uses what I call the "golden rule" of personal finance:

Total annual income □ Total annual expenses □ $$$ for our goals

We'll fill in this equation over the next two chapters.

First, the Inflows

The first part of your financial plan is your income (the second part is your expenses, covered in Chapter 5). What do you expect to earn over the next 12 months, month by month? If you earn a salary or regular income, log into your bank account and find the amount that hits your bank account each paycheck. This is the number you want to use for your planning. Also look at how often you get paid. Is it once per month, every two weeks, twice per month, or nine months of the year? If you get two paychecks per month, the amounts might look different each time.

Note: if you're paid twice per month, that's 24 times per year. If you're paid every two weeks, that's 26 times per year. Two paychecks can make a big difference so you want this to be accurate.

Enter your income into the space below or use a spreadsheet to map it out. You can also use my template in the Financial Adulting toolkit at **financialadultingbook.com**.

Income Source	Amount per Paycheck	How Often	Yearly Amount	Monthly Amount
Example: Salary	$2,122	24 times	$50,928	$4,244
Total				

If you expect to get a raise or plan to ask for a raise and aren't sure what that will look like, use a paycheck calculator (there's one in the toolkit!). This will estimate the amount you'll see reflected in your paycheck. Don't forget to take out what you pay for your benefits and 401(k), health savings account (HSA), and/or flexible spending account (FSA) contributions (we cover these medical expense accounts in Chapter 10). You can start using this new number in the months you expect to see the pay increase.

We've mapped out the first part of our financial plan. Just a heads-up: this is usually the more simple and exciting part.

But there's a lot more to our inflows than what we are currently earning. Many of us want to make more money. I'm all for that! Earning more can make your expenses more manageable, make it easier to save for your goals, and/or allow you to have a greater impact. Not to mention, in many cases, earning more would mean you're being compensated fairly for the work you're already doing.

Income Source	Jan	Feb	March	April	May	June	July	Aug	Sept	Oct	Nov	Dec	Annual Total
Example: Salary	$4,244	$4,244	$4,244	$4,244	$4,244	$4,244	$4,244	$4,244	$4,244	$4,244	$4,244	$4,244	$50,928
Total													

For the Love of Money: What About Partners?

If you share finances with a partner (even just some expenses), and they are willing, it probably makes sense to include them in the plan. When you add them to your plan, you can keep their numbers completely separate or integrate them (while still seeing who earns and spends what). In the next chapter when we add expenses, I show you a few ways to do it. Add your partner's income to the lines in the previous exercise.

Side Hustles

Side hustles used to be a form of supplemental income or a way for people to start a business on the side before it grew big enough to take over their full-time job. More and more, side hustles or second jobs are needed in order to just get by and pay the bills. When you earn income through your own business, freelancing, or a side hustle, you want to set aside money for taxes. Each business is unique, but putting aside 30% of your profit in an online savings account "tax fund" is a good place to start. I prefer to do this as a percentage of income. Depending on what your expenses look like, that percentage can vary, so calculate an estimate for your business. When any income comes in, transfer that percentage directly to your tax fund.

The Gender Wage Gaps

In case you missed it, there are very real and problematic earning gaps for women and even more so women of color, mothers, and women with disabilities. The Equal Pay Day calendar puts these gaps into context by showing how far into the next year each community would have to work in order to earn the same amount a white, non-Latino man earned in 12 months. In this chart you'll see the date accompanied by the pay gap in dollars.

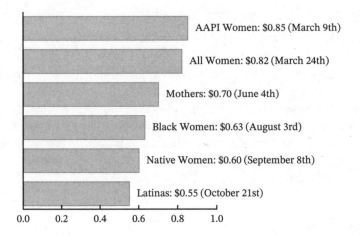

AAPI Women: $0.85 (March 9th)

All Women: $0.82 (March 24th)

Mothers: $0.70 (June 4th)

Black Women: $0.63 (August 3rd)

Native Women: $0.60 (September 8th)

Latinas: $0.55 (October 21st)

Source: Data from Equal Pay Today.

Some Takeaways

BIPOC women experience the compounding effect of intersection-ality. These gaps get even worse when a woman of color is also a mother, has a disability, or is transgender. Women with disabilities earn $0.72 for every $1 a man with a disability earns and people with disabilities earn only $0.68 for every $1 a nondisabled person earns.[1] Transgender women's earnings fall by nearly one-third after they transition.[2]

Men also experience wage gaps. Black men and Latinos earn $0.87 and $0.91, respectively, for every $1 a white man earns.[3] The pay gap is $0.95 for gay men and $0.77–$0.88 for bisexual men.[4]

Closing the Wage Gap

If we stay on our current path, we won't see pay equality for another 257 years.[5] *Woof.* The wage gap is a major contributing factor to the gender and racial investing and debt gaps. And this compounds year over year. Raising the minimum wage, mandating paid parental leave, and providing affordable high-quality childcare (which we covered in Chapter 2) help to close both the wealth and wage gaps. Here are some additional ways to close the wage gap.

Pass Policy for Equal Pay

It's been illegal to pay men and women differently for performing the same work since the passing of the Equal Pay Act of 1963. But it can be challenging to prove the work is equal. According to Margaret Scheele and Setareh Ebrahimian, attorneys at Fisher Phillips, a management-side law firm, who focus on pay equity, the real protections are at the state level. Many state laws have a more lenient requirement for defining who can serve as a comparator, such as equal pay for *substantially* similar or comparable work. Every state with the exception of Mississippi and North Carolina has some sort of equal pay legislation and new laws continue to help close the gap. For example, California now (as of January 1, 2021) has a pay reporting requirement where private employers with one or more employees in California, and 100 employees overall, must submit a pay data report to the state each year.

Perform Company Pay Audits

A pay equity audit means looking at current compensation and roles across gender and race/ethnicity to see that pay is fair – meaning, employees are receiving equal pay for substantially equal work. Setareh shared that she's definitely seen a trend of more companies conducting pay equity audits and it's not just to stay out of legal trouble. "A lot of companies want to know if there are pay disparities internally and how to address them because they are interested in attracting more employees, attracting better employees, reducing their turnover rate, and generally want to do the right thing."

Revamp Internal Hiring and Promotion Processes

There is often gender and racial bias built into internal company practices – from who gets promoted to staffing decisions and how annual reviews are conducted. Women often receive less feedback, get fewer high-profile assignments, have less access to mentors and sponsors, and are less likely to be hired. In a study on government jobs with 16 million participants, qualified Black women were 58% less likely to be hired than white men, and overall, qualified women were 27% less likely to be hired than qualified men.[6] An applicant named Jennifer is assumed to be much less competent than an applicant named John, even with the exact same qualifications. Studies show that even if Jennifer did get the job, she'd be paid less and would also be less likely to be mentored.[7]

Address the Unpaid Labor of Women

In the United States, women perform 4 hours of unpaid labor per day compared with men's 2.5 hours. That's almost 11 extra hours per week, 45 hours per month, and almost 550 hours per year. What would you give for an extra 11 hours per week? Economists have acknowledged that gross domestic product (GDP), the most common method to track an economy's health, has been leaving out the unpaid work of women for 80 years. By Chapter 4 of this book, are you surprised? Many of the policies mentioned earlier, like raising the minimum wage, paid leave, and affordable childcare, will help. On the individual level we can work to create equality in our homes, which will not only improve our own lives but, for those with children, will model a more equitable division of labor for them.

Negotiate What You Deserve

As part of closing the wage gap and increasing our income, we can also negotiate to get paid what we as individuals deserve. Whether you are working to remedy a pay discrepancy or are just ready for your next raise, here's how to negotiate your compensation.

Reframe the Negotiation

First and foremost, what is a negotiation? It's just asking for what you want. You might not realize it but you're negotiating all day, every day. When you and a friend decide which restaurant to go to, that's a negotiation. When you later decide which app to share, that's a negotiation, too. We can use these everyday low-stakes negotiations as an opportunity to practice asking for what we want.

What are some low-stakes ways to practice negotiating this week?

1. _____

2. _____

3. _____

You might have noticed that it's so much easier to negotiate and vouch for your friends than for yourself. This is something we can work to unlearn but even after working on this for years, I still feel it. What's helped me is to realize that I am negotiating on behalf of women everywhere. When you negotiate your compensation you are paving the way for other women to do the same, you are normalizing negotiating, you are gaining experience you can share with others, and you are doing your part to close the pay gap. That's powerful.

Understand the Double Bind

Women who negotiate (and studies show women are actually negotiating as much as men) can be viewed as unlikeable and are more likely than men to receive feedback that they are "intimidating," "too aggressive," or "bossy." This is the *double bind*. For women of color, this translates into the angry Black woman and fiery Latina stereotypes. Women are told to negotiate, but when we do, there are negative long-term career implications.

As a way to overcome the double bind, experts recommend that women negotiate communally, using words like "we" and "us" and framing your "ask" in a way that shows it's better for the team and company as a whole. Yes, I'm annoyed even writing this, but this is the world in which we're negotiating.

As a way to give companies the benefit of the doubt and hold them accountable, Claire Wasserman, the founder and author of *Ladies Get Paid*, is a big fan of saying, "I know you're a company that pays people fairly. I know you're a company that values gender and racial equity, so I'm sure we can come to a conclusion that works for everyone." And know that you're making the company better by asking them to pay you fairly. If you're interviewing at a new company, you can say this without knowing it's true (because how can you know?), but if you work there, you'll want to tailor the statement to be reflective of the reality at the company.

Know Your Market Rate

Let's be clear – your market rate is not the same as your worth. I think this idea that what we earn is what we're worth is one of the reasons talking about what we earn feels so uncomfortable. Our market rate is just the going rate for the type of work we do. That's it. And it typically comes in the form of a pay range (also called a pay band).

How do you find your market rate? Start by talking to friends and colleagues (especially white men) about what they earn. You can acknowledge the awkwardness and share how important pay transparency is for equal pay. Remember, you are giving them an opportunity to be an ally. You can also talk with people who used to work in your role. This can feel a bit less daunting, as they aren't sharing their current salary information.

Side note on pay transparency. Keeping salaries a secret hides pay inequities and discrimination. When we know what others are earning, we know whether we're being underpaid. It can feel difficult to talk about what we earn, but it's worth it. Share what you earn with coworkers and friends. Enter your salary info into databases like the Career Contessa Salary Project, Salary.com, Glassdoor, and PayScale so that the information is more readily available. Know that it is completely legal for you to share your pay with your coworkers and that it's illegal for your company to penalize you for it. That being said, it's important to acknowledge that it can be hard to prove if your company did penalize you for it. Pay transparency is a small part of a broader systemic solution, but information is a powerful starting point.

"Fun" fact: In 19 states it's illegal for an interviewer or future employer to ask about your salary history (including what you are currently earning). The reason? If most women are already being underpaid, this perpetuates wage gaps.

For more salary info, call up recruiters in your industry (they have all the insider pay info!) and do some online research. The more specific you can get about your role, location (it matters!), and level of seniority, the more accurate the range will be.

What's your market rate?

Ask Friends
and Colleagues

Talk to a
Recruiter

Online
Research

Know Your Walkaway Rate

The last thing you want to do is take a new job or stay in a job where you're being underpaid, only to resent the role and feel angry. Go into the negotiation with optimistic expectations but also know what you are *not* willing to accept.

Take time to think this through. Know the facts and compensation range the role warrants and also know yourself and your specific experience. Imagine yourself working in the job a month or six months down the line. What compensation will have you continue to feel valued in the role?

There is a lot of nuance to this. If you are pivoting careers, you might be excited to switch roles and know that you will accept lower pay as you gain experience in a new industry. Just know that women generally tend to undervalue their experience and expertise, which might apply more to the new role than you think.

What's your walkaway rate?

Prep Your Case

One of the most important things to bring into a salary negotiation is a list of your successes and accomplishments. You want to be able to share the value you've brought to the company (or previous companies) and, in some cases, show how you've already stepped into the position you want to be promoted to.

When you have a big success at work, you might think you'll never forget it, but over time, it's hard to recall all of the things you've done. You might even draw a blank: "What have I even been spending my time doing these last few months?" Keep a running log of your successes, big and small, so you can pinpoint projects where you've had an impact. When possible, use measurable data like a percentage increase in revenue, a decrease in expenses, how many participants were involved, and the project's timeline. You can also add these successes to your LinkedIn profile, CV, or resume.

Lauren Smith Brody, gender equity advocate and author of *The Fifth Trimester*, talked about the very valuable yet overlooked work that women take on more often than men, like informally mentoring a colleague, leading an employee resource group (ERG), or helping to train someone. Don't forget to include any additional unpaid work you do. Make it part of your routine to add a win or two to your list of successes each week.

Not only will this serve as a great resource, it's also a nice confidence boost!

Example Success Log

Date	Success	Impact/Challenges You Overcame/Other Notes

You can download a digital version from the Financial Adulting toolkit.

Toot Your Own Horn

You know that amazing success log you started? It's time to share it with people (specifically, your colleagues).

If you aren't used to sharing your successes, it can feel uncomfortable at first, but I promise it gets easier – and over time your boss will come to expect it. Pop into their office this week (in person or on Zoom) and share a success. You can update them on a project that's going well or share an exciting result you and your team achieved. Then build the habit of doing it at least once per month or quarterly, depending on the relationship.

Side note on imposter syndrome: Imposter syndrome is feeling like you do not deserve your success and accomplishments because they are due to luck and you'll be discovered as a fraud. Sound familiar? Women experience imposter syndrome more than men and this is intensified for women of color. According to clinical psychologist Emily Hu, "We're more likely to experience imposter syndrome if we don't see many examples of people who look like us or share our background who are clearly succeeding in our field."[8] You can imagine the implications this has on what women earn. It's helpful to understand that this is very common and might be impacting your confidence in a negotiation or even taking on a more high-profile project.

The term *imposter syndrome* has become more and more controversial because it "directs our view toward fixing women at work instead of fixing the places where women work," says Ruchika Tulshyan and Jodi-Ann Burey in a piece for the *Harvard Business Review* (*HBR*).[9] They go on to encourage companies and managers to create a culture that addresses systemic bias and racism so women, and especially women from underrepresented communities, experience imposter syndrome less and less.

Negotiate; Don't Stop with *No*

If you want a promotion, your manager should know about it. You can even ask specifically what it would take to make it happen. If during your research you found out you are being paid less than your male colleagues or below market rate, bring that up. Given all the publicity and work being done around equal pay, it can work really well to call the issue out directly. "In my research it has come to my attention that I'm being paid less than my peers for my role (or even my male peers)."

Lauren encourages everyone, before going into even the simplest negotiation, to understand that closing the wage gap and promoting and retaining women is the best thing for everyone, including the economy. A recent study showed that if there were equal representation in the workforce, the U.S. GDP would go up by 5%. Read an article like that right before any negotiation and you'll go in thinking, "Yes, we deserve this!" Now that's a pump-up.

Claire encourages us to push ourselves outside of our comfort zone but not so much that we've twisted ourselves into a pretzel to become someone else. "You still have to be you."

When I hear the word "no" in a negotiation I can feel very shut down. But the word "no" is actually a sign to continue the conversation. If your boss can't give you a raise at this time, try to understand why. By getting curious rather than shutting down, you might find helpful pieces of information that you can use to support your manager in making your case.

It's a Year-Round Process

We often think of these salary conversations as a once-a-year or once-per-promotion cycle occurrence. The pressure is on, and they can feel really formal and nerve-wracking. But the truth is, we want to be having these conversations throughout the year.

Claire recommends trying to have these types of conversations on a quarterly basis. "It doesn't mean you're necessarily having a conversation about getting a raise. Maybe you check in to see how you're doing, to ask if you're on track for your promotion, or even more broadly talk about how the company is doing or what growth and up-leveling could look like for you." This is also a great way to find out about any leadership development, mentoring, or shadowing programs that the company may offer or reimburse.

Other Important $$$ Things You Can Negotiate

Our base salaries are really important because future raises, bonuses, and 401(k) matching are usually calculated as a percentage of them. That being said, there are many other parts of our total compensation that we can negotiate and should factor in when comparing opportunities.

Georgia Lee Hussey, CFP and the founder and CEO of Modernist Financial, encourages us to "look at and really understand the whole package, including benefits, especially when you're negotiating. There's so much money in there that is often ignored." And you can negotiate for whatever is most beneficial to your personal goals.

- Relocation budget (reimbursed expenses for a move to a new place)
- Paid leave (this should always be a benefit but it's not always the case)
- Vesting (how quickly stock compensation or 401(k) matching become yours)
- Flexibility (control over your schedule or ability to work around other priorities in your life)
- Bonus structure/commission (compensation tied to performance)
- Professional development expenses (this could look like a training or coaching program or part-time MBA)
- Equity (common in startups – ownership of the company in the form of options, restricted stock units, or performance shares)

Your Financial Adulting Action Items

☐ Map out your monthly income for the next 12 months.
☐ Help close the wage gap. You can find a comprehensive list of what you can do in the Financial Adulting toolkit.

☐ Practice negotiating with low-stakes situations in your everyday life.

☐ Prepare and negotiate (it's a year-round process!).

☐ Keep a running list of your successes (make sure to share them with your team).

Woohoo! Now you have your money inflows mapped out and are on your way to increasing them. Next up, we talk about your money outflows, or your expenses. This is the last piece we need to put together your financial plan!

CHAPTER 5

Your Money Outflows

You have your goals and your income; now it's time to move on to your expenses. To make a plan for your expenses (or outflows), there are few things you need to do.

Map Out Your Expenses

First, think about the next 12 months. Are there expenses you expect to come up this year that didn't last year? For example, you might be planning to move to a different apartment, know you have a trip planned over the summer, have a best friend's wedding in six months, or plan to send more money back home. Jot these down or download the spreadsheet in the Financial Adulting toolkit.

Write down any new upcoming expenses.

_____

_____

_____

_____

_____

Are there any experiences or expenses you'd like to incorporate into your plan this year that you didn't last year? Maybe you would love to get a gym membership or want to be able to take a vacation (or an extra vacation). I call these lifestyle upgrades and there's nothing wrong with them. These are things you'd like to work into your plan. Write them down here.

Write down any lifestyle upgrades or new expenses you'd like to incorporate.

_____

_____

_____

_____

_____

Next, let's look at your current expenses or what's actually happening with your money. Start by listing each of your expenses in the space provided. You can put them into categories later if you'd like. To make it easier, you can look at previous bank and credit card statements to jog your memory.

Looking at a few recent statements will help a lot, so you can start there, but to be most accurate, you'll want to scan through the past 12 months. This way, you don't forget about an annual credit card fee or that you always buy yourself a gift on your birthday.

Important: This is not going to be perfect. You can always add in things you forget and we'll talk about a process for adjusting these numbers as your life changes.

List out all of your current expenses.

_____	_____	_____
_____	_____	_____
_____	_____	_____
_____	_____	_____
_____	_____	_____
_____	_____	_____
_____	_____	_____
_____	_____	_____
_____	_____	_____

Add Numbers to Your List

Now we're going to add numbers to each of the expense items on your three lists. What will each cost over the next 12 months? Write down each of your expenses and how much each cost you per month. If it's a one-time thing, you'll put the total in one month (the month you incur the expense). If it's a daily, weekly, or monthly expense, you'll put an amount in every month.

Don't forget to add everything up in the right column (the year's total). Seeing what each expense costs you for the year brings a lot of clarity (sometimes nausea) because we see the true impact it has on our financial life. This can also help us see if there are any expenses we'd rather trade for others.

I like using a spreadsheet because I have the worst handwriting (anyone who's seen it will agree) and also because it's easier to change and adjust without redoing everything.

Some tips:

- For some expenses, you might not be sure what they will cost. Do some research, think back to what similar things cost in the past (look at those previous bank and credit card statements), and give your best estimate. It's much better to estimate and get it wrong than to have nothing there at all.

- For the expenses that vary, like utility bills, I start with the same amount as that month the previous year and add a bit extra because prices usually go up (*ugh*, inflation). So if summer months typically come with a higher utility bill, that's reflected in my plan.

I know this takes real work *but* it's truly worth it. Believe me. If we don't have an accurate and clear picture of our spending, the rest of our plan won't be accurate and we won't know how much we can spend and save for our goals.

For expenses that are bit more tricky to calculate the monthly cost, use this chart.

Expense	Amount per Time	How Often	Yearly Amount	Monthly Amount
Example: Groceries	$100	Weekly	$5,200	$433.33

Multigenerational Living

Dasha Kennedy, the founder of The Broke Black Girl you met in Chapter 2, describes multigenerational living as a living arrangement between two or more generations. One in four Americans live in a multigenerational household and it's most common in BIPOC households.[1] Multigenerational living can eliminate thousands of dollars in expenses and make other financial goals possible. It can also support parents and grandparents who don't have financial means. There are so many ways it can work and benefit the entire family.

For Dasha, multigenerational living made a huge impact in her life. She shared that in the Black community, the homeownership gap makes it harder for families to financially survive on their own, let alone thrive. Dasha's grandmother was the first in her family to own a home. When Dasha was born, four generations were living in that home. When she was a young single mother, she was able to live in that home again and save up before moving out on her own.

Become Aware of Your Spending

When it comes to our expenses, we have a few things (okay, a lot of things) working against us. As a result, many of us would rather not know what's happening with our money. I get it, ignorance can feel like bliss. If you think you'd benefit from more awareness around your spending (hint, most of us would), here are some tips:

- **Keep a money journal.** Write down (or type out) everything you spend in a physical journal, an app, or my personal favorite, notes on your phone. You can grab a template in the toolkit!

- **Spend in cash (when possible).** Paying for things in cash usually feels a lot more "real" and painful than swiping a credit card. It's important to note that this isn't the case for everyone. If cash feels more like Monopoly money to you (you know who you are!), skip this step.

- **Unsave or don't save your credit card information.** If you have to manually type in your credit card info (rather than it syncing automatically), it adds an extra step and forces some awareness when you make a purchase.

Expense	Jan	Feb	March	April	May	June	July	Aug	Sept	Oct	Nov	Dec	Annual Total
Example: Student Loan Payment	$250	$250	$250	$250	$250	$250	$250	$250	$250	$250	$250	$250	$3,000
Total													

- **Try the 48-hour rule.** Wait 48 hours before buying anything that's not part of your regular spending. You might find that you don't even want it when the impulse wears off.

- **Unsubscribe from sales emails.** If you are always tempted to buy things from your favorite store when you get the 40% sales email, unsubscribe. Why torture yourself? If you aren't ready to take this step, at least have the emails go to a separate folder so you don't see them in your inbox.

- **Do a quick gut check before making a purchase.** What's my current mood? How long have I wanted this item? You might start to notice a trend in when and where you make your impulse purchases.

The Pink Tax

If you're a woman, you pay a pink tax. I spoke with Liz Grauerholz, a sociology professor who studies social inequalities (including the pink tax!). She describes the pink tax as "the practice of charging women more than men for identical services and products." This discrepancy applies to clothes, toys, and healthcare products, among many other things.

According to the New York City Department of Consumer Affairs, women's personal care products cost 13% more than the equivalent men's products and are actually smaller in volume.[2] The pink tax cost the average woman $2,294 in 2021.[3] If we invested that amount annually in the market, that would be over $100,000 in 20 years.[4] I'm enraged. Are you?

Liz shares some things we can do but stresses that "the burden shouldn't rest on the individual consumer to force change. It's important for communities and states to enact policies dictating fair pricing."

- Support companies with gender-neutral pricing and companies that take a stand against the pink tax (they are out there!).

- Buy more gender-neutral products when shopping for toys, razors, shampoos, deodorant, and other personal care products.

- Avoid the dry cleaner's as much as possible. End of story.

- Compare prices when shopping (this goes for personal care products but also when buying cars and mortgages).
- Talk to your state representatives, local retailers, and on social media and speak up when you see price discrepancies. In certain states you can report it.
- Question unfair pricing when you see it. Liz admits this is hard to do but says you can start by getting curious. At your hair place you might ask, "What's the price of a basic cut?" and then "Is that the same for men and women?" They might make all kinds of justifications but you've brought it up, and that's a win.

Set Up a Sinking Fund

Large irregular expenses are one of the most common ways our financial plans get derailed. A big expense like a vacation, the holidays, or your quarterly homeowner's association (HOA) fee can make cash for the month tight or not workable. Then you have to pull money from your rainy-day fund or put the expense on a credit card to deal with later. It can feel like we're always taking two steps forward and one step back. *Blah.*

The good news is there's a solution that works – enter sinking funds. Sinking funds get their name because they are money we set aside just to sink (or spend). A sinking fund is meant to be spent on something specific; it's different from your rainy-day fund, which is money set aside in case of an emergency.

For example, if I know I plan to spend $750 in December for Chanukah, I can set aside $62.50 per month or $31.25 twice per month in a holiday fund; $31 per paycheck feels way better than $750 all at once. And when December rolls around, I have $750 in my account waiting for me to spend. Sounds good, right? Here's how to set up your sinking funds.

Make a List

List out your large irregular expenses. Large is relative, and irregular means that they don't happen every week or month – this can even be something that's happening in a year or two. Keep it as simple as possible at first (you can always add more later). Include expenses that aren't workable (or don't work well) with your current income. They might have given you trouble in the past or you know you don't have room in your regular paychecks to cover them.

Some common ones: travel, the holidays, annual subscriptions or expenses, tuition, camp, birthdays, shopping, moving, medical bills (sometimes your deductible), family care expenses, and vet bills. If you notice that a random thing comes up every quarter but you're not sure what it will be, set up a catch-all sinking fund for that. Some like to use sinking funds to build room for some spontaneity in their budgets. If you set money aside each paycheck, and a random fun thing comes up, you will have money set aside to say yes to it.

If you're like me and this concept makes you really excited, yay! But don't go too wild and create a bazillion sinking funds. Start simple, with one or two to get the hang of it; you can always add more from there.

List out some potential sinking funds.

1. _____

2. _____

3. _____

4. _____

5. _____

Price the Expenses Out

Write down how much each of your large irregular expenses costs (or make an estimate) and count the number of paychecks you have until you want to use the money. Divide the cost by the number of paychecks and *voilà* – that's the amount you want to set aside per paycheck.

You don't have to contribute to your sinking funds once per paycheck if a different frequency like monthly or weekly works better for you. Some who have larger bills like rent, mortgage, or loan payments come out the first of the month might prefer to have their sinking funds come out once a month after the second paycheck. Or if the per-paycheck numbers feel daunting, some find that breaking them up into weekly transfers can make it seem more manageable.

You can see how it's easy to feel like you have extra money to spend (or save) with each paycheck when some or all of it is already accounted for by these upcoming larger expenses. This gets us in trouble.

Sinking Fund	Total Cost	# of Periods Until You Want the Money	Transfer Amount
Example: Chanukah Fund	$750	12 months	$62.50

Give Them a Home

The next step is deciding where the money from each paycheck will actually go. I'm a fan of opening separate online savings accounts (a.k.a. high-yield savings accounts) for each sinking fund. That way, each dollar has a clear job and you can see all of the accounts with their respective nicknames when you log in. This all should be completely free and – bonus – the money earns a bit of interest.

Most importantly, your sinking funds are out of sight, out of mind. Even though we can transfer the money over in a few days, it feels less accessible because it's not an immediate transfer like the money in our savings accounts attached to our checking and we usually don't check in on it as frequently. You can find a list of my favorite accounts in the Financial Adulting toolkit (**financialadultingbook.com**). These accounts are also a great place to keep your rainy-day fund!

Do you already have an online savings account? If not, where will you open one?

_____

_____

_____

Make Them Automatic

Once you have your accounts set up, arrange for an automatic transfer to be made to each of your sinking funds each paycheck (or whatever frequency you choose). When it's time to make a purchase, like paying for a flight for an upcoming trip, you can transfer over the amount from your sinking fund to your checking account.

Adding Sinking Funds to Your Financial Plan

I have a sinking funds section as part of my expenses in my financial plan. Each sinking fund has its own line item and I include the amount that goes to the fund each paycheck (rather than the amount I spent). That's because the money transferred to your sinking funds is reflected in your bank account balance (even before you spend it). You can keep track of how much you've spent from your sinking funds in another area so you can stay on plan and adjust your monthly transfer amount if what you expect to spend changes.

Have you set up automatic transfers? If you aren't ready to do this yet, come back to it once your plan is looking good. Have you added your sinking funds to your expense list?

_____

_____

_____

Plan for Pitfalls

The following are some common expense planning pitfalls and how you can avoid them.

Making Your Plan Too Complicated

When you make a plan, watch out for being a bit (or very) overzealous with the categories. I've been there. For example, you might decide to break out your food expenses into groceries, lunch, dinner, takeout/delivery, snacks, and drinks categories. That can end up feeling very overwhelming and tedious to track. Start with a simple "food" category or two categories: "groceries" and "takeout/delivery." You can always break things down into more detail once you get the hang of it or find that more detail in a certain area would be helpful.

Unrealistic or Too-Optimistic Planning

After seeing that you spend more than you'd like on Lyfts, you delete the app and vow never to take a Lyft again. This might work for a week or two but going cold turkey or not including an expense that will most likely come up again just sets us up to fail. For most of us, really restrictive plans don't work. And even if you're one of the few who can make it work, restrictive plans rob us of a lot of fun.

Try to make the estimates as realistic as possible. If you want to make changes, that's great. Usually it works best to let yourself ease into them. It takes time to build new habits.

Excluding "Small" Things

Sometimes in an effort to keep things simple, we decide to leave out the "small" expenses. These can't make a difference, right? Sadly, they can. Depending on how many there are and how often they happen, leaving them out or always rounding down can make the difference between meeting our goals and not. I know it's annoying but we need to include them.

The same goes for guessing at our expenses. Most of us have a tendency to guess lower than reality (hey, we're optimists!) and if we're doing this with a lot of expenses, it can really add up. It's okay to guess-timate for things you're unsure of but if the information is available, take the time to look up what the expense actually is.

Planning for Four-Week Months

If you plan your expenses as if there are four weeks in a month, you're going to be over budget. There are 52 weeks in a year, so by figuring that each month has four weeks ($12 \times 4 = 48$), we're missing four weeks or assuming that during those four weeks we spend no money at all. That's not going to work out well. Let's say you spend $150 per week on food. Instead of saying $600 per month ($150 × 4), you'll want to plan for 4.33 weeks in a month (52 weeks/12 months). Or to be most accurate, you can look at the calendar each month to see how many weeks there are that month. The extra $50 ($650 vs. $600) might not seem like much, but over the year that adds up to $600 that we're not accounting for. And that's in just that one category.

Time to Incorporate Your Goals

Now that you have your income, expenses, and sinking funds mapped out in your financial plan, it's time to add a section for your goals. I like my goals to be the first section after my income so my goals are top of mind (literally). For the goals section, refer back to your plan in Chapter 3. There will be a line for each goal and the amount you are putting toward that goal each month. You can also include a sum of all your goals so you can see what you are contributing toward all your goals each month.

Putting It All Together

You now have everything you need to put your financial plan together. Your plan will calculate this monthly and for the year. For your plan to work, meaning that you're "in the black" or there's enough money coming in to cover your expenses and goals, this equation has to equal 0 or more than 0.

Goals	Jan	Feb	March	April	May	June	July	Aug	Sept	Oct	Nov	Dec	Annual Total
Example: Rainy-Day Fund	$250	$250	$250	$250	$250	$250	$250	$250	$250	$250	$250	$250	$3,000
Total													

Total annual income – Total annual expenses (including sinking funds)
– $$$ for our goals = 0

If the amount remaining is positive, you have some extra left over after your expenses and your goals. If the number is negative, you don't have enough income coming in to cover the expenses and goals you included. Now, for most people, this number is negative at first – sometimes very negative. It was for me. That's okay. It's much better to

Your Annual Financial Plan

Total Annual Income		Total Annual Expenses (including sinking funds)		Total Annual Goal Contribu- tions		What's Remain- ing or Missing
Example: $50,000	–	$40,000	–	$10,000	=	0
$	–		–		=	

Your Monthly Financial Plan

Total Monthly Income		Total Monthly Expenses (including sinking funds)		Total Monthly Goal Contribu- tions		What's Remain- ing or Missing
Example: $4,167	–	$3,333	–	$833	=	0
$	–		–		=	

know this and have the chance to try to do something about it than to not know and stress as you see your credit card debt increase.

Also, the first version of your plan is usually pretty inaccurate. Until we live our plan for a few months and see how it compares to our actual expenses, it might not reflect reality. If over time you find that the numbers are accurate and you aren't able to put as much toward your goals as you'd like, that's also okay. We'll cover some strategies in the next chapters and if you haven't read it yet, *The 30-Day Money Cleanse* has some amazing tools to decrease spending without giving up the things you love (there's a link in the Financial Adulting toolkit).

For the Love of Money: Financial Planning with Partners

If your partner's finances affect you, include them in your financial plans. I find that one of the most effective ways to do this is by having expenses broken out into three sections: one section for each person plus a section for expenses that are funded or assigned jointly.

Keeping things broken out this way in your financial plan spreadsheet can hold you and your partner accountable for what's yours. If you have kids, each kid can have their own section as well.

Money can be a sensitive topic (or let's be real, one of the most sensitive and stressful topics) to talk about with a partner. If you don't have a lot of experience or haven't had a great experience with these conversations, here are some ideas:

- **Start with the fun part.** What are your goals? What do both of you envision and want for the short term and long term and what does that mean financially? If you haven't yet, go through the exercises in Chapter 3 together.

- **Go below the surface.** Instead of sharing how mad you are that your partner went over budget again (believe me, I've been there), share *why* that stresses you out. Are you worried about paying off your debt? Are you afraid you'll end up like your parents who filed for bankruptcy? Talking about *why* something matters or upsets us can help get to the real issue rather than feel like an attack.

- **Do some problem-solving.** If you notice that certain things continue to be stressful over time or there are certain areas that your plans get out of whack, take a step back, play detective, come up with some possible solutions, and test one out. Maybe you need a new sinking fund category or maybe your budget isn't realistic for both you and your partner.
- **Set a spending threshold.** Decide together on a number or threshold for spending. For anything above that amount (that's outside of your normal bills), you talk about it first. For example, you might decide that you talk about any purchases over $50 together first. This limits the number of surprises that show up at the door.
- **Share about your upbringing and culture.** Sharing about our upbringing and culture helps our partner understand where we're coming from. Share how your family interacted and currently interacts with money. What's the first money conversation you remember having or your first money memory?
- **Know your money personality.** Brian Walsh, a CFP and PhD in personal finance with SoFi, shared that knowing his own money personality (a money avoider) made it easier for him to make a system with his wife. While he enjoyed being involved in the overall strategy, she was much more adept at executing it given her money personality. Once they shifted roles, things went a lot more smoothly.

Pay Yourself First

If you've tried to put money toward your goals (paying down debt, saving, investing) in the past and were unsuccessful, you might be feeling skeptical that it will work this time around. I understand that. Here's why this time is different.

Many of us (I used to be one) wait and see what's left over at the end of the month before we save. When we do it this way (unless you are one of the few unicorns who can do this – you know who you are), there will never be any money left over to save. Some expenses (or many expenses) always come up. It happens over and over again.

In order to save for our goals, we need to pay ourselves first. That means setting up an automatic transfer to get the money out of our checking accounts to wherever we want it to go. This way we're treating paying ourselves like we would any other bill.

If you were able to make your financial plan equation work, take your goals plan (how much, how often, and where) and set up automatic deposits for each of your goals. If you're worried about the automatic transfers, add calendar reminders that tell you when and how much will be coming out of your checking account. Even if your financial plan needs more finesse, it's important to start. Set up a small transfer (even $5) to your top-priority goal (or two goals). You can come back and increase the amount after your plans come together.

How will you pay yourself first?

How Much?	How Often?	Where?
Example: $250	Monthly	Rainy-Day Fund (high-yield savings account)

If You Need It – the Health and Safety Budget

If you're really struggling to make your budget work, or you really need to decrease your spending as much as possible, let's talk about a health and safety budget. Tiffany Aliche, The Budgetnista and bestselling author of *Get Good With Money* you met in Chapter 2, shares that when we experience some type of financial trauma like losing a job (or impending loss of a job) or face a high unexpected expense, "our knee-jerk reaction is to try to figure out how to maintain our current lifestyle. But it should actually be to protect ourselves" and our health and safety.

To create your health and safety budget, ask yourself what expenses you need to maintain your health and safety. Tiffany gives the example of an inhaler for someone who has asthma. If I don't have this inhaler, will I be unhealthy? Will I be unsafe? If it's a yes, it's part of the health and safety budget. Your cable bill, on the other hand, is probably not important for your health and safety.

List out the expenses that you need to maintain your health and safety.

_____   _____   _____

_____   _____   _____

_____   _____   _____

_____   _____   _____

_____   _____   _____

Then Tiffany suggests "calling the other providers you pay and letting them know you might be late or delayed." Some will offer hardship programs and others won't, but "you are your first priority, not your bills or expenses."

Whom do you need to call to tell them you might be late or delayed or to inquire about financial hardship programs?

1. _____

2. _____

3. _____

4. _____

5. _____

Set Up Your Net Worth Tracker

I mentioned in Chapter 4 that your financial plan also includes a current snapshot of where your money is and what you owe. We're going to put that together now. Our net worth is a fancy way of saying what we have, minus what we owe. When someone says the word "millionaire" or "billionaire," they are referring to someone's net worth.

First and foremost – our net worth has absolutely nothing to do with our worth as a person. We too often conflate the two. And with good reason – it's part of our culture and our society. If the term *net worth* carries too much weight for you, feel free to rename it. You can call it your "numbers," "totals," or even something more fun, like your "treasure count."

Here's how to set up your net worth tracker. You can calculate it in the space in this section or by using the downloadable version in the toolkit.

Start with What You Own

First, list all the things you own (also called your assets). For clarity purposes, I like to give each account or item its own line. It's a handy way to keep track of which accounts you have and where. Some examples of the things you may own:

- Bank account balances
- The value of your investment accounts
- The market value of your home
- Your car (if you own, not lease it)
- Personal property like jewelry, art, wine, and furniture
- Anything else you could sell that has value

Then add them all up. This amount is your total assets.

Things You Own/Your Assets	Amount
Example: Bank Account	$550
Total Assets:	

Add Up What You Owe

Then list all the things you owe (also called liabilities). I like to give each credit card or loan its own line item. Here are some examples of things you may owe:

- Credit card balances
- Mortgage
- Car loan
- Student loans
- Personal loans
- Money you borrowed from a family member

Then add them all up. This amount is your total liabilities.

Things You Owe/Your Liabilities	Amount
Example: Credit Card Balance	$1,000
Total Liabilities:	

Calculate Your Net Worth

Then all that's left to do is to subtract what you owe from what you own. This is where you stand right now. Where it really gets fun is that we'll update this number once per quarter and you can see the progress you've made.

Assets	–	Liabilities	=	Net Worth
Example: $10,000	–	$1,000	=	$9,000
	–		=	

Why Does It Matter?

Updating your net worth each month can be really motivating and help you see your progress. Fun is good! It also keeps us honest about our progress (since it provides a full picture of our finances) as our financial lives get more and more complicated. I might see my bank balances increasing and think that I'm making headway toward my goals, only to find that my credit card balances are also increasing. If I track my net worth, I'll see that it isn't actually increasing even though individual account balances are. And finally, keeping track of your net worth also gives you a great financial snapshot and then you don't have to keep a running list of your accounts in your head.

For the Love of Money: Protect Your Assets

Lauren Hunt, divorce attorney extraordinaire, firmly advocates for a **prenup** (a prenuptial agreement) if you're getting married, a **postnup** (postnuptial agreement) if you're already married, or a **cohabitation agreement** if you're living together and not married. These agreements describe your wishes for your assets (and living situation) in the case you get a divorce or break up.

Lauren recommends starting with any specific worries you have and working to address those first. From there, you can add in additional terms to address any side items that appear. There is usually one person in the relationship (which, surprise! usually happens to be the woman) who would experience more financial insecurity in the case of a divorce or breakup.

While many of us agree that these are really important conversations and agreements to have, we dread bringing up the topic. How unromantic is it to plan for divorce before we even get married? I know I thought this!

Lauren offers an important reframe. "To me, when someone is asking you to sign a prenup, it's really saying that if we hit a rocky point (which every marriage does), we want to be able to stay focused on saving the marriage." That's actually really romantic when you think about it!

I asked Lauren a lot of questions about setting up bank accounts with a partner. What I didn't realize is that if you have one of these agreements in place, it really doesn't matter how you set it up because you are protected by the agreement. So you can set up your joint finances in whatever way suits your fancy. Lovely!

If you don't have an agreement in place, be very conscious of what the laws in your state say.

Your Financial Adulting Action Items

- ☐ Map out your expenses for the next 12 months (this is a one-liner but it's a biggie!).
- ☐ Test out some strategies to become more aware of your spending.
- ☐ Do what you can to avoid the pink tax.
- ☐ Create sinking funds for your larger irregular expenses.
- ☐ Put the pieces of your plan together – income, goals, expenses, and sinking funds.
- ☐ If you are looking to decrease your expenses and align your spending with your values, do The 30-Day Money Cleanse.
- ☐ Set up a health and safety budget if you need it.

☐ Pay yourself first.

☐ Set up your net worth tracker.

☐ If you have a partner, understand what would happen financially in the case of a divorce or breakup. Consider getting a prenup, postnup, or cohabitation agreement.

You've now mapped out your goals, income, and expenses. and put the pieces all together. You have a completed (but not final) financial plan. That's a huge accomplishment! If it doesn't look how you had hoped, you're not alone and that's okay. I have strategies for you in the next chapter, and we're also going to talk about using your money for doing good in the world.

CHAPTER 6

Consumer Activism

Next we're going to talk about consumer activism. The exercises in this chapter will increase the positive impact you have in the world with your money, which also typically has the wonderful side effect of decreasing the amount you spend.

What Is Consumer Activism?

Consumer activism means using your dollars to support or vote for things you believe in. It also means boycotting (or *not* using your dollars to support) companies that have values or take actions that are in opposition to what you want to support. The idea is that when we buy or don't buy something, our group buying power can influence companies to change their practices and policies.

Consumer activism can mean buying (or not buying) your everyday products or services from companies that believe and support the same values as you. It can also be in the form of giving to nonprofit organizations doing work that's important to you, and there are also opportunities to invest our money in ways that have an impact (we cover investing in Chapter 8). In order to become a consumer activist, we need to decide what our activism looks like.

Some Consumer Activism Inspo

For me, it's always helpful to learn and get inspiration from what others are doing. Sometimes this whole process can feel very abstract and overwhelming but Tanja Hester, author of *Wallet Activism*, maintains that it's worth it: "The collective good needs you." I've included Tanja's framework for making financial decisions in the following section. I also interviewed Georgia Lee Hussey, the founder and CEO of Modernist Financial whom you've already met, and Kara Perez, the founder of Bravely Go. All three are conscious consumers, activists, and financial educators.

It's important to note that this is what their criteria looked like at this point in time, and, just like yours, their criteria may change and evolve.

From Tanja: She gives us four guiding questions to ask before making a decision in order to make "choices that promote real change." Use this framework for your biggest, most impactful choices.

1. **For whom?** Does the proposed action serve those who truly need the change, because they have the most disadvantages, or does it largely serve those who already have lots of advantages?

2. **Can everyone do this?** Is this choice that I'm considering something everyone can do? And, if everyone did it, would that be sustainable? If not everyone can do it, what does that tell me?

3. **Is it too cheap?** Is something priced so low that it could not possibly have been produced or couldn't be offered without exploitation of people, the planet, or both?

4. **What am I funding?** What type of world am I helping create if I contribute profits to the entity offering something?

From Kara: Here's how she defines her process.

1. **What's the best choice for the planet?** Because we all need the planet.

   Kara asks herself questions like "Where are they sourcing their materials? Are they using recycled ocean plastic? Where are they producing this? What does the packaging look like?"

   She not only looks at the item itself but also thinks about how hard it will be to get the item to her door in Austin, Texas (and how much gas will be used). "Maybe there's a company doing the exact same thing that's closer to me."

2. **What's the best choice for underrepresented communities?**

Kara says, "Each community has its own needs and challenges; buying criteria that work for a single, queer white woman in LA might not work for a parent on the Cherokee Nation in Oklahoma. I think it's important for people to make ethical decisions within their own framework and reality." Kara asks the following questions to see if she can actively send money into certain communities: "Are any of these companies I'm looking at women-owned or BIPOC owned? How much are they paying people? How do they treat their workers?"

3. **What's in my budget?**

Then she looks at prices and her budget. Maybe she can't get everything she needs from a more expensive place but she can pick and choose for certain things.

From Georgia: Here's how she focuses her spending.

- For Georgia, company labor practices and workers' rights are number one. She shares, "I just want people to be treated fairly. It's ultimately about relationships and kindness."

- When possible, she shops small and local (avoiding big-box retailers). When you spend $1 at a local business, $0.68 stays in your local economy versus $0.43 for a large retailer.[1] But because labor practices and workers' rights are her number one, she shares, "if I am on a road trip and there is no local coffee to be had, I will happily spend my money at Starbucks because Starbucks pays for f***ing undergraduate degrees and healthcare."

- She also supports companies with headquarters in her area because it keeps a lot of resources local.

- For clothes, she buys secondhand or consignment pieces. She shares, "Fast fashion gives me hives." Otherwise, she has one or two pieces per year made by a local fashion designer. "He's made me clothes that I'm still wearing 15, 16 years later. It's not cheap but it fits me perfectly, is exactly what I want, and it supports a local maker." If you want to check him out, his website is Adam-Arnold.com.

Your Consumer Activism Criteria

Think about what's important to you. What criteria will you think about before supporting a company?

What are your consumer activist criteria?

Consumer Activist Criteria	Ranking
Example: Woman or BIPOC-Owned	1

Rank each of your criteria in order of most important to least important. If that's impossible, it's okay if there are some ties.

It's important to note that it's a tremendous privilege to be able to make choices with a consumer activist lens. Many people can't choose a more expensive option because the company is making better choices. Many don't have time to do this type of research given work and caregiving schedules. If you don't have this privilege, it's important to take care of your own needs first. It's okay to pick and choose where you can be a consumer activist. It's okay to start small and work your way up.

Sometimes Not Buying Anything at All Is the Best Option

During our interview, Tanja shared that she often bristles at the phrase *consumer activism* because it frames us as a consumer. It's easy to forget that sometimes the best strategy for our wallets and the environment is to just not buy anything at all.

She gave the example of buying beautiful "eco-friendly" steel containers to replace the plastic ones in our kitchens. "Now we are throwing out the plastic containers and buying new products, and steel is incredibly resource-intensive to make." I did this exact thing and didn't realize that I was double-spending and making a less environmentally friendly decision.

Sometimes a quick pause and gut check before we buy something can help. If, after you do a gut check, you decide that you do need to buy something, ask yourself: "Can I buy it used?" or "Can I use something I already have?"

Use Your Voice

In addition to voting with your dollars, you can use your voice. If there's a brand you love but wish they were doing things differently and better, tell them! On the other end, you can champion companies that are doing things that line up with your values. When a company hires a Black CEO or switches to compostable packaging, that's something we can shout from the rooftops to show that we care.

Do a Consumer Activism Spending Audit

Now it's time for your first spending audit. Look at each of your expenses (from Chapter 5) through your consumer activist lens and assign each a number on a scale of 1–5, with 1 being *not* aligned with your consumer activism criteria and 5 being *completely* aligned. If the 1–5 scale feels overwhelming, you can start with a simple Yes or No.

Where to do this: If your spending plan is in a spreadsheet, you can add a column to the left of each of your expenses. If you wrote your spending plan in the book, write the number next to it in a different color. I've also given you room to do it in this section. I included the total spend amount for the year so you can see how much of your money is going to each category. This can help you prioritize, as you may want to make changes first where you're spending more money.

You can find a list of resources to do consumer activism research in the Financial Adulting toolkit.

A lot of our consumer activism won't be a clear yes or no. Companies are big and complicated entities made up of many people, past actions, and future actions. There's a lot of gray in here so get ready for a very imperfect journey.

Expense	Annual Spend	Consumer Activism Rating
Example: Bath Products	$150	5

You might not think your rent has a consumer activism rating, but Tanja reminded me that living close to work or public transportation changes your commute and the climate impact. You can also take your research further and look at your spending as a whole. How much of your spending goes to highly aligned items versus spending that doesn't? If you want to support BIPOC-owned businesses, what percentage of your spending goes there? Or if it's important that companies pay a living wage, how many on your list pay at or above $15 per hour? You can look at each of your expenses individually and then as a whole to get a more comprehensive picture.

Remember, this is all about research and evaluating – no changes to be made yet.

Make Note of Anything You'd Like to Shift

Going through a spending audit can be *very* eye opening. There might be things we know we'd like to shift ASAP and others that are less urgent or more on the cusp. You might decide that you want to support local bookstores instead of buying from Amazon, or discover that only 5% of your expenses go toward women-owned businesses.

In the following exercise, make a list of each of the spending items you'd like to shift or, if you don't want to rewrite them, put a star next to them in your financial plan or highlight them. Wait to act on any of these until the next exercise.

1.	6.
2.	7.
3.	8.
4.	9.
5.	10.

Take It Step by Step

If you're feeling overwhelmed by where your money is going and the changes you want to make, I was (and often still am) right there with you. If you're feeling nauseous by what you found from your research, I know. But the good news is that it's much better to know and be able to make changes than to not know what your dollars are supporting (although it sometimes doesn't feel that way!).

Now it's time to make a plan, and it's okay to take it step by step. We'll always be learning. As Tanja says, "It's not about perfection. It's not about shaming yourself. It's doing what we can."

Cancel Anything You Don't Need

The first, easiest, step to take is to cancel any expenses for things you no longer want. This could be a bill or subscription that doesn't align with your criteria and is something you don't think you'll miss. Canceling saves you money right away because you're eliminating expenses. You can cross these off your to-do list first.

Make a Commitment to Switch over One Recurring Item per Month

On the list of expenses you'd like to change, how many (that you didn't want to cancel) are recurring? What's great about recurring expenses is that once we do the research and make the switch, our spending will continue to go to those places indefinitely. You can commit to switch a recurring expense once per month (or even more frequently if you want). For example, I switched where I get my eyebrows done (something I do once every six weeks) to a local Black-owned salon. I also now get my shampoo and conditioner from a certified B-Corp.

Some of Our Spending Is Meta

Some of our expense items won't show us the full picture. For example, we might shop at a certain grocery store, but we're also making many smaller spending choices while shopping there. For the grocery store (and other places like it), you can make a commitment to researching the brands you buy on a regular basis. If you go to the grocery store every two weeks, you might research one new item each time you go. You might start with your salad dressing this week and your breakfast bar the next.

It Doesn't Have to Be All or Nothing

When we get into all-or-nothing thinking it can become easy to feel so unmotivated that we do nothing. When I get in this mindset, I catch myself thinking things like, "What's the point, anyway?" All we can do is commit to doing better and better over time. I talk about tracking your progress in Chapter 14, which helps keep motivation up!

What's your consumer activist plan? List out what actions you are going to take and by when. I recommend mapping out your action items for the next three months or so.

Action	By When
Example: Research one new food item each time I grocery shop	Next grocery trip on Monday

Don't Forget About Banks

Where we bank is a financial decision that votes for our values over and over again. This is something Tanja feels very strongly about. "Nobody is talking about ethical banking and it's actually much more impactful than ethical investing. There is a direct line between the money in your savings account and fossil fuel lending."

Let me explain. One of the ways that banks make money is by lending out the money we've deposited. They pay us for the money in our savings account (let's say 0.01%), lend the money out (let's say for 7%), and keep the difference.

"So you know the Dakota Access Pipeline?" Tanja says. "You don't like it. You hate it. Well, it's funded by Chase and Wells Fargo using the money in your checking and savings accounts."[2,3] There are some resources to check how your bank stacks up in the Financial Adulting toolkit. Tanja shares that you can also search your bank's name with the terms *ECOA violation*, *FHA violation*, and *lending discrimination* to see if they are a repeat offender.

How does your bank stack up?

_____

_____

_____

Black-Owned Banks

Due to racial discrimination, the Black community hasn't had access to banking products and services either at all or in the same way that white folks have. Many banks didn't accept Black customers and still today, racial discrimination happens so frequently that there is a hashtag dedicated to "Banking While Black" that describes instances of tellers calling 911 for a customer wanting to cash a check, bank employees using racial slurs, and Black customers being denied service.

Black-owned banks were created to serve the Black community and are at least 51% Black-owned. Many are also actively working to close the racial wealth gap. They play an important role in fighting systemic racism and discrimination in the financial sector. By switching to a Black-owned bank, you are supporting that mission and giving the bank a better chance to thrive and grow. You are taking a stand for financial inclusion and equality.

How Do I Choose My Bank?

It's important to take your own banking needs into account. If you bank from your phone, make sure the bank has a user-friendly app. If you use the ATM on a regular basis, understand how ATM fees work.

Any bank you choose should be FDIC- or NCUA-insured, which means that if something were to happen to the bank, your money would be protected (for anything up to $250,000).

If you send money back home to family in other countries, those types of international transfers might not be possible with all banks or might come with a much higher fee at some banks than others. This is where tradeoffs in our decisions come in. Sending money back home is an act of consumer activism in itself. You might decide to stick with your current bank to make that happen for a lower cost, but the tradeoff is worth it to you.

Like with anything in our finances, switching doesn't have to be all or nothing or right away. If it feels overwhelming to switch over everything, start by opening a savings or checking account with a new bank.

What are some things that are important to you in a bank as far as how you bank? Feel free to take notes here as you do your research.

_____

_____

_____

_____

_____

If you'd like more info on how to open a bank account and the different types of accounts, head to the Financial Adulting toolkit.

Cultivate a Practice of Giving

If you have the opportunity and financial privilege, your spending plan should include giving. This could be by giving to nonprofits, mutual aid organizations, family members, or other individuals. It could be by giving money, but also donating goods and services and/or your time. Money isn't the only resource we have to give.

We can get caught up in all the details around giving, but just doing it is more important than exactly how we do it. Tanja shared, "It doesn't matter if you do a bunch of small donations, bigger chunks, spread it around different places or combine it into one place – just give." This approach was honestly a relief. She shares, "Most nonprofits are doing so much incredible work with limited resources. These are people and organizations who really care." If you want to do some research before giving, you can use GuideStar and Charity Navigator to evaluate nonprofits.

Through my work and personal financial life, I've found that giving is a lot like saving. If you wait until you think you have enough money, you'll never get started. If you want to start giving, choose an organization that is doing work you're passionate about (you might already have one in mind!), start with a small automatic contribution, and you can work your way up from there.

That being said, it's important to take care of yourself first. If you are struggling financially, it's important to wait to give. If you are paying off high-interest credit card debt or trying to build your emergency savings, I'd recommend you wait to start giving.

Also check if your employer matches donations. It's a great (and often overlooked) way to double your contributions without increasing how much you give.

Do you want to make an adjustment to your giving plan (or create your giving plan)? How much and how often will you give? Remember to keep your motivation in mind.

How Much/How Often	Where
Example: $200/month	Room to Grow

For the Love of Money: Consumer Activism with a Partner

If you make a lot of your financial decisions with your partner, you will want to bring them into the consumer activism conversation. If they aren't on board at all, start with changes that mostly impact you. When you want to incorporate some joint changes, make sure to share with your partner why the change is important to you. If they are hesitant or are fully against it, try to understand why. For example, maybe they aren't up for switching banks because of the time and hassle. Is there a way you can support them in making the transition? Or maybe they're worried that making a switch to a more ethical brand will cost more money. Can you show them how it works within your spending plan and that eliminating a different expense makes up the difference?

Update Changes in Your Spending Plan

You'll notice that in most chapters and in many of the financial actions we take, there will be updates to your spending plans. As you cancel any expenses, you can remove them from your plan going forward. If the last section had you revamp your plan for giving, make sure to update that as well.

Your Financial Adulting Action Items

- ☐ Create your consumer activist criteria.
- ☐ Conduct a spending audit.
- ☐ Make a consumer activism plan for your spending.
- ☐ Evaluate where you bank and potentially make a switch.
- ☐ If you have the opportunity to do so, create your giving plan. If your company matches employee donations, make sure to get your donations matched!
- ☐ Update these changes (spending and giving) in your financial plan.

You are now a consumer activist. You know what spending is important to you and what types of companies you want to support with your business. As consumer activists we can always grow and do better. This will be something we revisit on a regular basis throughout our money journeys (I show you how in Chapter 14). Now, we're going to move on to how to make your money grow. It's time to talk investing!

CHAPTER 7

Work Optional (a.k.a. Retirement)

Retirement can sound like a snooze-fest because unless you're close to retiring, you are saving for something that is very far away. It's hard to say no to money now to reap the rewards much later. But the benefits are big.

The Power of Compound Interest

When it comes to investing (for retirement and otherwise), especially when we're starting early, there's a beautiful phenomenon called **compound interest** that helps our money grow exponentially. Look at this chart:

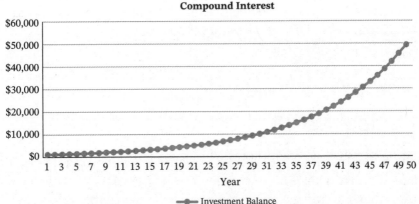

Oh, it's beautiful! How it works: You invest $1,000 and it grows by 8% each year. Over the past 30 years the S&P 500, which is often used as a proxy for the market, has had an annual return of 8.29% (adjusting for inflation). After the first year you have $1,083, by year 15 you have $3,302, and at year 50 you have $53,631 (over 53× what you started with).

"Fun" poll: Would you rather have a penny that doubles for 30 days or $1,000,000?

Drumroll . . .

On day 30 the doubling penny would be almost $5.4 million. Well, that escalated quickly.

The rule of 72 states that your estimated return divided by 72 is how long it takes your money to double. What!? So in this case, using 8.29%, your money would double every nine years. Not bad.

TLDR (but please always read): The earlier you start, the more time you're giving your money to compound and grow exponentially.

What Does Retirement *Actually* Mean?

Retirement means work is optional. *Work optional* is a term I learned from our friend Tanja Hester (her first book was titled *Work Optional*). Retirement is often associated with an age, but work optional is the point in your life at which you no longer need to work to pay your bills.

You have saved enough money (in what may be called a nest egg) that you can live off your investments. Your income is made up of a combination of your investment returns (or investment growth and dividends) and selling the investments themselves.

Where Do We Keep This Magical Nest Egg?

One of the first ways we invest is via our 401(k). It's a great place to start and a great place to learn about investing. A **401(k)** is a company-sponsored retirement plan. If we have a 401(k) plan with our employer, we can elect to have a certain percentage of our salary taken out and contributed to this plan.

At the very least, we want to maximize our company **401(k) matching** because it's free money our company gives us for investing in our own retirement. Wait, what? Yes, free money. Well, not *actually* free – it's part of your total compensation and if you're not maximizing your match, you're leaving money on the table.

401(k) Matching

If your employer offers 401(k) matching, you will typically see it offered as a percentage of your salary – let's say 3%. That means that if you contribute 3% to your 401(k), your company will match it (i.e., double it). If you contribute 4%, your company will still contribute 3%. If you contribute 1%, your company will contribute 1%. If you earn $75,000, your company match can total $2,250 (3%). That's a 100% return on your first $2,250 of contributions!

Does your company offer 401(k) matching?   ☐ Yes   ☐ No

If so, how much (usually a % of salary)? _____

How much are you contributing? _____

Even if your employer doesn't match, there are major tax benefits to contributing to a 401(k).

1. The amount you contribute can reduce your taxable income. Off the bat, you're paying less in taxes and this could even put you in a lower tax bracket.

2. The investments grow tax-free. In your non-retirement accounts, you have to pay taxes on your profit (more on this in Chapter 8); in your retirement accounts, you don't. These accounts grow and compound for many years, so not paying taxes on this profit will end up saving you a *lot* of money. Depending on the type of account, you may have to pay taxes when you take the money out of it (more on this soon).

If Your Employer Doesn't Offer a 401(k)

- You can open an IRA (individual retirement account) on your own.
- If you run your own business, you can open a self-employed retirement plan.
- If you work for a nonprofit, you may have a 403(b) that will function very similarly to a 401(k).
- If you work for the federal government, you may have a Basic Benefit plan (a pension) and a Thrift Savings Plan (TSP), which operates a lot like a 401(k). State and local government employees receive similar options with different names.
- If you are a teacher. it's more complicated. I sat down with Dan Otter, the founder of 403bwise, a nonprofit that helps teachers better understand their retirement plans and advocates for access to lower-cost investment choices. I have a must-read guide for you in the Financial Adulting toolkit.

More 401(k) Deets

You elect a certain percentage of your salary to go to your 401(k). The maximum amount you can contribute per year is $20,500 in 2022 (or $27,000 if you are over age 50). The deadline to contribute is December 31st of that year.

It might sound like no fun to have your employer take out part of your paycheck before you even see it, but it feels less painful than it sounds because it's coming out pretax. With your 401(k) you receive a set of investment options to choose from. Some plans have better options than others.

You can withdraw as much money as you want after you're 59½, but if you take money out before then, you pay a 10% penalty (plus the taxes owed). There are exceptions that allow you to take money out without a penalty or you can take out a loan from yourself, but generally, if possible, I like to think of this money as untouchable. We're letting it work its magic.

More IRA Deets

An **IRA (individual retirement account)** is a plan that you can open up on your own (without your employer). You can contribute up to $6,000 in 2022 (or $7,000 if you are over 50 years old). The deadline to contribute is the same as the tax deadline (typically April 15th). This gives you a few more months than a 401(k).

With an IRA, you can invest in anything available to you in your **brokerage account**, which is an account that allows you to deposit money and buy and sell investments. I talk about how to choose one in the next chapter. You can even open a **self-directed IRA** and invest in real estate and alternative investments (anything outside of stocks, bonds, and cash).

The same withdrawal rules apply but vary slightly, depending on whether it's a Roth or Traditional IRA (see the chart in the next section).

What the Heck Does Roth versus Traditional Mean?

Roth and Traditional are essentially tax designations that apply to 401(k)s and IRAs. With a **Roth** account you pay taxes now. With a **Traditional** account you pay taxes when you take the money out. In both accounts, the investments grow tax-free.

Which is better?

"Fun" fact: If your tax rate now is the same as your tax rate when you retire, there is *no* tax difference between what you will owe with a Roth and Traditional account. Cool, right? Yes, I know. My sense of cool is quite warped.

Let's say you earn $100,000, contribute 15% to your 401(k), your income tax rate is 30% both now and when you retire, you're 30 years old, plan to retire at 67 (in 37 years), and you earn 7% return on your investments each year. To keep it simple, let's also say you never earn a raise (I know, that's not cool, but this is pretend, so bear with me).

If you contributed to a Roth 401(k), you'd have $1,683,543 after 37 years. Nice! You wouldn't have to pay any taxes on that money when you take it out. If you contributed to a Traditional 401(k), you'd have $2,405,061 after the same period *but* you'd still have to pay 30% in income taxes when you take the money out. Apply a 30% tax rate to $2,405,061 and you get $1,683,543. The same number!

Generally, if you think you're in a lower tax bracket now than you will be when you plan to take the money out (i.e., you think you'll be earning more then), then it makes more sense to pay taxes now. Important caveat: This assumes tax rates look similar to what they are now when we retire, but we don't actually know what they will be. Paying taxes now can avoid some tax risk in the case taxes go up.

Contributing to a Traditional IRA has another benefit. It can reduce your tax bill now (depending on your income and if you are offered a 401(k) plan at work). More on this in Chapter 11.

There are some other differences between the two. With a Roth IRA, you can take out the amount you've contributed penalty-free. Roth and Traditional 401(k)s have some penalty-free reasons you may take out funds, but ideally, you leave the money in and let it grow!

The Backdoor Is Open

There is a rule that you can only contribute to a Roth IRA if your income is below a certain amount (this does not apply to a Roth 401(k)). Your **MAGI** (**modified adjusted gross income**) must be less than $144,000 for 2022 if you're single and $214,000 if you're married filing jointly.

But if you earn more than the limit and still want to contribute, don't worry. You can do what's called a "backdoor Roth IRA" (for now. . . there is proposed legislation to change this). It's a completely legal way for you to contribute to a Traditional IRA and roll it into a Roth if you earn above the income limit. Another win for high earners.

Here's a summary of the differences between Roth and Traditional IRAs and 401(k)s.

	Traditional IRA	**Roth IRA**
Funded with	Pre-tax $	After-tax $
Contribution limits for 2022	$6,000 ($7,000 if age 50+)	$6,000 ($7,000 if age 50+)
Taxes	Contributions may be tax-deductible; taxes are paid when money is taken out	Contributions are not tax-deductible; no taxes are paid when money is taken out
Generally best for those who believe their tax rate will be	Lower in retirement	Higher in retirement
Income limits	None	$144,000 single; $214,000 married filing jointly (see backdoor)
Required minimum distributions	At age 72	None
Withdrawing $ before 59½ years old	10% penalty on all withdrawals (and income tax)*	The amount contributed can be withdrawn penalty-free; otherwise, 10% penalty*

*Both Roth and Traditional IRAs offer the same penalty-free withdrawal exceptions including up to $10,000 for a home, qualified education expenses, and health insurance premiums, among others.

	Traditional 401(k)	**Roth 401(k)**
Funded with	Pre-tax $	After-tax $
Contribution limits for 2022	$20,500 ($27,000 if age 50+)	$20,500 ($27,000 if age 50+)
Taxes	Contributions may be tax-deductible; taxes are paid when money is taken out	Contributions are not tax-deductible; no taxes are paid when money is taken out
Generally best for those who believe their tax rate will be	Lower in retirement	Higher in retirement

(Continued)

	Traditional 401(k)	Roth 401(k)
Income limits	None	None
Required minimum distributions	At age 72	At age 72
Withdrawing $ before 59½ years old	10% penalty on all withdrawals (and income tax)*	The amount contributed can be withdrawn penalty-free; otherwise, 10% penalty*

*401(k)s may offer exceptions to the withdrawal penalty, including medical bills and permanent disability. Look at the specifics of your plan.

Show Me the Money – How Much?

Lauren Anastasio, a CFP and director of financial advice at Stash (you met her back in Chapter 5), says 15% of your income is a great retirement savings goal for those looking to retire in their mid-to-late 60s and want to maintain a similar lifestyle. We love simple guidelines!

Another general guideline I've heard many times is that you can calculate how much you need to retire by taking the amount you want to earn in retirement and multiply it by 25. So if you want to earn an annual "salary" of $75,000 in retirement, you'd want to have $1.875 million saved. This assumes you take out (or withdraw) 4% of your nest egg each year and need the funds to last for 30 years.

The thing is, when it comes to planning for retirement, there are a lot of variables, many of which we don't and won't know. Like, "How long will I live?" and "How much will life cost then?" Meaning, what will inflation or the rise of prices have been? "How much will my investments grow each year?"

So we do as much as we can and hope for the best.

Just kidding. LOL. What we do is we (or handy online calculators) make very educated assumptions and we check in on our plans each year.

Head to your Financial Adulting toolkit for links to my favorite retirement calculators. I recommend looking at a few to get a range, given that each will use slightly different assumptions. This will tell you how much you need to retire and then how much you want to be contributing now (each year) to get there.

Some information you'll need to use the calculators:

- How much you already have saved for retirement
- Your age
- The age you want to retire
- Your monthly expenses (or how much you want to earn) in retirement

Using the Retirement Calculators

Don't be afraid to play around with the calculators and to try different assumptions. You might plan to retire by 65 but are also curious what it would take to retire by 50. Check out what you'd need in both situations.

When you use some retirement calculators, they'll assume that your spending in retirement will be 70–80% of your current spending. This is an old assumption based on people paying off their homes by the time they retire. Adjust this spending number to what you want or plan to be spending in retirement. This is personal and you set the terms.

Are All Calculators Created Equal?

Rachel Sanborn Lawrence, CFP and lead financial planner at Ellevest, is a fan of calculators that use **Monte Carlo simulation**. Wow, flashback to my corporate finance class in college. This means that instead of running one scenario that assumes a perfect 7% return each year (with a 50% success rate), Rachel runs 1,000 scenarios and chooses a retirement amount where 700 cases are successful (a 70% success rate). What's success? When it comes to retirement, success means you are able to cover your expenses all the way up until the end of your life. Doing this makes your plan more conservative, and you may end up with more money than you need in retirement, but Rachel says (and I concur), "That's a really good problem to have."

Enter in your numbers (or estimates of your numbers) for one to three of the retirement calculators in the Financial Adulting toolkit. Record your results here.

Calculator Name	How Much to Retire	How Much to Contribute
Example: Calculator #1	$2,500,000	$1,600 per month

The Results

If you use the calculators and realize you're behind (or way behind), that's the way it is for most of us. If you haven't started saving for retirement yet or are far from your goal, don't fret (too much). Remember compound interest? Starting small is okay!

I'm a fan of the sneaky increase. You can up your contributions by as little as 1%. Then set a calendar reminder to increase 1% again in four to six weeks. Some 401(k) plans allow for an automatic increase on contributions to make this process easier for you.

If you're not feeling motivated by this faraway goal, look at your face with an age filter. Or look at an older relative and imagine you are them. No, I'm not kidding. A study out of Stanford showed that when participants looked at themselves at a future age, they allocated more than twice as much to their retirement accounts.[1] As you decide how much to contribute, imagine yourself in your 60s or 70s. Your future self will thank you. No, I mean it. Have your older future self thank your current self right now, immediately.

What About Social Security?

Social Security is a program created by Franklin D. Roosevelt to provide an income safety net to the elderly and unemployed. Many of us pay into Social Security over the course of our careers and then when we retire, we get a monthly check in return from the government. Currently, to receive Social Security in retirement you have to earn 40 "credits," which usually equates to about 10 years of work (and paying into the program!).

To get an estimate of what you can expect to earn, create an account at ssa.gov. While the future of Social Security isn't guaranteed, most financial experts I interviewed were hopeful it will be around for future generations' retirement. Regardless, Social Security income is not a replacement for saving for retirement – it's just a supplemental form of income.

Retirement Accounts Might Be Only *Part* of the Plan

In some cases you might need or want to supplement your retirement accounts with other investment accounts.

- **If you're maxed out.** If you want to contribute more than the max to your 401(k) and/or IRA, you can invest for retirement in your brokerage account (often called a taxable account). This may be because you don't have access to a company 401(k) and have hit the IRA max, want to earn more in retirement, are playing catch-up, or because you plan to retire early.
- **If you plan to retire early.** If you plan to retire before age 59½, you may want to save funds in a taxable (nonretirement) account in order to make withdrawals penalty-free. In many cases, you may be subject to an early withdrawal penalty when you take money out of your 401(k) or IRA prior to the age the IRS chooses. So, having another investment account can give you access to your funds without penalty if you're lucky enough to stop working before then.

Lauren recommends opening multiple investment accounts or bucketing your investments so it's very clear what money is for which goal. You might have retirement money in your investment account but also money for different savings goals (for us, that's the kids' bar mitzvahs!). That way it's very clear what each dollar is for and, depending on the time frame, you might invest the money for each goal differently.

Retire Early, You Say? Tell Me More

The Financial Independence/Retire Early (FI/RE) movement has gained a lot of popularity with people looking to reach work-optional life before traditional retirement age. When I first started my money journey, the FI/RE movement was just becoming trendy. I saw a bunch of bros eating beans out of cans to save money and thought, I'll pass. I stayed far away.

More recently, I've been inspired by other personal finance experts claiming the FI/RE movement in a very different way. I talked to Kiersten and Julien Saunders from rich & REGULAR, a lifestyle brand that inspires the Black community to build wealth, about their journey to FI/RE. Here's their advice.

> *It does not have to be deprivation. It doesn't have to be rigid. It's whatever you want it to be. More expenses means less saving now and higher expenses to cover in the future. It affects the timeline.*
>
> *Traditional FI/RE calculators assume that your expenses will be the same all the time, or have a very specific period where they'll increase (usually at 65) or they decrease over time. This assumes that life isn't happening to you in the interim. If somebody gets sick or you need to pay for something unexpected, it changes. The idea of a number is more of a North Star for us. It's more of a guideline than it is THE goal. It's very similar to weight on a scale. You fluctuate but stay within a certain range.*

Kiersten and Julien also warn about the flashy "win big" stories of people who go from $0 to $10 million overnight by investing in something like Bitcoin or NFTs (more on what these are in the next chapter).

Many more people have lost a lot of money this way. The far more helpful story is the one where someone saves and invests for 10 years and is able to retire comfortably. It's less sexy but it's real and it's something people can replicate.

The Gender and Racial Retirement Gaps

While some have the goal of retiring early, for many, retiring at all is nothing more than a pipe dream (Kiersten and Julien call this a "retirement crisis"), and a disproportionate number of those who won't be able to afford their retirement are women and people of color.

Half of all U.S. households are at risk of falling short in retirement.[2] 54% of Black Americans and 61% of Latinos shared that risk, compared to 48% of white Americans.[3] Rachel shared that women retire with two-thirds the amount of money as men.[4] Due to the wage gaps and disproportionate representation in low-wage jobs and additional debt, for many there just isn't enough money to save for retirement. This affects not only their ability to save but also how much they earn in Social Security later in life.

There's also a lack of access and eligibility to employee-sponsored retirement plans. As you now know, company 401(k)s allow for more than three times the contributions than IRAs. Over two-thirds of white workers have a company retirement plan option, compared with 56% of Black and 44% of Latino workers.[5] Those who do have access might not be able to contribute due to eligibility issues, if they've been at the company less than a year or are working part-time. Those without company-sponsored plans might not have the ability to open an IRA because they are unbanked or underbanked.

What you'll start to see is that everything is connected. Social, racial, and gender disparities touch every aspect of someone's financial life. This has a compounding effect on financial well-being, livelihood, access, choices, health, and freedom, among many other things.

Investing Jargon

The money in your retirement accounts needs to be invested to grow. Before we talk about choosing your investments, let's start with some of the jargon. I wish I could be chosen to rename all the investing jargon – it would be much more fun and straightforward. Maybe our investment portfolio could be called a sundae and our asset allocation is the mix of flavors and toppings. If you dig this, Vanguard, you know where to find me.

But for now, the best I can do is teach you to navigate the current language. And that's all it is; it's like learning any new language. When I hear someone speak in French, I have no idea what they are saying. Once I learn some words, I can start to decipher. Actually, I tried to learn French and I failed, so maybe that's not the best example, but you know what I mean.

Risk

Risk gets a bad rap, but good risk equals more return and return means growth for our money. One of the reasons so many of us are scared to start investing is that we believe we could lose all our money. And by *we* I mean me, too. I was very wary of getting started.

The worst drop in the market in my lifetime (that I can remember) was in 2008, during the Great Recession. So let's look at what would have happened in that terrible scenario. Let's say that you bought $10,000 worth of the S&P 500 (an index of the largest 500 publicly traded companies in the United States) when the market was at its highest in October 2007 (buying at the highest point is also the worst-case scenario, so I'm making this example very juicy). At its lowest point in the Great Recession, you would have lost 57% and been left with $4,322 (which is terrifying).[6] But if you held onto it, as of September 24, 2021, you would have had $28,424 (almost three times your initial investment!), or an annual return of over 7%.

This is why it's so important to invest for the long term. When we don't need the money right away, we can wait out drops in the market before selling. We saw this again more recently during the pandemic in March 2020. There were a few really bad weeks in the market but if you waited it out, things went your way in the end.

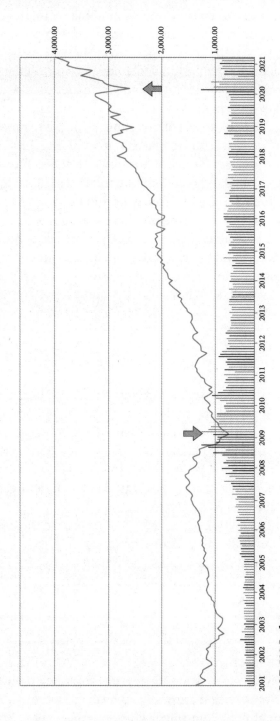

S&P 500 Index
Source: Yahoo! Finance.

Important fact to remember: You don't actually make or lose money until you sell your investment. I talk more about this in Chapter 8.

Our risk tolerance is our personal tolerance for risk. Understanding it can help us decide what to invest in and get an idea of how we might react if the market were to drop or get volatile.

The truth is, the riskiest part of investing is that we're human. Fear is real and when we're fearful we make emotional spending decisions like selling when our investments are down. Believe me, it might sound easy to avoid making emotional financial decisions, but in the moment, when you're seeing the frenzy on the news, there can be an urgency to try to cut your losses before there's nothing left.

This is where a financial planner, money coach, or accountability partner (I talk more about them soon) can help keep you from making a mistake and losing a lot of money. Because, remember, we haven't lost money until we sell. Risk has a bad rep, but really it's our behavior that gets us in trouble.

Asset Allocation

An asset is something you own and your asset allocation is your mix of investments (or mix of the things you own). The mix we're usually talking about is of stocks, bonds, and cash (all different asset classes). Typically, stocks are viewed as the most risky, then bonds, with cash being the least risky. This is correlated to their return. Stocks have unlimited upside, bonds have a fixed rate of return, and cash earns whatever you can get in your savings account.

"Fun" fact: In reality, cash is *losing* value because the cost to buy things goes up over time (hello again, inflation).

There's another asset class called "alternatives," which I mention in the next chapter. This is a catch-all bucket for anything other than stocks, bonds, and cash.

Stock

There are two ways to invest in a company: owning **stock** or investing in their debt. When you own a share of stock, you own a piece of a company (albeit a very small one). You might also hear this called "shares" or "equity." Use it in a sentence: "I own stock in General Motors through an ETF, which is one of 12 Fortune 100 companies with a woman CEO" (For a definition of an ETF, see the upcoming "Fund" section).

Bond

When we buy a **bond**, we're essentially lending someone money – usually a company or government. And in return, we get our money back plus interest. There is an agreed-upon interest rate, which is why a bond is also called a fixed income investment (we get back a fixed amount). Use it in a sentence: "10% of my retirement portfolio is invested in bonds."

You might hear the term **money market fund** thrown around. These are funds specifically invested in short-term U.S. government bonds called Treasury bills or "T-bills" and are very low risk. These are a type of bond or fixed income investment.

Diversification

Diversification means not putting all of your eggs in one basket. One of the best ways to get rid of unnecessary investment risk is to invest in a variety of companies, sectors, and geographies.

When you invest in one individual company or industry, there's a risk that the price will go down if something were to happen – for example, if you own stock in airline companies (a specific sector) and then a pandemic hits that halts almost all air travel (like we saw in 2020). Or you own the stock of a specific company and its CEO is charged with sexual harassment.

When you're invested in a fund (defined in the next section) you're invested in many companies. If something happens at one company, in one industry, or a certain geography, it can affect the share price (the value or price of a share) but on a much smaller scale.

Fund

Also called **mutual fund**, **index fund**, or exchange-traded fund (**ETF**). A fund is a type of investment that's made up of pooled money from investors (a.k.a. us!). This pool of money can be invested in stocks, bonds, or a combination of both. I've also heard a fund aptly described as a basket of investments. There are differences between mutual funds, index funds, and ETFs, but for our purposes (and honestly, my purposes, too), they aren't important. If you want to know the differences between them, I've included a link in the Financial Adulting toolkit. There is *so* much investing information out there. Part of being a financial adult is knowing what you don't need to know.

Funds are a great way to diversify (see the previous "Diversification" section) because by owning one share you can own stocks or bonds in hundreds of companies. Index funds and ETFs are types of low-fee mutual funds.

Portfolio

Saying **portfolio** is a fancy way of saying "your investments." Use it in a sentence: "I want to check what's in my portfolio." Then you log into your investing account to see what's going on with your investments.

Figure Out Your Asset Allocation

Choosing how your assets are allocated is probably your most important decision as an investor (or so some very smart people say). For retirement, Georgia Lee Hussey says, "If you are younger than 50 and you intend to retire at the standard 65 age range, please God, buy equities and not a lot of bonds. You have so much more risk you can take, because there's a lot of time until you need the money."

There's a general quick calculation to figure out your ideal asset allocation for retirement. Take 120 and subtract your age. That's the percentage of your retirement portfolio that should be invested in stocks rather than bonds. For example, if you are 30, 120 − 30 = 90% stocks and 100% − 90% = 10% bonds.

This is a simplistic calculation for your asset allocation and assumes you can handle fluctuations in your account without reacting and that you plan to retire at the typical retirement age (in your mid-60s). This

120	–	Your Age	=	% Stocks
Example: 120	–	30	=	90%
120	–		=	

100%	–	% Stocks	=	% Bonds
Example: 100%	–	90%	=	10%
100%	–		=	

is a personal decision. Some people prefer to have more of their portfolios in equities (me!) and some prefer less risk. The general takeaway is, if you're far away from retirement, you have the opportunity to take on more risk (and get after that growth). If you want to level up or there's some nuance to your situation, head to our Financial Adulting toolkit for some asset allocation quizzes.

You can also check out some target date funds (more on these in the next section) and see what their asset allocation is for someone retiring around the same time as you. You'll notice that as you get older (and closer to retirement), your portfolio becomes less invested in stocks and more invested in bonds. Knowing what we do about risk, our portfolio becomes less and less risky as we get closer to using the money. Brilliant.

This asset allocation helps us decide which types of funds to choose. For retirement, we'll want to choose at least one stock fund and one bond fund, or a fund that does this for us.

Research and determine your retirement asset allocation.

Asset Allocation for Retirement	Example
% Stocks	95%
% Bonds	5%
% Cash	0%
Total	**100%**

Target Date Funds

Even if we start out with our ideal balance of stocks and bonds, investments move and we get older (*sigh*) so our asset allocations will get out of whack. We can **rebalance** or **reallocate** (jargon alert!) our investments to fit our ideal balance on our own once per year, or we can invest in target date funds. Target date funds are typically named based on the year we plan to retire. So if you plan to retire in 2055, the target date fund will typically be called something like "Target Date 2055."

Target date funds take the work out of rebalancing for us because they reallocate as we get closer to retirement. As long as the expenses are low, and the allocation matches what you calculate for yourself, these are a great one-stop shop for retirement investing.

Based on your expected year of retirement, the fund makes sure your assets are allocated among stocks and bonds according to the risk associated with your retirement date. As you get closer to retirement, the allocation becomes more heavily weighted in bonds.

Georgia says, "I love a good target date fund. Just make sure it's cheap. Keep it under 0.25%." She adds, "Cheap and easy is extremely valuable in financial planning because it's less likely that we are going to let anxiousness impede our vision. And honestly, it's just about f***ing doing something and then stop worrying about it. There's a lot of analysis paralysis in this industry. I think that's intentional to funnel people into buying crap they don't need." Don't you love her?

Those who aren't fans of target date funds usually point to their high expense ratio (coming up in the "What About the Fees?" section). So if you can find a cheap one, great.

Choosing Our Retirement Investments

Target date funds are just one way to invest and might not even be an option in your 401(k) plan. Start with your list of what's available and do some research on each of the fund options. If you are investing your IRA, you will have many more options. Here's what to include in your research.

First, the Name

I know it sounds silly, but some of these funds have such long names. Some even have corresponding roman numerals – like "Obnoxious Investments Fund III." Eye roll.

Find the **ticker symbol** or the letters and numbers used to identify that particular investment. That way when you're doing your research, you know you're looking at the right fund. For example, the Vanguard Target Retirement 2055 fund's ticker symbol is VFFVX. That's much easier to type into Google. Go ahead and google it. If it's a target date fund, make sure the year matches or is closest to your retirement date (they typically round to the nearest multiple of 5 like 2045, 2050, 2055, etc.).

What's in the Fund?

You'll find a few (or a bajillion) sites that can give you more information about the fund. Start by looking at what types of investments this fund holds. Is it a target date fund, a fund filled with U.S. stocks or foreign stocks? Does it specify a certain industry or company size? How does it fit into your asset allocation? Hopefully more and more 401(k)s will include ethical funds like ESG funds, which are funds that screen for company environmental, social, and governance practices. I talk about these in detail in the next chapter.

You can also look at how the fund has performed over the past 10 or 20 years. Past performance doesn't guarantee future performance by any means, but, as Rachel says, "it's the best information we have to move forward with." Yep.

What About the Fees?

Every fund will have a fee in the form of an **expense ratio**. If you can't find it on the page, hit ctrl F or Command F and search "expense ratio." This will be a percentage fee that you are charged each year for owning the fund. It's kind of sneaky in that you won't have to send payment anywhere but the money will just be withdrawn from your investment account.

If the expense ratio is 0.15% and your retirement investments are $50,000, you're paying $75 per year. Some funds have high expense ratios. It depends on the type of fund but I typically consider anything above 0.5% to be high and I try to invest in funds with expense ratios well below that. Tony Molina, Product Evangelist at Wealthfront, says that for the big broad indexes (like the S&P 500 or Dow Jones Industrial Average), you can typically get an expense ratio of 0.08% or lower. Another way to look at this fee? If you are paying a fee of 1% and your portfolio earned 8% that year, you only get to keep 7% of those earnings.

Now it's important to note that when it comes to your 401(k) there are limited options and major tax benefits (I talked about them previously) so I give the funds a bit more leniency as far as expense ratios (especially once you've maxed out your IRA).

Take some time to research the funds available to you in your 401(k) or IRA. Take note of your research here. Remember, you'll want to find a target date fund or at least both a stock and bond fund. You can also mimic the investments in a target date fund if you want to create it yourself. Most will have a U.S. stock fund, an international stock fund, a U.S. bond fund, and an international bond fund. Circle your top choices here.

	Example	**Fund #1**	**Fund #2**	**Fund #3**
Name/Ticker Symbol	Fidelity S&P 500 Index Fund/ FXAIX			
Expense Ratio (%)	0.015%			
What It's Invested in/Asset Allocation	100% Equity/ S&P 500			
ESG Criteria (if any)	MSCI Rating of A			

If you are feeling pressure, I get it. But the good news about choosing investments in your retirement account is you can always switch them as you learn more or your situation changes.

Where Does Asset Allocation Come In?

If you aren't using a target date fund, you're creating your own asset allocation using a stock and a bond fund (or multiple stock and bond funds). Let's say you decide you want 90% of your retirement money in stocks and 10% in bonds. What does that actually look like? If you have $25,000 invested, you'd want $22,500 invested in stock funds (90%) and $2,500 invested in bond funds (10%). How do you actually make that happen? You have two options:

1. After doing some research you might realize that you aren't happy with what you're currently invested in. You can sell what you have and invest in your new funds at a 90/10 split. Going forward, you can have your contributions go toward the same 90/10 split. There aren't taxes associated with buying and selling retirement investments, so this method is very workable. Just make sure there aren't other fees associated with buying and selling.

2. If you are happy with your current investments, but you're just looking to change your asset allocation, you can change your contributions to build toward that ideal ratio. Let's say you are more heavily invested in bonds than you'd like. You can put all future contributions toward equities until you get to your 90/10 ideal asset allocation.

The market moves so over time our asset allocation can and will get out of whack. I talk about how and when to **rebalance** our portfolios in Chapter 14.

How will you get to your ideal asset allocation? Write down your plan here.

_____

_____

_____

Look Out for Other Fees

There are other fees to be aware of when it comes to investing. If you hire a financial advisor (typically 0.5–1.5% of your portfolio's value per year) or robo-advisor (0.25–0.35% of your portfolio's value per year) to manage your retirement account, that fee will be on top of what you are paying in fund expense ratios.

There might also be administrative fees like a quarterly or monthly cost to enroll in your plan. In retirement accounts there aren't usually trading commissions (fees for buying and selling funds), but that's something to look out for as well.

> Are there any other fees in your retirement accounts? Are you paying an advisor or robo-advisor? List out all the fees you're paying here.
>
> _____
>
> _____
>
> _____

Set Your Investing Up to Be Automatic

Now that you know how much you want to be contributing and what you want to invest in, you can log into your retirement account and set it all up. In your 401(k), you will change your contribution percentage as well as your investment choices. If you aren't sure how or where to do this, reach out to your HR or benefits representative.

You can also set up IRA contributions to be automatic, which takes the work out of making contributions and makes it more likely that you'll actually do it.

> Okay, it's go time! Log in and set up your retirement contributions. What percentage of your salary will you contribute? And what investments will those contributions go to?
>
> _____
>
> _____
>
> _____

Some Frequently Asked Retirement Questions

What Is 401(k) Vesting?

Sometimes your 401(k) matching is not all yours right away. Rude, I know! But this is a way for your company to incentivize you to stay. There will be a vesting schedule that tells you how much of your match is yours each year. If your 401(k) match vests over three years, the first third will be yours in the first year, then you receive another third in the second year, and you get the rest the final year. This happens each year with new matching contributions. When you log into your 401(k) website you should be able to see the vested amount and the total amount. The vested amount is the amount you'd be able to take with you if you left your job today.

Should I Roll Over My 401(k)?

It's generally a good idea to roll over old 401(k)s. There's nothing technically wrong with leaving money in your previous 401(k) *unless* there's less than $1,000 in the account (see the following "fun" fact). Otherwise, the money is yours, and it sits there. Here are some reasons to roll it over:

- **Communication issues.** Your company will most likely leave you out of communication about plan changes and updates.
- **It's a lot to keep track of.** Having a bunch of retirement accounts just makes things more complicated. Rolling your account over into your IRA or current 401(k) keeps things simple to track.
- **Better investment options.** Your new plan might have better options or, if it's an IRA, it essentially has unlimited options.
- **Lower fees.** If the account has any administration fees or the fund options have high expense ratios, you'll want to roll it over.

"Fun" fact: In certain cases, your employer can move the money from your 401(k). If you have less than $1,000 in your account, an employer is usually allowed to cash it out and cut you a check. You will pay the 10% early withdrawal penalty and any taxes owed if it's a traditional 401(k). If your 401(k) balance is between $1,000 and $5,000, your employer is allowed to roll it over into an IRA. In those cases, you'd want to make the decision before your employer does! If you have more than $5,000 in the account (from contributions at that job), your employer has to leave your money alone.

When you're ready to do it, head to the Financial Adulting toolkit for some pointers.

Should I Choose an "Aggressive" Investing Plan?

If you're young and your company asks you to choose an investment strategy, you most likely will want to choose the aggressive option. I know, I know. Who wants their money invested aggressively? Aggressive sounds horrible and it makes me so mad that that's the way it's described, but more risk (when it's good risk) means more return. And we want this retirement account to grow like a beautiful tree for you.

Saving for College with 529 Plans

Choosing to save for your child's college expenses is a personal decision and it's important to prioritize your own retirement first. Lauren says it's difficult, but she asks parents who are saving for their children's college expenses and not their own retirement, "How do you feel about the potential to be a burden to your children?" because that's the reality. There are student loans available to pay for school and parents can even help pay for those loans or support children in other ways when they can. You'll always have the option to finance an education, but there's no such thing as a retirement loan.

If you have the opportunity to set money aside for your child's future education, 529 plans allow for tax-advantaged investing, a lot like a 401(k) or IRA. You put money in and it grows tax free (no capital gains tax!). When you take the money out to use it for qualified education expenses (see the Financial Adulting toolkit for an extensive list of them), you get to use the money tax free. Depending on the state you live in and your income, some contributions to your 529 plan may be tax deductions. (Sadly, that's not the case in my state.)

Some important things to know about 529 plans:

- You can open one in most states, even if it's not your own. If your state offers tax deductions for contributions, you'll want to open a 529 plan in it.

- You can change the beneficiary. If you contribute to a 529 plan before your child is born, you can put it in your name and change it later. If your child ends up not using the funds, you can transfer them to another child or to someone else.

- You can make automatic contributions so you can set it and forget it.

- If you use the money for expenses that don't qualify, you will get hit with a 10% penalty and pay taxes on the capital gains in the account.

- Watch out for fees. The plans can be free to open and you should be able to find low-fee funds.

- When applying for financial aid, 529 plans are counted as parental assets.

So how much do you need? When my first son was born, I calculated what we would have to contribute to his 529 plan starting the first month of his life to pay for four years of private college tuition by the time he turned 18. To hit that goal we'd have to contribute over $1,000 per month (for 18 years!).[7] What about a public in-state institution? $552 per month. That's just absurd. We don't contribute that amount, but we do what we can. Even though the number will be really high, don't forget about compound interest. This money may have a long time to grow. Also remember, having some money set aside is better than nothing. Every amount will help.

I have a calculator for you in the Financial Adulting toolkit that will tell you exactly how much you want to be contributing now to pay for some or all of your child's education.

Run some different scenarios with the calculator in the Financial Adulting toolkit. How much do you want to set aside each month for 529 investing, if any?

	Example: Four-year in-state public tuition	Scenario 1:	Scenario 2:
Total Amount	$134,261		
Monthly Contribution	$300/month		

Other Investing Benefits You Might Get Through Work

Georgia made me giggle when she said, "The HR benefits booklet is a glory." But she's 100% right. Your company may offer you an HSA plan (which I talk about in detail in Chapter 10), employee stock purchase plan (an opportunity to buy discount stock), restricted stock units (company shares), or stock options (if you work at a startup). In addition, companies are now offering all types of different employee perks. These might be benefits you missed when you started working there because you were too busy hitting the ground running or maybe they've added new benefits since you joined. Go take a look and see what benefits you can use.

Your Financial Adulting Action Items

☐ Maximize your company match (if you have it).

☐ Understand your retirement account options, whatever they are. (Teachers: don't miss your special callout!)

☐ Run some retirement calculators to decide how much you need and what that means you want to contribute each year.

☐ Set a calendar reminder if you want to increase your contributions over time.

☐ Revisit the ways we can close the gender and racial financial gaps (covered in detail in Chapter 2).

☐ Figure out your asset allocation (there are more calculators in the toolkit for that).

☐ Research and choose your investment options.

☐ Create a plan to get to your ideal asset allocation.

☐ Make your retirement investing automatic.

☐ Roll over any 401(k)s you have with previous employers (or consolidate IRAs).

☐ If you're a parent, caregiver, or it aligns with your goals, set up a 529 plan to save for a child's college or other education expenses.

☐ Understand and maximize your work benefits, if available.

Okay, now that you're set up for retirement, let's talk about all other types of investing, including how to become an investor who grows their money and does good in the world. We'll learn from the experts and I'll walk you through it all step by step.

CHAPTER 8

Become an Investor for Good

We've covered retirement; now it's time to talk about investing for everything else. We can also choose to invest our money in ways that (mostly) aren't harmful and can even support the values we believe in.

Investing is an important part of being a financial adult because remember our friend, compound interest? It enables our money to grow exponentially. That can provide freedom in our choices and help us reach our goals. Not to mention, we won't miss out on thousands, tens of thousands, or even millions of dollars over the course of our lifetime.

Only half the people[1] in the United States invest, and women tend to invest 40% less than men, on average.[2] These numbers are even lower for communities of color. In 2019 only 34% of Black people and 24% of Latinos owned stocks, compared with 61% of white people.[3]

The Opportunity to Invest Is a Privilege

The problem is manyfold. It's not just that the stock market has been inaccessible for women and communities of color for centuries (although that's a big part of it). In order to invest, you need to have funds to invest. When 54% of the country is living paycheck to paycheck and 40% have less than $400 saved, investing is not something that's reasonable or feasible for most.[4] When Black and Latino families have eight times and five times, respectively, less net worth than white families,[5] that has a tremendous impact on their ability to invest. Having the opportunity to invest is a privilege.

And for the time being, if you have the privilege to be able to invest or expect to in the future, this chapter is going to get you set up. Not only do we need you set up to invest and grow your wealth, we want you talking about it. You're modeling it for others.

The Culture of Investing

What comes to mind when you hear the word "investor"?

If you think Warren Buffett or [insert other gray-haired white guy], it's not surprising. The investing world has been created for and by men. "Look at the brand symbol of the industry, it's a bull," says Sallie Krawcheck, the co-founder and CEO of Ellevest. That says a lot in itself.

The investment industry is very white and very male; 79% of financial advisors are white[6] and only 23% of certified financial planners (CFPs) are women.[7] That's a problem. If you look at bank CEOs, they are all white men, now with the exception of the first woman CEO at a large bank, Jane Fraser at Citigroup.

Emily Green, the director of Private Wealth at Ellevest, explained, "The banks are talking about diversity but white men are still slated to be the next CEOs. Banks and financial companies are going to need to hire people at all ranks who will be able to help create products and services that work for people other than white men." Instead of the industry working to fix how women are, they need to change what the banks do to serve women, and people of color. And that's not going to happen until there are women and people of color at all levels working in these organizations.

My Investing Story

Despite all my privilege and finance background, I still didn't feel like an investor. I wasn't part of the club. I felt like I should know more before starting. When I heard a colleague talking about his brilliant investing idea, I didn't think twice (or listen to my gut) and jumped on the opportunity. Turns out, he didn't know what he was talking about and I lost thousands of dollars (a large part of my net worth at the time).

I decided – never again. Never again will I depend on someone else to understand and invest my money. I'm going to figure this out.

I'll let you in on a little secret. Many people (even the *very* confident-sounding ones) don't know what they're talking about when it comes to investing. People are very quick to share their investing wins without sharing their investing losses.

Yet investing doesn't have to be that complicated. I mean, I'm going to break it all down for you in one chapter of a book. Plus, studies show that women are actually better investors when we do invest because we tend to trade less and have a more long-term focus. A Fidelity study showed that women investors earn 0.4% more per year than men (others show higher numbers).[8] Compounded year after year, this can amount to a big difference.

The best way to change investing culture is to get more BIPOC, women, and especially BIPOC women investing. And why do we want to change investing culture? It will make investing truly inclusive, so more women and BIPOC women will be able to build wealth. And we know what it means when more women are wealthy. All good things for everyone. So that's what we're going to do.

Before You Get Started

Before you put money toward investing goals, you want to make sure you've checked some important financial boxes:

- ☐ You have cash on hand in case of an emergency (i.e., a rainy-day fund; see Chapter 3).
- ☐ You have maximized your company 401(k) matching (covered in Chapter 7).
- ☐ You are investing for retirement in tax-advantaged accounts (Chapter 7).
- ☐ You've paid off high-interest credit card debt (more about other debt later in this chapter).

If you haven't checked these boxes, that doesn't mean you can't put *some* money aside to learn to invest. We learn by doing. Just like you would buy a ticket to a conference to learn more about a certain topic, you can set aside $5, $10, or even $100 to learn about investing.

I just wouldn't prioritize investing as part of your savings on a regular basis over the aforementioned goals. It comes down to security and protection (i.e., the rainy-day fund) and what's actually costing and earning you the most money.

What Is Investing?

Investing just means buying something with the goal of selling it later for more money. Investing in stocks, bonds, and real estate is just one way to do that. With retirement investing, the goal is to save up enough money to retire (not need to work). Any investing outside of that could be to grow your money for a specific goal like buying a house or sending your kid to college, or you might not even be sure.

Your **return** or **profit** on an investment is how much it earned. If you bought an investment for $100 and sold it for $150, you earned $50 or a 50% return on your original investment.

Return on investment = (Sale price – Purchase price) ÷ Purchase price

A 50% return sounds awesome but the timeline is also important. Did you earn that in one year or over 30 years? This is where **annualized return** comes in. This makes it easier to compare what you earned with other investments. A good return is relative. Yes, it's great to earn a 10% return but if the market went up 25% that year, it's not *as* great because you could have done much better.

Realized versus Unrealized Gains

When the value of your investment goes up, your profit (or the amount it went up) is called a gain. If you haven't sold the investment, that amount is called an **unrealized gain**. It's not realized because it's actually not your money yet. The investment value can still go up and down.

When you sell the investment and the profit (plus the original amount) is in cash in your account, that's a **realized gain**. Currently, you only pay taxes on realized gains.

Long-Term Investing Wins the Tax Game

In your retirement accounts (and other tax-advantaged accounts like a 529 plan – we covered them in the previous chapter– and an HSA, discussed in Chapter 10) you don't pay taxes on your **capital gains** (which is a huge gain for us, pun intended). In our nonretirement accounts we do. When we buy and sell an investment within a year, we pay **short-term capital gains tax** on the growth, which is the equivalent of our income tax rate. So if I earned $50 on an investment when I sold it, and my income tax rate is 30%, I'd owe $15 when I file my taxes.

If we hold our investments for over a year before selling, we pay **long-term capital gains tax**, which is 0% if you are single and earn under $41,675, 15% if you earn $41,676 to 459,750, and 20% if you earn over $459,750 in 2022. Let's say I earn $50,000; my $50 capital gain is now taxed at 15%. I'll owe an additional $7.50 at tax time.

What If You Lose Money?

I know, I'm so optimistic. So far I've only talked about making money. When your investment goes down in value, that's a loss. If you still own the investment, that's an **unrealized loss**. Once you sell your investment at a loss, the amount your investment went down is a **realized loss**. Losses decrease our taxes.

Okay, cool-cool-cool. But you might be wondering, where does this magical investing happen?

The Three Ways to Invest (from Least to Most Expensive)

When it comes to actually investing your money, there are three ways you can do it. Here's the high-level overview, along with pros and cons of each.

On Your Own

To get started, you'll need a brokerage account, some money (it can be a very small amount), and your investment choices. That's only three things. Not too bad, right? You are the one who logs into your brokerage account and buys and sells the investments.

PRO: It is the least expensive option. You are not paying an advisor's management fee. Georgia Lee Hussey says that up until you hit about a million dollars in investments, doing it on your own works great and can keep your costs low, letting the magic of compound growth work for you.

PRO: It is great for control freaks. You can choose from any and all investments available to you under the sun. Nothing happens to your money without you initiating it.

PRO: It is accessible to those who are ready to invest. As long as you meet the account minimum (which can be very low), you're in.

CON: We're not always rational with money. Having some barrier, like a person we can call or software we can trust, between us and our money can keep us from making emotional decisions. Talking to a person doesn't mean you have to hire a financial advisor. I talk about other financial professionals you can hire to mitigate this con later.

CON: You're doing the work. Rebalancing is on you. Checking in is on you. The truth is, you should be checking in regardless of how you invest, but with the other ways you have some more support.

With a Robo-Advisor

A **robo-advisor** is a digital platform that invests your money for you for a management fee (usually 0.25–0.35%). Typically, you'll open an account, answer some questions about your goals, timeline, and risk tolerance, and the robo-advisor will invest accordingly. Some you might have heard of are Ellevest, Wealthfront, Betterment, and SoFi.

PRO: They do the work. You answer the questionnaire and voilà! Your money is managed for you. Set up some automatic contributions and you can be very hands-off.

PRO: Most robo-advisors invest your money in low-fee index fund investments. I'm a fan!

PRO: Robo-advisors are accessible to those who are ready to invest. Your money is being handled by "expert" software for a low price and that can give you peace of mind.

PRO: They may offer the opportunity to talk to a CFP. You may have a person to reach out to if you get nervous during a market dip or have a question.

PRO: Many offer tax-loss harvesting, which can save you money in taxes. Tax-loss *wha?* Remember capital gains and losses? Well, robo-advisors sell your investments for a loss and buy similar **securities** (jargon for tradable investments) to keep your overall portfolio composition the same for the lower price. This locks in the loss (now a realized loss) and saves you money in taxes while not sacrificing your investments. This is something that happens digitally – it's not something you'd want to spend your time replicating on your own.

While this sounds very cool, I have been skeptical about how much savings this actually generates. Tony Molina was able to share that "while there is no way to quantify what tax-loss harvesting is going to do for someone (it depends on market movement and specific investments)," for Wealthfront, "the average client typically gets back at least three times the value of our 0.25% fee in the benefits of tax-loss harvesting – about 0.75%." If you harvested losses of $3,000 and your income tax rate is 30%, you are now paying $900 less in taxes.

CON: That fee. It's small but it's a fee nonetheless. What does that mean in real dollars? Take 0.25% (.0025) and multiply it by the amount of money you have invested. If you have $10,000 invested, that's $25 per year.

CON: You could replicate the portfolio on your own. Many robo-advisors choose simple low-fee investment options for you, which is great and one of the reasons I'm a fan of them. But at the same time, you can also replicate what they are doing on your own. It just takes more work on your end.

CON: There may be no person to talk to (this is a pro for some and a con for others). If there is support available, you are probably not going to be talking to the same person every time.

CON: There is not much of a barrier to emotional investing decisions (very similar to investing on our own). Having a better understanding of how investing works can really help with this (for investing on your own, too!). Tony says, "Know that you will have to deal with the downturn as well as the upturns in passive investing. You'll get hit hard in the downturn but know that you're going to come out ahead." It helps to keep this in mind.

Hiring a Financial Advisor

Hiring a human (vs. software) to manage your investments for you.

Side note: *In my first few years as a money coach and educator I was very disheartened (and actually horrified) by financial advisors. I saw a lot of harmful things happen with my clients and in my community and I believed the entire financial advisory industry was a scam. Later I learned that there is a key differentiator between these horror stories and helpful financial advice. Ready for it . . .*

Fiduciary versus suitability standards. *If an advisor is bound by fiduciary standards, they are required to put their clients' interest above their own. Broker-dealers (usually advisors through brokerage companies) only have to fulfill a suitability obligation, which means they are only required to recommend what is suitable and not harmful for you. This blows my mind. The rule is that they don't harm you?! You want to make sure any financial advisor you hire is bound to fiduciary standards. We have resources to find fee-only fiduciary advisors in the Financial Adulting toolkit.*

PRO: There is more support. Some people really want to be able to call their person up and talk about their investments or calm their fears when the market is down. And they are happy to pay more for that (four to five times more).

PRO(ish): They can help you get more nuanced. You might think that hiring an individual (which costs more money) will mean you get more nuanced financial planning to meet your needs. You might even expect the advice to include your holistic financial picture. This is the ideal scenario and usually only happens once you have some very considerable wealth. You'll want to get clear on what support you will be getting when you interview potential advisors.

CON: This is the most expensive option. Advisors typically charge a percentage fee to manage your funds (usually 0.5–1.5%). If you have $100,000 invested with a financial advisor and their fee is 1.5.%, that's $1,500 per year. Another way to look at it? If your portfolio earned 6% and you paid a 1.5% fee, you're now only keeping 4.5% of that profit. That being said, it's best to work with a **fee-only** advisor who doesn't sell you products to earn commission.

Tony shares, "If you are high net worth, some advisors will be able to put you into alternative assets not available to everyone else. Otherwise, you're paying a higher fee just to talk to someone. There's no competitive advantage." Georgia says that "investment management is highly replicable. We have all the evidence we need to know how to invest well. There are some differences in philosophy but they are just nuances."

CON: This option is inaccessible to most. Many advisors only take on clients who have a certain amount of money to invest (they call this their minimum). Minimums can range from $50,000 to $1,000,000 so for most, hiring a financial advisor is not a possibility.

CON: They may try to sell you expensive products you don't need. Another thing that gives advisors a bad rep is that *fee-based* (different from fee-only) or commission-based advisors can hawk products – specifically, products that earn them commissions (a conflict of interest that I've had an issue with for the entirety of my career). These products might be in the form of insurance products (more on this in Chapter 10) or expensive funds with high expense ratios, load fees (a percentage fee you pay to purchase the fund), exit fees (a percentage fee you pay to sell the fund), and 12b-1 fees. This is another con that can be eliminated by working with a *fee-only* fiduciary.

Regardless of which option you choose, you want to understand what's happening with your investments. If you are working with an advisor, you want them to be open to educating and listening to you.

Which way to invest is the best fit for you right now?

_____

_____

_____

But Wait, What's a Financial Planner?

A CFP or **certified financial planner** is technically a type of financial advisor (I know, it's confusing). Financial planners do not always manage your investments and usually have a more holistic view of your finances (outside of just your investments and insurance). They go into the details of your entire financial plan. Brian Walsh, a CFP with SoFi you met a few chapters back, calls financial planners the quarterback or coordinator of your finances. They can offer second opinions when you talk to specialists in any given personal finance area like investing, insurance, or tax and estate planning.

Even for those early in their careers and money journeys, Georgia believes a financial planner is still valuable. She says, "It's really beneficial to see somebody for a couple hours just to give you the lay of the land and tell you which benefits to choose. And then you're good for two years." Financial planners have different models. Some meet with you to make a plan for a few hours and you're set. And others serve more as long-term accountability partners throughout the year (and everything in between).

You want your financial planner to be a CFP, fee-only, and a fiduciary. I've included my favorites in the Financial Adulting toolkit.

"Fun" fact: These titles aren't cut and dry. There can be overlap between financial advisors and financial planners. Some CFPs are also financial advisors (who invest your money for you) and others are strictly financial planners (who put together a financial plan but don't invest your money for you). I say this over and over but regardless of what option(s) you choose, you always want to know how the people who are educating you are getting paid and what you are paying in fees. There are some resources in the Financial Adulting toolkit that will help you vet financial professionals.

TLDR (just kidding, definitely read the whole thing): The personal finance and investing spaces are continually changing and becoming more accessible for new investors. If you want more support, you can also hire financial or money coaches – someone to help you create goals, overcome setbacks, and break through the barriers holding you back from those goals – as well as a financial planner to support you in investing and looking at your entire financial picture.

What You Need to Get Started

If you are interested in getting started on your own or are curious about what it would entail, you'll need to open a brokerage account.

What Is a Brokerage Account?

A brokerage company is a firm that enables you to buy and sell investments. When you open up a **brokerage account**, you can then transfer money into the account and buy and sell investments there. There are many brokerage companies. Some you might have heard of are Vanguard, Fidelity, Charles Schwab, TD Ameritrade, E-trade, and there are many more (this list is by no means exhaustive).

How Much Money Should I Invest?

If you've never invested before, you might have a chunk of savings you want to invest and/or a monthly amount you'd like to put toward your investments. You can go back to Chapter 3 for help in prioritizing which goals should come first and how to break down your goals into monthly targets. You can test out different amounts in your financial plan (or happiness allocation). There's a common investing myth that you need a lot of money to invest. Depending on how you decide to do it (coming soon), you can start with as little as $5.

Can I Invest Before I Pay Off My Student Loans (or other debt)?

The short answer is yes. A few things to consider here. First, what's the best use of your money? If you can expect to earn 7%, on average, adjusted for inflation in the market, and your student loans have an interest rate of less than that, then it makes more sense financially to invest than to aggressively pay down your student loans. Lauren Anastasio and Brian agree with this 7% cutoff and Rachel Sanborn Lawrence prefers 5%.

The tricky part is, we have no way of knowing what the market will look like in the years you invest instead of paying down your debt, so it's not a cut-and-dried answer. Is it ever? To make decisions easier, I like to look at the numbers. The following chart shows what kind of trade-off we are talking about.

Let's say you have $10,000 in student loans, with an interest rate of 5% and a $250 monthly payment. In scenario #1, you pay $750 toward student loans and in scenario #2 you pay $250 toward student loans and invest $500 with an interest rate of 7%. You can run a similar comparison with your own debt information (there's a template in the Financial Adulting toolkit).

In 14 Months	Scenario #1	Scenario #2	Difference
Debt Paydown	$10,000	$2,997	
Debt Balance	$0	$7,003	
Investment Balance	$0	$7,314	
Net Worth	**$0**	**$311**	**$311**

In 44 Months	Scenario #1	Scenario #2	Difference
Debt Paydown	$10,000	$10,000	
Debt Balance	$0	$0	
Investment Balance	$6,246	$25,144	
Net Worth	**$6,246**	**$25,144**	**$18,899**

Another important thing to consider is your relationship toward your debt. Some feel very comfortable and happy having student loans and making the monthly payments, where others want to pay them down as soon as possible.

Time Is *Very* Important

Understanding your goals for the money you are investing is important because of time. When you need the money will determine whether you should be investing it in the first place and how risky those investments should be. For any money you need in the short term (the next one to three years), you will want to keep that in cash (like a high-yield savings account).

After we're covered for the next three years, Brian recommends breaking down the remaining investments into goals for the next three to seven years (a medium-term bucket) and longer than seven years (a long-term bucket). For medium-term goals he says, "It's a balancing act. There's no perfect answer because it's long enough where I want it to grow, but it's short enough where a market decline could have a bad impact. It's typically a mix of stocks and bonds." For the long-term goals, he usually recommends that everything (or almost everything) be invested in stocks because that's the best for long-term growth.

When we invest for the long term we have the opportunity to wait out the market dips because we don't need the money for anything pressing. It's a much more powerful and much less stressful place to be. In some cases we may not even know what the money we are investing is for. That can be a good sign that we don't need the money in the near future. Can you hear the major privilege in this? I hope so.

Are You Ready to Level Up Your Risk Knowledge?

There are two types of risk, systematic and unsystematic. **Systematic risk** is the risk that the entire market can go down. This can happen when there's a recession, a global pandemic (oh, hey, 2020), or even when there's bad news. Following is a chart showing the total stock market over the past 30 years. Overall, the trend is far upward (yay long-term investing) but there are days or months where the market is down. Systematic risk is inevitable, unsystematic risk is not.

Unsystematic risk is the risk of loss in a certain industry or for a specific company (during the pandemic when no one was traveling, airline stocks took a big hit). Or when a company announces that their profit will be lower than expected, their stock price may go down. By investing in many industries and even more companies, we can mitigate this risk. And this is why investing in one company's stock

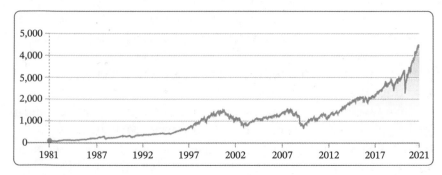

S&P 500 Index
Source: Yahoo! Finance.

is more risky than buying a fund that holds 3,000 companies, where the movement of one company or industry won't have too much of an impact on the whole.

The Types of Investments

In our brokerage accounts we can invest in anything that's **publicly traded** (jargon alert), meaning an investment that the general public can buy and sell via their brokerage accounts. Each investment that is publicly traded has a **ticker symbol**.

Funds are a great way to diversify because they are invested in all different things (each has their own mandate or description of what they invest in). By buying a share of a fund, we can be invested in hundreds of stocks or bonds, or a mix of both. You can separate funds into two categories: actively and passively managed.

Actively managed means that there is an investment professional (really a team of professionals) choosing the investments. **Passively managed** means that the fund mimics an index so it's essentially managed by a computer (there are people too but far fewer). Examples of indexes are the S&P 500 (the largest 500 publicly traded companies in the United States) and the Dow Jones Industrial Average (a.k.a. "The Dow," which tracks 30 large companies). Actively managed funds have higher expenses because you are paying for the team and expertise. You might assume that the investment professionals (actively managed funds) would earn higher returns, but it's actually really hard to beat the market.

"Fun" *very* **important fact:** Passively managed funds typically outperform their actively managed counterparts. Research shows that over the past 15 years, 86% of actively managed stock funds underperformed their respective benchmarks. Passively managed funds are less expensive and typically earn more profit – it's a win-win.

Rachel concurred and said that with equity (or stock) funds, passively managed is the way to go. She said that with some types of bonds you can argue that there can be added value with active management, but she still recommends passive management for bond funds. Rachel also shared that in "alternative assets" (anything outside of stocks, bonds, and cash), which are typically more of a focus for high-net-worth individuals, active management can be a differentiator.

What's in These Funds?

Outside of bonds versus equities, funds are often broken down by **sector** (industry) and/or size of the companies in the fund. As you can imagine, with a fund that's only invested in one sector, you are much more exposed (jargon alert) to anything happening in that sector, but at the same time, if it does really well, you will also earn more return than if you were invested in a bunch of other sectors at the same time.

Georgia says, "Invest in passively managed, low cost, broadly diversified funds – keep it super-unsexy."

What Does Broadly Diversified Mean?

It means that your portfolio is invested across a lot of sectors (e.g., tech, healthcare, etc.), geographic regions, and companies of different sizes.

Geographic locations are often broken down by U.S./domestic, international developed (e.g., Australia, Sweden, and Germany), and emerging markets (e.g., India, Mexico, and China).

Company size is determined by market capitalization, often shortened to "market cap."

> **DEFINITION: Market cap** is often used as a proxy for company size. You can look up a public company's market cap, which is calculated by taking their stock price multiplied by their total shares outstanding (tradable shares on the stock market).

Large-cap companies are large companies that are typically viewed as more stable and less risky, like Apple, Microsoft, and Johnson & Johnson. Small-cap companies tend to be more volatile but have a larger opportunity for growth (many you probably haven't heard of), and mid-cap are somewhere in the middle.

A broadly diversified portfolio will likely also include bonds and a bit of cash. It can include diversity in who issues the bond (e.g., government or corporate bonds) and the length of the term of the bond (short or long term). There's also a subsection of government bonds called "munis," which is short for municipal bonds issued by local governments.

Where Does Investing for Good Come In?

Emily says, "If you're not thinking about the impact of your investments, you're still making an impact, it's just a negative impact." That means thinking about where you're investing your money, and how that aligns with what you value personally. Think consumer activism for your investments.

Let's talk about options. ESG stands for environmental, social, and governance, and reflects criteria used to screen companies for their policies, the idea being that ESG funds are index funds and ETFs that only include companies that meet a certain level of criteria. Some funds exclude fossil fuels, gun manufacturers, tobacco companies, and companies that have had human rights violations. Others only include companies that have a certain number of women on the board and management team. And while there still isn't a governing third party, you can go to MSCI's (Morgan Stanley Capital International's) analysis tool to see how funds and companies rank on ESG factors.

Georgia shares that the most important thing to remember with ESG investing is that "it is not going to be perfect. It is actually going to be deeply, deeply imperfect. So bet on that. It's going to involve a lot of gray area."

Cleona Lira, the founder of Conscious Money, says, "Do not worry so much about the labels. Look more at the underlying companies that the fund is investing in. The top 10 holdings on a fund factsheet provide a lot of information." Other experts echoed this. Tanja Hester says it's important to be skeptical of ESG labels. You want to do your research to see what's actually in any given fund.

Georgia says that having a focus can help. At Modernist Financial, the primary portfolio has an environmental focus, predominantly centered on greenhouse gas emissions (and reducing them). She says if you add too many filters or factors you're considering, you're going to filter everything out and not have much left to invest in, which creates much more risk due to less diversification.

What's really cool is that a number of studies show that ESG funds are *outperforming* their non-ESG counterparts – so investing in them is a win-win. As there is more and more demand for these types of funds (from us financial adults), we'll see a lot more options come into the horizon. I keep a list of my favorites (and tools to research them) in the Financial Adulting toolkit.

What About Socially Responsible or Values-Based Investing?

Georgia shares, "It's important to understand that the movement for socially-conscious (a.k.a. values-based) investing comes out of religious institutions. We at Modernist don't offer "socially responsible" investment filters (though the name sounds like it would be a good thing) because, due to religious beliefs, these filters generally disinvest from companies that engage in stem cell research or produce abortion/ contraceptives for women's healthcare. As a progressive investor, that is not 'socially responsible' to me." She adds that "some elements of that analysis are really helpful," like screening for munition companies and companies that use child labor. "I really am grateful that religious communities laid that groundwork for contemporary ESG investing, I just don't subscribe to all of their recommended filters."

How to Choose a Brokerage Account

As you do your research, you'll find that not all brokerage accounts are the same and some will be a better fit than others. But again, at the end of the day, it's better to make a choice than not take action and miss out on time for your money to grow.

Read through this list, then set a timer for 30–60 minutes to do some research. When the timer goes off, make your choice. Nothing like a deadline! Here's how to choose a brokerage account.

Start with Recommendations

Now that you have a better idea of how you want to invest, keep that in mind in your research – meaning, you plan to focus on highly rated ESG funds, or funds in general. You want to start with a list of a few names. You can google, look to experts, or ask friends. We also have a list for you in the toolkit. When googling, be wary of top-10 lists. Sometimes companies pay to be on those, so you'll still want to do your own research.

When you have a list of names, take a look at customer reviews. It's important to see what people are saying who are actually using and experiencing the platform. Is it easy to get in touch with customer service? Do they have text support or do you have to hop on the phone? Do the investment options match how you plan to invest? Do customers like the website/app? How do you prefer to communicate? A lot of this is personal preference.

Look for a Low or No Minimum

Depending on how much money you are starting with, certain account minimums will be a dealbreaker. Many accounts have low or no minimums.

Make Sure There Are No Trading Fees

Back in the day when I started investing, you had to walk up the hill barefoot both ways to make a trade. Just kidding. But many brokerage accounts did charge a fee or commission each time you made a trade (unless you were trading their securities). The good news is, it's now easy to find accounts with $0 commissions, all the time. Trading fees are a dealbreaker.

Say No to Other Fees

Are there any other fees like a monthly or annual account maintenance fee? There are plenty of account options that don't charge any other fees, so this one is also a dealbreaker for me.

Do They Pass Your Consumer Activist Criteria?

Back in Chapter 6, you made your own consumer activist criteria. The financial services space is evolving (albeit more slowly than I'd like). There are new companies being founded and the more established brands are implementing changes to do better. You might not be able to find a perfect fit but you can definitely factor this in.

SIPC Insurance

Any reputable brokerage firm will be **SIPC insured**. This is similar to the FDIC insurance that we talked about in Chapter 6 in that if the brokerage firm goes under for any reason, your money is protected. That being said, it's very important to understand that being insured doesn't protect your investments from losses as far as ups and downs in the market.

Choose your brokerage account.

	Example	Brokerage Account #1	Brokerage Account #2	Brokerage Account #3
Investment Options	Plenty of low-fee funds			
Customer Reviews	Lots of 5-star reviews			
Consumer Activism Rating	3			
Fees/ Minimum/ SIPC Insurance	No fees, no minimum, yes SIPC insurance			
General Notes – Does this account fit your needs?	Highly rated app, auto transfers easy to set up			

Once you choose, you'll follow the brokerage firm's process for opening an account. It will feel very similar to opening a bank account.

What If I Don't Want to Do It Myself?

If you go the robo-advisor route, you'll open up your account through the robo-advisor (not through a separate brokerage), but your research will look similar. Research:

- The fees and other costs
- Investment options
- How they stack up with your consumer activist criteria

If you are interested in using a robo-advisor, do some research.

	Example	Robo-Advisor #1	Robo-Advisor #2	Robo-Advisor #3
Investment Options	All low-fee index funds; ESG option available			
Customer Reviews	4/5 stars; many reviews			
Fees / Costs	0.25%; no other fees			
Consumer Activism Criteria	3			
General Notes – Does this account fit your needs?	Overall seems like a good fit. Love the chat feature.			

If you hire a financial advisor, your brokerage account will typically be through their company. You can open an account with them directly or, if you already have an account, you will transfer your investments over to them. Before hiring a financial advisor you'll want to ask or find out:

- Are they an RIA/fiduciary?
- Do they have any other credentials?
- Are they a fee-only advisor or do they get paid to sell you products?
- What's their investment philosophy?
- What does your gut say about the interaction? Did you feel heard? Was it a judgment-free conversation?
- Did they take the time to explain what's happening with your money?

Take notes here.

_____

_____

_____

What About the Apps?

Apps can be added to your research – you'll want them to meet the same criteria (i.e., no fees). They are another type of brokerage account that may add some different features, education, and gamification, like investing your spare change or social media components to encourage conversations around investing.

Another thing you'll see in many of the apps is the opportunity to invest in **fractional shares**, meaning instead of spending $1,000 for a share of Tesla stock, you can buy a portion of a share for $5. The goal of many of these apps is to make investing more accessible and fun, and you know I'm all for that.

Choosing Your Investments

There isn't one perfect investment choice for you. There are thousands of books, millions of articles, and entire TV channels that talk about investing 24/7. Two people can completely disagree on strategy and both make good money. At the end of the day, you want to be invested and have your money growing.

Start with Asset Allocation

We calculated your asset allocation for your retirement investments in Chapter 7. The asset allocations for your other investments are a different story. In the Financial Adulting toolkit you can find some of my favorite resources for finding your ideal asset allocation.

Answer the questions in the calculators with the specific money you are looking to invest in mind. You'll probably answer the questions differently if you are investing the money you plan to use to buy your house in 7 years than your retirement money that you don't need for over 20 years.

Record your asset allocation results for a couple calculators.

	Example	Calculator #1	Calculator #2	Calculator #3
Stock %	85%			
Bonds %	10%			
Cash %	5%			
Total	**100%**			

Now On to the Funds

You're ready to choose some investments. Some of the calculators in the Financial Adulting toolkit give specific fund recommendations or genres to get you started. You researched funds for your retirement in Chapter 7. You'll do the same thing here (just with lots more options) and if you decide to, you can now add your ESG criteria. If you need some funds to get you started, I have a list in the toolkit.

Great! Now research these criteria for three to seven funds.

	Example	Fund #1	Fund #2	Fund #3
Name/Ticker Symbol	SPDR SSGA Gender Diversity Index/SHE			
Expense Ratio	0.2%			
What It's Invested In/ Asset Allocation	Companies with greater gender diversity/100% equity			
ESG Criteria (if any)	MSCI Rating of AA			

A Couple of Things to Note

- If the fund is tracking an index, Tony recommends looking at the tracking error. How good of a job is it doing at tracking the index it's supposed to track?
- If adding the ESG component feels overwhelming and will keep you from getting started, no judgment. This is something you can come back to later.

Purchasing or Selling an Investment

You've come so far! To purchase or sell an investment, you might think you just hit buy or sell. Maybe in some of the apps, but it might not be that easy. Here's how to purchase an investment and some frequently asked questions.

The Ways You Can Purchase and Sell

The easiest way is to make a **market order**. That just means you'll purchase (or sell) the investment at the market price at that time. This is what I now do and I recommend it for everyone, unless you find it fun to try to earn a few extra cents per share.

Only if you're interested: You can also use stop and limit orders to name your price. Specifically, a **limit order** has you purchase a share at a named price or better and a **stop order** activates a market order when the investment hits a certain price. To make it more "fun" you can combine them in a **stop limit order**. At the levels most of us are investing, it's not worth the extra work and time to do these fancy orders for a few cents.

Choosing the Number of Shares

When you purchase an investment you typically have to enter in the number of shares you want to buy. Take the amount you want to invest and divide it by the share price. If you have $100 to invest and the share price is $35, then you can buy two shares. The extra cash waits until next time.

It Won't Happen Immediately

I share this so you don't freak out while your money is in limbo. It takes time for an order to execute and the shares to show up in your account. Don't fret when it's not immediate. You can come back and check in a day or two (depending on the platform) and the shares will be there.

Should I Choose to Reinvest Dividends?

Some companies pay **dividends**, which means they share profits (in cash) with their investors (a certain amount per share). If you don't choose to reinvest your dividends, the cash will sit in your account. If you choose to reinvest your dividends, the cash will be used to purchase more shares. Dividends are great if you are looking for some income (side note: they are taxed as income!) so they are a great tool in retirement. While we're growing our money, it typically makes sense to reinvest.

How Do I Know What's a Good Price?

Want to know a little secret? No one really knows. Not even people who do this for a living. Yes, you'll hear buy low and sell high. Sounds easy enough, right? But in practice you can't know when the market is at its peak or low. Constant investing over time (either per month or per paycheck) is the way to go.

Am I Buying at the Right Time?

This is pretty similar to the last question in that no one really knows, but it's helpful to understand some terms you'll hear thrown around. A **bull market** means stocks are going up or whoever said it thinks stocks will go up. A **bear market** is the opposite; things are going down. A **bubble** means that prices are high (things are overvalued) and will eventually "pop" or go back to a much lower level. A **correction** is when there's a drop in prices because things were overvalued or too high.

Do I Invest All My Money at the Same Time?

If you have a chunk of money, should you invest it all at once? There are mixed reviews. **Dollar-cost averaging** means that instead of investing all of your money at once (and getting one price), investing over time at different prices will reduce your risk of buying in when the stock price is high. This happens naturally when we invest on a regular basis, like every month or every paycheck, which is great.

To do this with a chunk of money, you could, as an example, invest a quarter of it (25%) every week until it's all invested. This takes some extra work. *But* research shows that it usually turns out better to get all of it invested at once because over time markets tend to go up.[9] When something is easier *and* better for our money, that's a win-win. Plus, you're less likely to forget to invest.

When Do I Sell My Investments?

Sell your investments when you're ready to use the money for whatever goal you've been saving for. Yay! Or maybe you are no longer a fan of an investment and are looking to make a switch to a different one. Just know that with investments outside of your retirement accounts, selling is a taxable event. If you made money (which I hope you did if you're selling it), you will pay capital gains tax.

Learn from Some Investing Experts

What better way to learn than to see how the experts are investing their own money? You're welcome.

Georgia Lee Hussey, CFP and founder of Modernist Financial: Georgia says, "I invest in passively managed, low-cost, and broadly diversified index-like funds and ETFs. I keep it super-unsexy." She recommends you do the same. "Keep it fast, easy, cheap, and automated and then move on to something more interesting like your giving plan or how to spend your money more intentionally" (like we covered in Chapter 6). Pretty cool that you know what all that means now, right?

Farnoosh Torabi, money expert and host of the *So Money* podcast: Farnoosh uses a robo-advisor for her personal investing and recently revisited her portfolio because her investments were keeping her up at night. She shared that "traditional financial advice says set it and forget it. But no, because when life happens, you need to check yourself and that includes your investment portfolio." When she set up her portfolio 10 years ago, she wasn't the breadwinner, she didn't have kids, and she was in a different place. Her emotions served her in that they led her to revisit her investments and rebalance her portfolio.

Emily Green, Director of Private Wealth at Ellevest: Even though she invests other people's money all day, every day, Emily has her money invested in a robo-advisor and has automatic contributions set up to her impact (or ESG) portfolio. Since she's 34 (at the time of the interview), her retirement accounts are mostly invested in equity funds and she said her nonretirement investments are pretty "aggressive" as well.

Tony Molina, Product Evangelist at Wealthfront: Tony shared a personal story of how his investing strategy changed. Before the pandemic, he and his wife were saving for a home as a more long-term goal. Then their priorities shifted, work from home became the norm, they had a baby on the way, and they realized they wanted to buy much sooner. They sold their investments earlier than they had expected (luckily the market was up) and took a tax hit on their realized gains. I share this story because we make plans, but plans change. Even though investing is for the long term, it's still your money and it's liquid. Our plans don't have to be perfect to get started.

How Your Investing Can Change as You Build Wealth

I spoke with Alex Lieberman, co-founder of *Morning Brew* (one of the daily newsletters I get and love). They also have a great personal finance newsletter called *Money Scoop*. Alex shared his personal investment strategy:

> *I've historically invested my money in a very practical way that fit my lifestyle. Meaning, I didn't have time to spend researching investments. Plus I have zero competitive advantage. I invested in funds that track the S&P 500. And over time, odds are that they would grow at 7 or 8% return each year, on average.*

More recently, since selling a portion of the Brew, *and being fortunate to accumulate some wealth, I've moved to working with dedicated financial advisors who manage the bulk of my money. I have a close relationship with them where they update me on how they are putting my money to work in a balanced portfolio that I would describe as pretty aggressive (as it should be for a 28 year old).*

Now that Alex has more time, he enjoys coming up with investment ideas (for a small portion of his portfolio) and talking through them with his advisors. He views them not only as managing his money but also as educating him about investing. He dedicates about 10% of his portfolio to alternative investments like real estate, private equity, angel investing, and crypto.

We talked about the higher fees he pays for a financial advisor. Here's how Alex thinks of them:

The average financial advisor charges somewhere between 0.5% and 1% of assets under management. To me, it becomes very clear over a period of time (let's call it a few years), whether they are able to outperform net of their fees. And if they're not, then that's when I start thinking about working with someone else. If they are, then that's great because I've created a space where I can feel confident that I am preserving my wealth, growing my wealth, and I have the space to learn."

How will he know if they outperform net of fees? He'll compare his portfolio with the advisor to a scenario where he invested in an S&P 500 fund or used a robo-advisor. I'm excited to check in with him on this in 2023. Maybe I'll include a follow-up in my next book.

Protect Yourself from Yourself

We're usually the number-one threat to our own investing success. Here are some ways to protect yourself from yourself:

- Remember – you haven't lost (or earned) money on your investments until you sell them.

- Don't watch your investments all day.
- Automate if you can.
- Don't try to time the market.

Some Other Things That Might Be on Your Mind

What the Heck Is Bitcoin?

Understanding Bitcoin is not necessary to understand investing, but it's everywhere, so you might still want to know what it is. Bitcoin is a form of **cryptocurrency** (the most popular form of "crypto"), which is digital currency not tied to any banks or government (traditional money is part of the fiat system). Bitcoin is created and trades on a decentralized system known as blockchain.

You can invest in different cryptocurrencies like Bitcoin and Ethereum, but you can also invest in diversified crypto ETFs. Farnoosh got started investing in the space by investing in an ETF of companies that work in the space more tangentially or that support crypto technology. Even though she chose a more diversified crypto investment rather than choosing one of the currencies, she shared that it's still very risky and only makes up a very small piece of her investing portfolio.

You might have also heard the term *NFT*, which stands for nonfungible token and is a photo, video, or other digital file stored on a digital ledger that people trade.

Is Individual Stock Picking Like Gambling?

Individual stock picking (also called speculative investing) can be fun for some investors but it doesn't have to be part of your strategy. While I sometimes have FOMO when people make it big off of a certain stock, I also remember the big losses we don't hear about but that happen more often. I am happy with my long-term 8% return I get with diversified index funds.

Brian says you should only consider speculative investing once you have your financial foundation in place (those boxes checked!) and even then he recommends keeping it to 5% or less of your portfolio. Georgia calls this "hunches and fun" and recommends keeping it to 2–5%. She says, "Let's not bet your whole future on whether you think Tesla or Bitcoin is going to make it or not, because these markets are too small and volatile to make them a large part of your portfolio. You want this to be money you are okay with losing."

Your Financial Adulting Action Items

- ☐ Understand that investing is a privilege.
- ☐ Check some important financial boxes before you get started investing.
- ☐ Start to get comfortable with investing lingo (this takes time!).
- ☐ Choose how you want to invest – on your own, with a robo-advisor, or if you want to hire a financial professional.
- ☐ If you want more support, look into hiring a financial planner or money coach.
- ☐ Research, choose, and open your brokerage account or robo-advisor account (if applicable).
- ☐ Research and choose your investments (including ESG funds).
- ☐ Decide how much you can and want to invest.
- ☐ Learn strategies from investing experts.
- ☐ Start investing. Make it automatic when possible.
- ☐ Use strategies to protect yourself from yourself.
- ☐ Adjust your financial plan for the amounts you are now investing.

Huge congrats! You are now an investor who not only grows their money but also does good (or you're ready to start as soon as you check those financial boxes). Your money is officially working for you! This is just the beginning of your investing journey. Continue to ask questions, get support, and normalize investing conversations with friends. That's how we'll change investing culture.

Next up, we're going to talk about a different type of investment, a real estate investment – a.k.a., buying a home.

CHAPTER 9

Buying a Home

Whether you're thinking of buying your first home or a rental property, you're investing in real estate. There are many things to consider and navigate as you decide whether it makes sense for you to buy a home and then go through the process. Here we go!

Buying a Home – How It Works

Most of us won't be able to (or want to) pay the entire price of the home in full (commonly referred to as paying in cash). Most home buyers pay a chunk of money up front (in the form of a down payment) and finance the rest using a specific type of loan called a mortgage.

Before we talk about the home-buying process, it's important to answer a few questions.

Rent versus Buy?

Ah, the "American Dream." Own a home with a two-car garage and a white picket fence and you're on your way to happiness, right? Not quite. There are many misconceptions about homeownership. A big one is that it makes financial sense for everyone to own a home and paying rent is a "waste of money." Homeownership doesn't make sense for everyone and there are many factors to consider before taking the leap.

THE HOMEOWNERSHIP GAP

The United States has a long history of racism in real estate (remember the FHA and redlining from back in Chapter 2?), which, in addition to a whole lot of other discrimination in our financial systems, has led to a racial homeownership gap. In 2019 the white homeownership rate for people 35–54 was 73%,[1,2] Black homeownership was 50% (a 20%+ gap), and Latino homeownership was 52% (a 20%-plus gap). Tiffany Aliche, our friend The Budgetnista, says, "Homeownership is a cornerstone for wealth and the statistics show that homeowners have more wealth than those who don't own homes."

Not only are there fewer Black and brown homeowners, research shows the homes that Black and brown people do own are automatically devalued by 23%, which equates to $48,000 in equity per home.[3] Tiffany says, "If you say my house is worth $48,000 less than it is, that's $48,000 I don't get to pass on to my heirs. Multiply that across all Black families and that's $156 billion taken from the Black community.[4] That's a big part of the wealth gap." Devalued homes reduce wealth (and intergenerational wealth) and also affect someone's ability to borrow, refinance, and sell the home for a higher value. It also takes funding away from schools, infrastructure, and public safety in Black communities via property taxes.

Timing

Consider how long you plan to stay in this home. There are costs involved with buying and selling a home. The longer we own a home, the longer we give it time to appreciate (or increase) in value and the longer we give it to lessen the burden of those up-front and back-end costs.

Your Budget

Your budget can determine how long you want or are able to stay in a certain home. If there's a neighborhood you really want to live in but it doesn't work with your budget *yet*, you might want to wait to purchase so that when you do, you can see yourself living there for a long time.

Or if you plan to have kids or expect parents or other family to move in with you, you may want to wait to purchase a home that can accommodate your growing family.

Your Goals

The financial piece of the home purchase is really important, but it's not everything. A lot of people purchase a home not because it's the best use of their capital (i.e., cash) but because it's something they want. It's important to them. Maybe they want to have a place to call and make their own. Or maybe it provides a sense of financial security to not depend on the rental market.

> Use a rent vs. buy calculator (my fave is in the Financial Adulting toolkit) to see what makes the most sense for you financially at this point in your life. Write down your results here.
>
> _____
>
> _____
>
> _____

How Much Will This Cost?

Have you heard the term "house poor"? It's a sad phrase for a very common situation where homeowners spend all (or most) of their savings to purchase their home, plus a large portion of their income goes to their mortgage (and other home-related expenses). It's not fun or comfy, so we want to go in with our eyes wide open.

The Down Payment

This is the most well-known expense associated with buying a home. It's also the largest and most daunting (by far), which explains why it gets so much attention.

With a conventional mortgage, if your down payment is below 20%, you'll likely pay private mortgage insurance (PMI), which is usually 0.5–1.5% of the cost of the mortgage each year. Not having to pay PMI is ideal, but putting 20% down also makes purchasing a home potentially out of reach for many, especially in the short term.

There are some other reasons you might want to consider a larger down payment. Putting more money down can:

- Make your offer look more competitive, especially in a hot real estate market

- Mean a lower monthly payment, which can make monthly costs more affordable

- Typically mean a lower interest rate, which will save you in interest costs

- Make it easier to secure a mortgage (the loan is viewed as less risky)

Estimate your down payment. If you're not sure, come back to this later. You can also download our house budgeting spreadsheet from the Financial Adulting toolkit.

Cost of the Home	×	Down Payment %	=	Total Down Payment
Example: $250,000	×	20%	=	$50,000
	×		=	

Mortgage Closing Costs

Closing costs are the expenses associated with the mortgage and closing on (finalizing) the purchase or sale of the home. The exact amounts will vary by state, the cost of your home, the mortgage, and whom you hire. Head to the Financial Adulting toolkit for a closing cost calculator, which will give you an idea of what they will be in your area, given your mortgage size. Some closing costs may include:

- Title insurance
- Prepaid expenses (interest and taxes)
- Wire fees
- Loan origination fees
- Additional taxes and fees
- Escrow fees
- Broker fees (for sale of a home only)

Wait, what are escrow fees? Escrow fees are fees that go toward setting up your escrow account. An escrow account is an account created and held by a third party where you put your earnest money (also called a deposit) until your home purchase closes. These funds are applied toward your down payment. Then, a separate escrow account managed by the company servicing your mortgage can be set up (and may be required). It will usually use part of every monthly payment to fund property taxes and insurance out of the account.

Estimate your closing costs (using a calculator in the toolkit) here.

_____

_____

_____

Other Closing Costs

But that's not all . . . here are some other potential closing costs.

- Home inspection
- Homeowners insurance
- Real estate attorney
- Private mortgage insurance (PMI)

Add up estimates for other closing costs.

Home inspection	$
Homeowners insurance	$
Real estate attorney (if applicable)	$
PMI (if applicable)	$
Total Other Closing Costs	$

Life Insurance

This one might come as a surprise but if you are buying a home with a partner, life insurance can be an important purchase if one person wouldn't be able to afford the payments on their own. Life insurance can protect them from having to sell the home or default on the mortgage if something were to happen to their partner.

If you are buying a home on your own, you may still want to purchase life insurance. If something were to happen to you, whoever you leave the house to would be responsible for the mortgage payments (and all other costs). If you want them to be able keep the home and not have to sell it, life insurance might be needed for them to do that. We talk life insurance in detail in Chapter 10.

Will you want to get life insurance (if you don't have it already)? Get a cost estimate.

Home Emergency Fund

When we own our own homes, we can no longer call the landlord when something breaks. This is a big adjustment (at least it was for me). If your dishwasher breaks or something happens with the AC, you're going to have to foot the bill. To prepare for these inevitable home repairs, you will want to create a new rainy-day fund for your home in addition to your regular rainy-day fund, or you can increase the amount you keep in your original rainy-day fund to cover unexpected home costs.

> How much do you want in your home emergency fund?
>
> _____
>
> _____

Property Taxes

Property taxes are an annual tax that will vary by where you live and the assessed value of your property. The assessed value of your home is often not the price you paid for it (which is called the appraised or market value), but a value placed on it by the local government for calculating taxes.

The amount you owe in property taxes will change every certain number of years when the property is reassessed or if there is an increase in property taxes in your town. How often your taxes will be reassessed varies by city.

> Estimate your property taxes based on the budget for your home and your neighborhood/area. If you're not sure, you can come back to this later.
>
> _____
>
> _____

Updates, Renovations, and Decor

When you purchase a home, you'll likely want to start adding your personal touches or notice that some aspect (or many) of the home wants some love and attention. Updates (like painting), decor costs (like lighting and furniture), and any renovation expenses should be included in your home plan. These costs can be significant if you are investing in a fixer-upper or if many things arise from the home inspection.

It's hard to know how much you'll want to spend on updating a home until you meet it. You can include an estimate here that you can always update.

_____

_____

_____

Maintenance Expenses

If you are buying a co-op or condo, or live in a development, you'll likely have a monthly maintenance fee or HOA (homeowner's association) fee. This is money that the building or community uses each month for cleaning, staff, amenities, and reserves for larger projects. Even if you are buying a house, there can be monthly or quarterly maintenance fees associated with neighborhood upkeep, such as maintenance of common lawn areas, sidewalks, sewer lines, or streetlights.

When you see a price that feels too good to be true, check out these fees. Sometimes they are so high it's like adding a rent payment on top of your mortgage.

If you are moving from an apartment to a house or even to a larger home, it's important to account for any additional costs that you didn't have before. Will your utilities be higher? Do you now have a lawn to take care of? An annual chimney cleaning? Will you need to buy more furniture?

What are your estimated maintenance or HOA costs?

_____

_____

Costs of the Move Itself

Once you've purchased your home, you'll need to figure out how to get all your stuff there. This is an expense we often forget about or underestimate. Depending on how far you have to move and how much stuff you have, moving costs will vary. When making your plan, get estimates from some reputable movers in your area to see how much you should save up or account for.

How much do you expect the move to cost?

_____

_____

Incorporate These Costs into Your Plan

Add Up the One-Time Costs

If you decide to buy a home, this is your home savings goal. If it feels astronomical and far away, I get it. If it's important for you to become a homeowner sooner, adjust your expectations. Or if your wishlist is nonnegotiable, you can increase the time it will take to reach the goal (for now).

What are the total one-time costs?

	Scenario #1	Scenario #2
Down Payment	$	$
Mortgage Closing Costs	$	$
Other Closing Costs	$	$
Home Emergency Fund	$	$
Updates, Renovations, and Decor	$	$
Cost of the Move	$	$
Total One-Time Costs	**$**	**$**

Incorporate the Ongoing Costs

For the ongoing expenses, we go back to our friendly financial plan (or happiness allocation). You can estimate the ongoing costs and enter them into your plan to see if they're workable with your current (or estimated) income and other expenses.

What are the total ongoing costs?	Scenario #1	Scenario #2
Life Insurance	$	$
Property Taxes	$	$
Maintenance Expenses	$	$
Total Ongoing Costs	**$**	**$**

"Try On" Your Estimated Homeowner Expenses

This is brilliant (if I do say so myself) and often skipped over. One of the easiest ways to see how being a homeowner will feel financially is to "try on" your new expenses for size. Take the estimated monthly costs you calculated, including your mortgage, property taxes, insurance, and HOA, if applicable. If this is more than you are paying now for housing, transfer the difference to savings each month. For example, if the total will be $2,000 per month and you are currently paying $1,500, pay your bills as usual and transfer an additional $500 to savings. It's a win-win because you'll be saving up for your new home while also getting an idea of how this home will affect your spending plan.

Wait, I'm Discouraged; This Is Much More Expensive Than I Thought

I know. Saving up for a home is a really big goal. Know that your progress toward your goals doesn't have to be linear and it won't be.

Just because I'm saving $5 or $20 per paycheck right now doesn't mean that it will take me 10,000 years to save up for a home. Our progress can be exponential, especially as we learn new skills and get motivated by our results. And it's okay if it takes you some time to reach this goal! It's a big one.

Also, if you earn a commission or receive a bonus or lump-sum payment, putting aside a significant portion of that (if possible) can help you reach your homeownership goal.

Stay motivated: Keep an image handy of your home (or the home you want) on your phone or in your wallet. Look at it often. Before we bought our home I was working in a windowless basement in our apartment on the Upper West Side. I really wanted to work in an office with a big sunny window. This is the image I kept on my desk and in my mind as we searched for our new home. When we bought our condo there was a room with a big window and that's right where I put my desk!

Organize Your Finances Before Starting the Process

There are a couple things you can do in advance that will make your life *much* easier during this process. Believe me, I know. I didn't do them.

Check Your Credit Score and Get Credit Ready

Our credit score is typically one of the most important factors lenders consider when we're applying for a mortgage. Not only does it determine if we qualify for a loan (more details on this later), it can also impact the interest rate we're offered (which can matter *a lot* on a big loan). We'll talk credit scores in detail in Chapter 12. Increasing your score can take time, so the earlier you start making moves, the better.

Check your credit score. Where do you stand? _____

Simplify Your Accounts

During the mortgage process, you'll be sending over lots (and lots) of financial information, and then more follow-up financial information and then more follow-up financial information and . . . you get the idea. It's painful. The simpler your financial life, the easier this will be. Consolidate accounts where you can. Make a list of everything you have (and owe) and where, and know your logins and passwords.

Important: Do this *before* you apply for a mortgage. Moving money around and making account changes during the mortgage process will lead to much more paperwork and even more of a headache.

> What can you do to simplify your financial life before you start the home-buying process?
>
> 1. _____
>
> 2. _____
>
> 3. _____

Go on a Buyer's Budget

Fee Gentry, MBA real estate professional, founder of the Black eXp Network (a network of 3,700 Black real estate professionals and allies) and co-creator of the Agent Accelerator Academy, a 60-day course teaching agents to work with communities of color, recommends reducing expenses before the home-buying process; it is a win-win because it makes your spending look good for your lender and you'll also be saving more money. Not only that, don't make any major purchases and don't open a credit card, take out other debt, or refinance your student loans (which will affect your credit). This buyer's budget is all about keeping spending down and keeping yourself credit ready.

What will your buyer's budget look like? Was there anything you were planning on doing that you no longer will be doing?

_____

_____

_____

Understand the Types of Mortgages Available

Your mortgage is a big deal. For many of us, it's the largest loan we've ever received. Here are the key details of the different options.

- **Conventional loans.** A conventional mortgage is a mortgage with a bank rather than with the government. You will typically need a credit score of 620 or higher to qualify but exceptions can be made depending on your personal finance profile (like how much income you earn and cash you have in the bank). Below are some common types of conventional mortgages. "Jumbo" mortgages are larger than conventional loans and come in these same types.
  - **Fixed-rate mortgages.** These mortgages have the same interest rate for the entire life of the loan. You might see 30-year, 15-year, 10-year, and even 7-year fixed-rate mortgages. You don't have to worry about interest rate fluctuations. What you sign is what you get. It's typically more expensive (interest-rate-wise) to lock in an interest rate for a long period of time. Depending on how long you plan to live in your home or how quickly you plan to pay off your mortgage, it may be worth getting a mortgage for less time.
  - **Adjustable-rate mortgages (ARMs).** These mortgages have a fixed rate for a certain period of time and then the rate adjusts depending on where interest rates are at the time. A 10/1 ARM is an example of an adjustable-rate mortgage. The rate is fixed for 10 years and then adjusts each year going forward.
  - **Interest-only mortgage.** This is exactly what it sounds like. You're only required to pay off the monthly interest and don't

have to make payments toward principal. This one requires a *lot* of discipline to pay down any of the mortgage principal – discipline I don't have.

- **FHA loan.** These loans are backed by the Federal Housing Administration (FHA). You can generally qualify for an FHA loan with a credit score of 580 or above and your down payment can be as low as 3.5%. The catch with a down payment below 20% is that you'll usually be required to pay an MIP (mortgage insurance premium), which typically costs 0.45–1.05% of the cost of the mortgage each year and 1.75% for upfront MIP. If you are using the rent vs. buy calculator, make sure it factors in MIP, or you can add that to your mortgage interest rate as a proxy. You'll also want to add it into your ongoing costs in your budget. There are size limits on the loan, which will depend on your location.

- **USDA and VA mortgages.** These are two other mortgage options for those who qualify in rural areas or are military-qualified borrowers, respectively. Neither requires a down payment and the VA mortgage doesn't require mortgage insurance.

Outside of mortgages there are financial assistance programs available for first-time homebuyers.

- **Housing Choice Voucher (HCV) homeownership program.** This program provides monthly payment and down payment assistance to first-time homebuyers who meet specific income and employment requirements. You can learn more at hud.gov.

- There are also state and local programs that provide first-time home-buying assistance to veterans, those in specific industries (like teachers and service members), specific locations (like in rural areas), and at specific income levels. What's available varies by state (and county) but it's worth looking into!

Fee encourages us to ask the mortgage bankers lots of questions and to deep-dive watching mortgage tutorials on YouTube. I understand the tendency to want to get the process over and done with but I promise it's worth taking the time to really understand what's available.

Which mortgage makes the most sense for you? What will your monthly payment look like? How much are you paying in interest each month and over the course of the time you plan to have the loan?

	Option #1	Option #2	Option #3
Mortgage Type			
Monthly Payment			
Interest Rate %			
Interest Paid per Month			
Interest Paid Over the Course of the Loan (or how long you plan to own)			

Should You Go Digital or Analog?

Fee says that sometimes the digital mortgage companies work really well (they're convenient and can remove bias from the mortgage process) and that there are also benefits to working with a local provider (they're more familiar with how loans are written in that specific community and they work to compete with the "big" mortgage companies). I'm a fan of trying both and seeing where you get the best rate.

Fee says that in the same way you ask questions of your agent (I have a list for you in the toolkit), you can also ask questions of your lender, such as: "I'm concerned because I've heard that women or those in the AAPI community or senior citizens get discriminated against. Can you walk me through the process?" You can learn a lot from how they respond.

List out a few potential mortgage lenders. Choose a combination of digital lenders, local lenders, and bigger banks. Depending on what the process looks like in your area, you might want to get preapproved at this point. Your agent can help with the timeline!

1. _____

2. _____

3. _____

4. _____

5. _____

An Important Ratio to Lenders

Each lender has their own metrics they look for in a borrower. In addition to your credit score, lenders will also look at your **debt-to-income (DTI) ratio**. Your DTI ratio is calculated by taking the total amount of money you put toward debt payments each month and dividing that by your gross monthly income. **Gross monthly income** means your income before taxes and deductions are taken out. If you earn commissions or bonuses, those can go in there too. You can calculate your gross monthly income by taking your annual income and dividing it by 12.

Lenders look at two DTI ratios during the mortgage approval process. First, they look at the ratio of all your new housing costs to your gross income (**front-end DTI ratio**). These costs include your mortgage principal and interest, insurance, property taxes, and HOA dues (if applicable). Then they look at your new mortgage *and* all other monthly debt payments you make as a percentage of your gross monthly income (**back-end DTI ratio**).

Some lenders may have a DTI ratio limit with restrictions on lending to people above that limit. For example, a lender may want to see a DTI ratio below 35%, with no more than 28% going to your mortgage. That means that if you earn $50,000, your annual debt payments will need to be below $17,500 and only $14,000 of that can go toward mortgage payments. But lenders also take credit score and cash reserves into account and can make exceptions.

What's your DTI? If you prefer to use a calculator, head to the Financial Adulting toolkit.

Monthly Housing Costs	/	Gross Monthly Income	=	Front-End DTI
Example: $1,167	/	$4,167	=	28%
	/		=	

Monthly Housing Costs + Other Debt Payments	/	Gross Monthly Income	=	Back-End DTI
Example: $1,458	/	$4,167	=	35%
	/		=	

If you are looking to improve your DTI, a great way to do that is to pay down debt. We'll make a plan to pay off your debt in Chapter 13.

What About Discrimination in Lending?

Fee shared, "I see it every single time. Single women and people of color go through a different level of scrutiny by underwriters than let's say any married, straight white couple. I've had clients who are single women with an 800 credit score and $250,000 cash in the bank and then another million in assets saved, and the lender will come back with a higher interest rate than for some married dude who has a 650 credit score." And the same pattern is repeated with people of color.

It's the unfortunate reality and Fee says that all you can do is prepare for the extra level of scrutiny and have responses planned for any questions or pushback you get. For example, if you have student loans, be ready to share when they will be completely paid off and how you've never missed or had a late payment. She says a good agent should be able to help you prepare for this as well.

Understand Key Mortgage Jargon

Here is some jargon you'll want to know for the interest rate conversations:

- **Interest rate.** The amount you'll pay in interest each year on the mortgage. It does not include any fees or other mortgage costs you pay.
- **APR (annual percentage rate).** The total cost of borrowing money. It includes the interest rate, points (more on this next), mortgage broker fees, and any other charges.
- **Points (short for discount points).** Allow you to pay more upfront (in the form of a fee) to lower your interest rate. **Credits** are the opposite. They allow you to pay less up front in closing costs in exchange for a higher interest rate. Which should you choose? I always recommend running the numbers. If you pay $500 now to pay $15 less each month, it will take 33 months (2.75 years) to break even. If you are moving into a long-term home, it could be worth paying points up front to have that lower interest rate. If it's a shorter-term purchase, it might be worth it to pay less now and have a higher interest rate.

RATE	4.875%	5.0%	5.125%
POINTS	+0.375	0	−0.375
YOUR SITUATION	You plan to keep your mortgage for a long time. You can afford to pay more cash at closing.	You are satisfied with the market rate without points in either direction.	You don't want to pay a lot of cash upfront and you can afford a larger mortgage payment.
YOU MAY CHOOSE	Pay points now and get a lower interest rate. This will save you money over the long run.	Zero points.	Pay a higher interest rate and get a lender credit toward some or all of your closing costs.
WHAT THAT MEANS	You might agree to pay $675 more in closing costs, in exchange for a lower rate of 4.875%. **Now:** You **pay** $675. **Over the life of the loan:** Pay $14 **less** each month.	With no adjustments in either direction, it is easier to understand what you're paying and to compare prices.	You might agree to a higher rate of 5.125%, in exchange for $675 toward your closing costs. **Now:** You **get** $675. **Over the life of the loan:** Pay $14 **more** each month.

Three Scenarios of How Points Affect Interest Rate

Source: ConsumerFinance.gov.

> ### For the Love of Money: Buying a Home with Your Partner
>
> If you are going to be purchasing the home with your partner, Lauren Hunt (the divorce attorney we met in Chapter 5) recommends a prenup (if you're getting married), a postnup (if you're married), and a cohabitation agreement (if you're not).

Should I Pay Down My Mortgage?

Mortgage paydown will definitely come after building your rainy-day fund, 401(k) matching, paying down debt with a higher interest rate, and saving for retirement, but after that, it comes down to the opportunity cost of that money and your level of comfort with debt. This example can help you think it through:

Let's say you have a $350,000 mortgage, with an interest rate of 3.25% and a $1,523 monthly payment. In scenario #1, you pay an additional $500 per month toward your mortgage and in scenario #2 you pay your mortgage and invest the additional $500 with an interest rate of 7%. You can run a similar comparison with your own mortgage information (there's a template in the Financial Adulting toolkit).

After 4 Years	Scenario #1	Scenario #2	Difference
Mortgage Paydown	$53,436	$29,436	
Mortgage Balance	$296,564	$320,564	
Investment Balance	$0	$27,766	
Net Worth	**($296,564)**	**($292,798)**	**$3,766**

After 10 Years	Scenario #1	Scenario #2	Difference
Mortgage Paydown	$141,415	$81,415	
Mortgage Balance	$208,585	$268,585	
Investment Balance	$0	$87,047	
Net Worth	**$208,585**	**$181,537**	**$27,047**

You'll see that over time, investing outpaces the mortgage paydown, and in scenario #2, you'd have a net worth of $27,047 more after 10 years. Note: To keep things simple, I only included the mortgage and investment balance from new investments in the net worth calculation.

If you have a mortgage (or get a mortgage), figure out where paying it off falls on your goal priority list. Put additional money toward it accordingly.

_____

_____

_____

"Fun" fact: Some lenders offer free **recasting** of your mortgage once you've paid down a certain amount of *additional* principal on the loan. This means they recalculate (or recast) your payments using the lower loan balance. For example, if you have a $150,000 mortgage balance and pay down an extra $20,000 in principal, your payments after recasting are now based on a mortgage of $130,000. This allows your total monthly payment to go down. Not hating that.

Another "Fun" fact: If you have a 30-year mortgage, your mortgage is **amortized** over 30 years. Your payments stay the same each month but what the payments go toward changes over time. At first, your payments are more interest than principal because your loan is at its highest balance. Over time, as you pay down your principal, the payments go more and more toward paying down the loan balance than interest. You can check out an amortization calculator for more details in the Financial Adulting toolkit.

When Should I Refinance?

The short answer is, when the numbers make sense. If you can refinance for a lower rate, that's great. It costs money to refinance – sometimes thousands of dollars – so it's also helpful to calculate how long it will take for the monthly savings to pay off or break even with the fees. For example, if you are spending $1,000 to refinance and it will save you $200 a month on your mortgage, you break even in five months. There are some handy calculators to help in the toolkit! Refinancing can also help you lock in a lower interest rate if your mortgage is moving to an adjustable rate in the nearish future.

Run a refinance calculator (if you already have a mortgage). How many months will it take to pay off? Do the numbers make sense?

Cost to Refinance	/	Monthly Savings	=	Time to Break Even
Example: $1,200	/	$200	=	6 months
	/		=	

Are there other benefits to refinancing for you?

_____

Another Way to Invest in Real Estate – REITs

If buying real estate feels too far out of reach or it's not quite a fit, there are other ways to get the benefits without a lot of the risk or costs. Real estate investment trusts (REITs) are companies that invest in real estate. By owning a share of a REIT (essentially a real estate fund) you own the properties in that REIT. Instead of purchasing a property of your own, you can buy a share of a REIT for $100 and own a piece of hundreds of properties.

Research some REITs.

	Example	REIT #1	REIT #2	REIT #3
Name/Ticker Symbol	Vanguard Real Estate ETF / VNQ			
Expense Ratio	0.12%			
What It's Invested In/ Asset Allocation	Invests in REIT stocks / 100% equity			
ESG Criteria (if any)	MSCI Rating of A			

Your Financial Adulting Action Items

- ☐ If you are a woman or BIPOC, know that you will most likely encounter discrimination during the homebuying process.
- ☐ Decide whether it makes sense for you to purchase a home financially, but don't forget to weigh subjective factors as well.
- ☐ Estimate the one-time cost to buy a home as well as the ongoing costs.
- ☐ Incorporate the estimated costs into your financial plan. Are they workable?
- ☐ "Try on" your estimated monthly homeowner expenses to see how they feel.
- ☐ Start saving (if you haven't already) for the larger one-time expenses.
- ☐ If you are buying a home with a partner, protect yourself with a prenup or cohabitation agreement.
- ☐ Add your mortgage to your goal priority lists, if it's not there already.

☐ Run a refinance calculator and/or see if it makes sense to recast your mortgage.

☐ Research some REITs.

This chapter was a biggie. You are now clear on whether or not it makes sense for you to buy a home. If it does, you now know the *true* cost and you are also a whiz on everything related to mortgages. Whew!

Retirement investor – check! Investor for good – check! Real estate investor – check! The next section of the book is *critical*, yet something we tend to want to glaze over. First up, we'll talk about protecting yourself. I'm talking protecting your income, protecting your chosen family, protecting your health, protecting your home, protecting your car – all the protecting.

CHAPTER 10

Insurance

Insurance is painfully important – painful in that it's confusing and there's a lot to know and understand. And also painful in that not protecting yourself can be financially disastrous. I'm going to break down the different types of insurance with some expert help (as painlessly as possible).

I sat down with Jennifer Fitzgerald, the CEO of Policygenius, a platform where customers can compare and buy insurance policies (you'll find lots of their amazing resources in the Financial Adulting toolkit), and she ranked the types of insurance in order of priority. Only some may apply to your financial situation.

1. **Health insurance.** Medical costs are one of the biggest drivers of personal bankruptcy and home foreclosure. Everyone should be covered.

2. **Homeowners and car insurance** (if you own your home and own or lease a car). These are typically your biggest financial assets.

3. **Life insurance** (if you are a parent or someone depends on your income).

4. **Disability insurance** (to replace your income if something were to happen to you).

We're going to start with the most important and work our way down the list from there.

Health Insurance: What You Need to Know

You pay a monthly amount (a **premium**) to your health insurance company and in return they agree to pay for some or all of your medical bills.

Because health insurance companies pay for lots of people's medical bills they negotiate discounted rates with doctors and hospitals (which helps keep costs down). These doctors and hospitals are labeled **in-network**. Doctors and hospitals that don't have a negotiated rate are **out-of-network** and insurance companies typically don't cover appointments and expenses with those doctors (until you hit your **out-of-network deductible!**).

Some Key Health Insurance Terms to Know

Your deductible. How much you pay on your own before your insurance kicks in. If you have a $500 deductible and get charged $400 for a doctor's visit, you'll pay the $400 and all other charges up until you pay $500 in total expenses. Once you hit $500 in bills, the amounts you owe will depend on your insurance. Sometimes all expenses above the deductible are covered. Sometimes there's **coinsurance**, where you share the cost with the health insurance company (i.e., 80/20, where the insurance company pays 80% of your bills and you pay 20%). Typically, plans with higher premiums (higher costs) come with lower deductibles, and vice versa. Some plans have both an **in-network deductible** and an **out-of-network deductible**.

Your copay. Sometimes annual checkups and visits with certain doctors cost a flat fee called a copay. These may also be covered and cost you $0. Your copay could also be the amount you pay per visit after you reach your deductible. Other plans offer coinsurance (mentioned above) up until you hit your **out-of-pocket max.**

Your out-of-pocket max. There is usually an in-network and out-of-network max for the year. If you are thinking, "Are you kidding me with these terms, Ashley?" Sadly, no, I'm not kidding. The max is the most you can pay out-of-pocket in total (on your own).

Your in-network max is typically lower (sometimes much lower) than your out-of-network max. It's the max you'll have to pay with in-network providers. And the out-of-network max is the maximum you'd pay for providers that aren't in-network. The good news is, this is the most you will pay in healthcare expenses in any given year. Once you hit your out-of-pocket max, insurance covers the rest.

Important: Your deductible and out-of-pocket maxes reset each year. On the date your plan resets (which can vary by plan), you're starting from a $0 deductible and $0 toward your out-of-pocket max. In addition, the amounts can change from year to year and typically increase over time.

For the Love of Money: Family Health Insurance

There's typically a higher deductible and out-of-pocket max for a family (more than one person) than an individual. In addition, your monthly premiums (or payments) will be higher. If you are partnered up, you don't have to be on the same health insurance plan, but you might want to be if one plan has better copays, a lower deductible, or lower out-of-pocket expenses.

Where Do I Get Health Insurance?

Your employer. If it's available to you, you'll probably want to get health insurance through work. Usually there are a few options to choose from and companies subsidize part or all of the monthly premiums.

Healthcare.gov (or your state marketplace). If you work for yourself or a company that doesn't offer health insurance, or are unemployed, you can get health insurance through the government health benefit exchange. Depending on your income, you may qualify for a subsidy (or discount). If you are part of a professional organization or union, you may be able to get a less expensive policy through them.

Health insurance company. You can purchase health insurance directly from the health insurance company (rather than going through the exchange). If you are going to get a discount on health insurance, it may be worth it to go through the exchange and reapply each year.

Medicaid. If you earn below a certain income level, you qualify for Medicaid. The requirements vary by state. It's a government-funded program so the costs are lower or free, yet you can still choose your insurance provider.

Medicare. If you are over 65, you qualify for Medicare, which is also a government-funded program so costs are lower.

Your family. If your family or caregiver has an insurance plan and they're inviting you to stay or be added on, you are allowed to do so until you are 26.

COBRA. If you were recently laid off or left your job, you can keep your health insurance plan for the next 18 months using COBRA (stands for Consolidated Omnibus Budget Reconciliation Act of 1985 – quite the mouthful!). It's typically very expensive (because your employer is no longer subsidizing the cost). This option is more attractive if you've already hit your deductible or out-of-pocket max (or are close to it). You can also check your health benefit exchange to get something more affordable in between jobs.

When Can I Get Health Insurance?

Open enrollment is the window of time during which you can sign up for insurance or change your insurance. For the government exchange, open enrollment typically starts in early November and ends in mid-December. If you are getting health insurance through your company, you'll want to ask about specific dates, because they vary.

Qualifying life events like changing or losing a job, having a baby, or getting married allow you to sign up or change your insurance outside of the open enrollment period. You usually have 30–60 days to sign up or make any changes after one of these life events.

"Fun" important fact. You usually have 30–60 days to add a new baby to your health insurance, depending on your insurance plan. To do this you need your child's birth certificate and Social Security number. I know, I know – like you don't have enough to do when you have a newborn.

What About Double Insurance?

You are allowed to have two health insurance plans and many people choose to do so in order to get the best coverage available to them. One policy will be designated the primary insurance and the other will be the secondary insurance. The primary insurance pays claims first and whatever is remaining goes to the secondary insurance. If you qualify to join a parent's plan, a spouse's plan, or Medicaid coverage, you might consider the cost and benefit of having two plans.

How to Choose Your Health Insurance Plan

There are two main types of plans: HMOs (health maintenance organizations) and PPOs (preferred provider organizations). **HMO** plans are typically less expensive. You are assigned a primary care physician (**PCP**) and need to get a referral to see any specialist doctors. You can typically find PCPs everywhere, but there's usually one office for specialists in your region (all in one place). Depending on where you live, you may have to travel outside your city.

PPOs tend to have higher monthly premiums but you have more flexibility to see the doctors you want to see and there is usually coverage for in-network and out-of-network doctors (although out-of-network will typically be more expensive). PPOs can be high-deductible health plans (**HDHPs**) if the deductible is over $1,400 for an individual and $2,800 for a family. When you have an HDHP you are eligible for an HSA (health savings account – yippee!). Check out later in this chapter for more info on this).

As tedious as it can be to look through these plans, I recommend understanding how each plan works and then running your own numbers. How? Start with what you expect your medical expenses to look like. Do you anticipate any doctor's appointments outside of your annual physical and gynecology checkup? Do you have any upcoming procedures or plan to have a baby? Do you or a loved one you are responsible for have a chronic illness or disability? Is there a specific doctor or hospital you want to go to for care?

While we can't predict every medical expense, if you plan to have a baby or typically see a lot of specialists, you can probably plan to hit your deductible (at the very least). If you have or plan to have multiple people on your health insurance plan, go through this process for each person.

	Example	Plan 1:	Plan 2:	Plan 3:
1. What do I expect to pay?	$250 per month (premium) plus deductible			
2. What is the most I will pay per year?	$250 per month plus out-of-network out-of-pocket max			

Think through your prescriptions (and if they will be covered), your current health, potential procedures, any future baby plans, dependents' or partner's health needs, disability, chronic illness, and mental health. Add the annual premium you pay to both question 1 and question 2.

After going through these exercises you will have a much better picture of which plan makes the most sense for you. Brian Walsh (he's the CFP and PhD in personal finance with SoFi you met in previous chapters) shares that one of the biggest mistakes he sees is that people choose the cheapest plan or the plan they already have (just because it's familiar) and that this can get them in trouble when an unexpected medical expense comes up.

Don't Be Afraid to Fight

Sometimes you'll get a bill that completely surprises you or something you expect to be covered by insurance isn't. Don't be afraid to ask questions, negotiate, and try to understand why things look different from what you expected. There are plenty of mistakes or miscommunications that happen and you don't want to be the one who pays for them. I know. Who has time for this?

Always reference your insurance plan to make sure the numbers match your coverage (e.g., your copay, coinsurance, deductible, etc.). Keep records of your bills: what you paid, whom you spoke to, when, and what they said (sometimes there's a case number given). If you are double-insured, make sure they billed the other insurance too.

You can also negotiate your medical bills. *Wha?* Yep! You can negotiate with the insurance company or hospital/health provider, and some health insurance plans or hospitals have patient advocates or social workers who can help and negotiate on your behalf. All hospitals have to forgive expenses or provide financial assistance for people who live at or below the federal or state income level or experience hardship, but *anyone* can apply.

Big Exclusions: Fertility Treatments, Adoption, and Trans-Related Healthcare

Fertility treatments like IVF and egg freezing are not typically covered under health insurance plans and are very expensive (like tens of thousands of dollars). More and more companies are offering fertility coverage of some sort to help defray those costs. It's worth looking into and considering in your planning (and even your job search).

Typically, benefits that help to cover the high costs ($40,000-plus) associated with adoption are part of the fertility plan. It's important to note that the high cost and lack of insurance for fertility treatments as well as adoption costs disproportionately affect the LGBTQ+ community.

Many policies do not cover any trans-related healthcare at all. This includes any surgeries, hormone treatments, or anything that gets categorized as trans-healthcare. This has a tremendous financial impact for the transgender community and their families.

How Do I Ever Budget for This?

You know that healthcare expense guesstimate you made previously to choose your policy? You can use that as your medical budget for the year! If you know you are going to have a procedure or deliver a baby soon, you can call your health insurance company for an estimate. If you think you are going to hit your deductible or out-of-pocket max, make sure your budget accounts for that too.

There are some very "cool" medical expense accounts that can help (you now know my sense of cool is majorly warped but these really are wondrous accounts). An **HSA** (health savings account) allows any individual with an HDHP (high-deductible health plan) to put pretax money aside for medical expenses.

If you have an HDHP, in 2022 you can contribute up to $3,650 for an individual or $7,300 for a family (and $1,000 more if you're over 55) to pay for qualifying medical expenses. You don't have to use the money that year (or even in the next 10 years) and once your balance hits a certain amount (often $1,000–$2,000), you are able to invest the money in the account and have it grow tax-free. *Tax-free* – like your 401(k) and IRA!

You can set aside more money in your HSA than you need for medical expenses as a strategy to grow more money tax-free. HSAs are actually *double* tax-free because you never have to pay taxes on the contributions (as long as you use them for qualified medical expenses) and you don't pay taxes on the investment growth. Once you've maxed out your retirement accounts and paid off high-interest debt, it's a great option to keep the party going.

"Fun" fact: After you're 65 years old, you can use the funds in your HSA for anything, but if it's not for qualified medical expenses you have to pay taxes on that money (similar to how you would in your traditional 401(k) or IRA).

A flexible spending account (FSA) is similar in that it allows you to set aside pretax money for medical expenses; the biggest differences are that (1) your employer has to offer the plan (you can't open one on your own) and (2) the money in there is "use it or lose it." You can usually either roll over $550 into the next year or sometimes there's a 2.5-month grace period where you can spend (or try to spend) the remainder of the funds. The most you can set aside in an FSA account in 2022 is $2,850. Some employers allowed more to roll over to 2022 because of the pandemic.

You can also set up a separate sinking fund for medical bills in an online savings account. Once you know your out-of-pocket max, it's helpful to revisit your rainy-day fund with that lens. Can it cover you in a year you have much higher than expected (or the max) medical expenses?

Gather some important details about your insurance.

How much do you pay per month (monthly premium)? _____

What's your deductible? _____

What happens after your deductible is met? _____

What's your in-network max? _____

What's your out-of-network max? _____

What's your total expected cost this year? _____

Do you qualify for an HSA? _____

Do you have an FSA through work? _____

How will you fund your medical expenses?

_____

Do you want to add anything to your rainy-day fund? If so, how much?

_____

"Fun" fact: There's another type of FSA that allows you to pay for dependent-care expenses, like preschool, summer day camp, before- or after-school programs, nanny expenses, and child or adult daycare, with pretax money. A big discount! You can find the full list of qualifying deductible expenses in the Financial Adulting toolkit. Sadly, if your work doesn't offer this plan, you won't have access to it. You can set aside up to $10,500 each year. You lose any unused funds and will need to renew your enrollment each year (we learned this the hard way).

Don't forget to update your financial plan for these numbers!

Important note. If you plan to contribute to an HSA or FSA plan through work, you may want to remove or reduce the amount of medical expenses in your financial plan because you'll now have money coming out of your paycheck to go toward them.

Healthcare Costs and Medical Debt

Two thirds of people who file for bankruptcy point to medical expenses as a reason,[1] making medical debt the single most common cause of personal bankruptcy.[2] Not only that, half of all home foreclosures (where you can't pay your mortgage and lose your home) have some medical cause.

DEFINITION: Bankruptcy, often called chapter 11, is a legal proceeding for when someone is unable to pay their debts or their debt becomes unmanageable. Through the proceedings, you are able to get rid of part or all of your debt but it significantly impacts your credit score for up to 7–10 years (depending on the type of bankruptcy). Some very wealthy folks use bankruptcy as a way to clear their debts while keeping their mansions, but for most, bankruptcy is a necessary yet expensive and difficult process that affects their financial well-being for years to come.

The average family spends $8,200 (or 11%) of their family income on healthcare costs per year.[3] Black families spend almost 20% of their household income on medical costs.[4] These high costs can lead to medical debt; 27.9% of Black households, 21.7% of Latino households, and 17.2% of white households have medical debt.[5]

Health insurance impacts families' medical debt; 16.2% of fully insured households have medical debt, compared with 30.8% of households where not everyone is insured.[6] People of color make up the majority of the uninsured population.[7] Disabilities also impact the rate of medical debt; 26.5% of households where someone has a disability have medical debt, compared with 14.4% for households where no members have disabilities.[8]

What a Health Insurance Policy Means for These Gaps (and our wallets)

People need access to affordable health insurance and medical care in order to thrive (even, in many cases, to survive) financially.

As a result of the pandemic, there was one bill passed that went into effect January 2022: the No Surprises Act.[9] The gist is that the bill requires advance communication (72 hour's notice) if something will be out of network and if the patient doesn't have a choice (like in an emergency situation), the provider must bill for in-network rates. The bill also provides potential relief for health expenses.

Protecting Your Assets: Homeowners and Car Insurance

Next up on the list is protecting your biggest assets, which are most likely your home and/or your car.

Homeowners Insurance – What You Need to Know

Homeowners insurance protects you if something breaks in your home or there is damage to your home, if something is stolen, or if someone sues you for getting injured in your home. It even can cover the cost of a hotel and meals if you have to be out of your home.

One important thing you'll want to calculate is your **replacement cost**. If your entire home was demolished in a fire (keeping it dark for you), how much would it cost to rebuild your home and replace everything inside? That's the amount of **coverage** you want to get. **Liability limits** are the maximum the insurance company will pay out under each type of coverage. There are usually limits per claim as well as a total limit for the year.

If you live in an apartment, your building may have homeowners insurance for the outside and structure of the building. In that case you would only need to cover the replacement cost of everything inside the apartment.

Depending on where you live, you might want to purchase additional insurance for certain perils (a cause of damage) that aren't covered under your homeowners insurance. If you live in Florida, hurricane damage is not typically covered in your homeowners insurance so you'd need a separate policy. If you live in an area prone to flooding you will want to make sure you're covered in the case of a flood or purchase additional insurance.

Your **deductible** is the amount you pay on your own before the insurance kicks in; it resets each year.

If you are a homeowner, or plan to be, understand what goes into your homeowners insurance.

What's the monthly premium? _____

What's your deductible? _____

What's your total coverage? _____

Are there any exclusions?

_____

Are there limits to valuable property? If so, consider valuable property insurance.

_____

If you don't have homeowners insurance or are looking for a better policy, you can take note of your research here and compare rates/coverage.

	Policy #1	Policy #2	Policy #3
Monthly Premium			
Coverage			

What If I Rent?

If you rent, you'll want a similar type of policy called renters insurance. It was one of the best purchases I ever made. Instead of covering the structure of the building and things like appliances and fixtures, it covers the things you own inside the home like your furniture and clothing, and will also pay for your hotel and meals in case you're not able to live in your home. It even covers items you own if they were stolen while not in your home. Snazzy, right?

In order to determine how much coverage you need, imagine that your apartment was turned upside down and everything was dumped out. How much money would you need to replace everything? Similar to homeowners insurance, there will be a coverage amount (the cost to replace your items) as well as a deductible (the amount you'll pay out of pocket before the insurance kicks in).

If you live with roommates, that's no problem. Just make sure to add them to the policy. I made the mistake of splitting a policy with my roommate and didn't put her name on it. When she went to make a claim, they weren't able to help her. I still feel terrible to this day!

If you are a renter, do you have renters insurance? If not, get it. _____

How much coverage do you need? _____

What will the monthly cost be? Compare a few policies to get the best rate. If you have roommates, make sure to add them to the plan.

	Policy #1	Policy #2	Policy #3
Monthly Premium			
Coverage			

Car Insurance – What You Need to Know

If you have a car, auto insurance is essential. It covers the damage to you and your car or someone else and their car in the case of an accident, as well as any damage from other things like theft, hail, or falling objects (or at least it should).

Your car insurance **declaration page** will list everything that you are covered for. Make sure:

- It includes everyone who will be driving the car.
- The car information is correct.

- It's enough coverage (more on this later in the chapter).
- The liability limits are correct (the max the insurance company pays).

How Much Will Car Insurance Cost?

Some factors used to price your car insurance include your location, the amount of coverage (more coverage is typically more expensive), your age (young drivers under 25 years old often receive a higher rate), how much you drive, your car make and model (safety, the cost to repair it, and chances of it being stolen may be considered), your driving history, and your credit score.

"Fun" fact: People with no credit pay 67% more for car insurance than people with excellent credit.[10] In California, Massachusetts, and Hawaii, car insurance companies cannot charge you more if you have a low credit score. If you are not in one of those states and your credit score increases, contact your car insurance company to see if they'll give you a better rate.

Rates will vary by company because they all have different ways of calculating your risk. In the Financial Adulting toolkit you can find the average cost of car insurance by state as well as some other great car insurance resources.

How Much Car Insurance Is Enough?

Not having enough or the right coverage has been a fear of mine: you pay your premium every month, you get in an accident, and come to find out your insurance doesn't cover what you need. Understanding the types of car insurance quelled my fears.

Minimum limits. This is the minimum amount of car insurance required by your state. Most drivers will want more car insurance than the minimums. This may include personal injury protection, uninsured/underinsured motorist, and liability coverage (more on what these are shortly!).

Comprehensive and Collision. This one is a biggie. This covers the cost of repairing *your* vehicle in a crash (it doesn't matter who's at fault) or in the case of damage from a different cause (like a falling tree). Currently no state's minimum limits include comprehensive and collision. In the case of a crash, the minimum limits only cover the cost of repairs to the other person's vehicle.

Personal injury protection. This covers medical expenses for you and the others in your car (after an accident). This can include lost wages.

Uninsured/underinsured motorist. This covers damage caused by another driver who doesn't have insurance or not enough insurance.

Liability. This is if you are the one at fault in an accident. This can be liability for property damage or an injury.

If you have car insurance, how much coverage do you have in each area?

Type of Coverage	Amount ($) of Coverage

If you don't have car insurance or are looking for a better policy, you can take note of your research here and compare rates/coverage.

	Policy #1	Policy #2	Policy #3
Monthly Premium			
Coverage Types and Amounts			

What's an Umbrella Policy?

The coverage amount of an umbrella policy goes above and beyond the amounts you are covered for on your car and your home. So if those get maxed out by a large lawsuit, you are still protected. Umbrella policies are important in the United States because we have a very litigious culture. As Tiffany Aliche says, "Folks love suing" so as you have more wealth (that goes beyond your home and car coverage limits), adding on an umbrella policy can be a great idea. Brian recommends looking into an umbrella policy when you hit $500,000 to $1 million of net worth. The good news is, it's really inexpensive and can protect you when, as Brian says, "something major could cost you everything."

Life Insurance – What You Need to Know

For me, life insurance conjures up images of sleazy salespeople, big price tags, and jargon overload. Anyone else? Well, unfortunately, many of us need it. But there's also good news. I'm going to show you how to navigate the process so that you are in charge and get exactly what you need (and don't pay for more).

What Is Life Insurance and When Do You Need It?

Life insurance pays out a specific amount of tax-free money when you die. This is called the **death benefit**. In exchange, you pay a monthly (or annual) **premium** (the cost of the insurance). Typically, the higher the payout (or death benefit), the higher the monthly premium. Also, the more likely you will die (the older you are, the more health issues you have, if you are a man, or the more risky your hobbies), the higher the premium. Dark, I know.

Who gets the money? Your named **beneficiary** or whoever you put on the policy; this can be a partner, child, or other person of your choosing. If the insurance is active when you pass away, they file a claim to get the money. It's worth reiterating that the money is tax-free to them.

Life insurance is important if you have children or someone else depending on you financially; you might also want some if you bought a home with a partner and they rely on you for the mortgage. Lauren Anastasio (the CFP and Director of Financial Advice at Stash we met in earlier chapters) says it can also make sense for anyone with student loans (that won't be forgiven) or credit card debt so that those they leave behind will be able to cover those debt obligations. *But* if no one is relying on you for money, you don't need life insurance. Don't buy life insurance if you don't need it.

Do you need life insurance? _____

The Types of Life Insurance

There are two main types of life insurance: term and permanent. With **term life insurance** you choose your amount of coverage (i.e., the amount your beneficiary gets if you pass away) and in exchange, you pay a monthly premium for a certain number of years. You can typically choose 10, 20, or 30 years. After that time, you no longer have life insurance or pay for life insurance, the idea being that your child is now grown up and doesn't depend on your income, your house is paid off, or you have saved up enough money that your dependents are protected if something were to happen to you. For 99% of people, term life insurance is the best choice. It's also the most cost-effective choice.

Some people (including insurance salespeople) will harp on the "wasted" money going toward premiums if you are alive at the end of the term and there's no death benefit paid out for your insurance. I'd say being alive is a bigger win. Tiffany says it best: "In the end, life insurance is a risk management tool, just like car insurance. If you pay for your car insurance policy through the life of its term and you never use it, are you going to be mad that you never got in an accident so that you could have used your insurance? I don't think so . . ."

The other type of life insurance is **permanent insurance**. It gets this name because you pay into it and once you pay into it enough, it doesn't go away when you stop making payments. There are different types of permanent insurance. The most common is **whole life insurance**. **Universal life** and **variable life** are other types of permanent insurance. These policies are _very_ expensive, meaning they have very high premiums in relation to the insurance coverage you get, and insurance agents make a very high commission when they sell one.

There are a lot of fancy things insurance brokers may say to sell these policies to you. They'll talk about the cash value, fixed investment returns, the ability to borrow from your cash value, or even pretend it's a savings plan (yes, this happened to a client of mine). But if you were to take the amount you'd pay for this really expensive policy and compare it to a much less expensive term policy (we're talking 20–25 times more per month), and invest the difference, you'll have _much_ (and I mean _much_) more money in the end in the scenario where you purchased the term policy.

So this begs the question, are these permanent insurance policies a scam? I've been asking this for years. Lauren says that, while they aren't a scam, people should be very judicious prior to purchasing insurance. The important questions to ask are: Where is the money going? What is the cost breakdown? What benefit amount do I really need? What is the type of policy, insurance or investment? She says, "Unfortunately, they are often being sold to people that they're not appropriate for." I 100% agree. Shame on them.

So who should consider a permanent insurance policy? Lauren says they _can_ make sense in two cases. And by _can_ she means that it's something you can evaluate, not that it always makes sense. For those with:

- A high value illiquid (noncash) estate who are worried about the estate taxes that will be owed by those they leave behind. Georgia Lee Hussey (the CEO and founder of Modernist Financial whom you met in earlier chapters) gives the example of a family farm or multigenerational business where the assets being left aren't in cash.

- A child or family member who has special needs and will need expensive care throughout their life.

Brian shares that these circumstances account for less than *0.01%* of the population and that no one else should consider whole life insurance. So there you have it. If you aren't in one of those two scenarios, stick with a term life insurance policy. And if you are in one of those two scenarios, know that not all permanent policies are created equal. You'll want to work with an independent broker and do a lot of research (more on this in the next section).

If you have a permanent insurance plan and now know that it's not a fit for you, it's important to understand what happens when you cancel to decide whether it's worth it to cancel (it usually is, unless you've been paying into it for 10 years, as that's when the bulk of the fees are paid off). Also make sure to have your term policy lined up before canceling your permanent policy.

Does term life insurance make sense for you? Or are you in a unique scenario?

_____

Whom Should I Work with and How Do They Get Paid?

Jennifer recommends that everyone "find an independent agent or broker." What. Is. That? There are two types of insurance agents: **captive** and **independent**.

"Captive agents only work for a specific insurance company and can only talk to you about products from that specific company," Jennifer explains. This means there are fewer options and no price comparison. Common examples of captive agents are State Farm or Northwestern Mutual. Jennifer recommends going to an independent agent who can represent a range of insurance companies.

All insurance agents make a commission when you buy insurance. The commission for whole life insurance is much higher than for term life insurance, which is unfortunately why so many people are sold whole life policies that aren't a fit.

Jennifer recommends the following:

- Compare at least three term life options. The policies should be for the same coverage amounts (the same amount of insurance) and for the same time period.
- Ask why the agent chose these insurance companies for you.
- Ask for or look up the insurance companies' AM Best rating to see that they are reputable (you want to make sure they will be around for a long time!).

How Much Life Insurance Do I Need?

Great question. Luckily, there's a calculator for that (in the Financial Adulting toolkit). There's also a pricing guide. Lauren recommends starting with your goals. Are you looking to cover your funeral expenses, pay off your debt, or have the money to support your kids through college? As fun as it sounds, think through the scenario if you were to pass away. How much would you want your partner, dependent, or children to have? How much would you want to give your children's guardian to raise them? How much would your sibling or friend need to pay off your mortgage if you're leaving them your home?

If you are looking for more of a general guideline, experts generally recommend getting 10–15 times your income in coverage and choosing a plan that covers you up until you retire. But I highly recommend working through a calculator as well.

How much life insurance do you want? _____			
	Policy #1	**Policy #2**	**Policy #3**
Monthly Premium			
Coverage Amount/ Time Period			
AM Best Rating			

What If I Get Life Insurance Through Work?

Some companies offer a certain amount of term life insurance as a benefit, either at no additional cost or for a small fee per paycheck. You can definitely factor this amount of insurance into your planning, but it's important to consider what happens when you leave the company. Are you able to continue the policy? If not, it's important to have a separate policy as well. You can always increase your private policy to make up for the difference. But if five years have gone by, the cost to increase your policy will be higher and it might have been more cost efficient to start with the total coverage amount five years earlier.

Disability Insurance

Disability insurance does not get enough air time. More than one in four of today's 20-year-olds can expect to be out of work for at least a year because of a disabling condition before they reach the typical retirement age. *Yikes.* Brian says he talks to clients more about disability insurance than life insurance because the odds of getting sick or injured and not being able to work when you're young are higher than dying.

Disability insurance protects your income in the case you are unable to work. You pay a premium to the insurance company and in the case you are unable to work due to a disability, they will pay you a certain percentage (typically 60%) of your salary or income. How long they pay depends on whether it's short-term or long-term disability insurance.

Short-Term versus Long-Term Disability Insurance

The main difference between short-term and long-term disability insurance is the length of time you have coverage. **Short-term disability** is for the short term. It typically kicks in after a couple of weeks and can provide you with income up until a year. **Long-term disability** is for the long term. It covers your income from usually around the year mark until retirement. Finally, financial terms that make sense!

Unless you get short-term disability through work (many do), it's usually not a cost-effective insurance to have. If your workplace doesn't offer a short-term disability policy, you can protect yourself for the short term with rainy-day fund savings.

> What disability insurance do you get through work? List out the terms of the policy or policies here.
>
> _____
>
> _____

How Much Does Long-Term Disability Insurance Cost?

Unfortunately, the cost of long-term disability insurance can be hefty. It can cost 1–3%[11] of your income per year. If you have long-term disability insurance available through work, it can often be much cheaper. I had the opportunity to carry over a long-term disability insurance policy through my last job. If you have that chance, do it!

"Fun" (but actually really not fun at all) fact: Disability insurance costs more for women since they have filed more disability claims. This is heavily skewed due to childbirth and pregnancy, which wouldn't be the case if we had mandatory paid leave. _Ahhh_. Rant over. Some insurance companies offer a gender-neutral rate.

Important: An "own-occupation" policy will pay out if you can't work in your current job, even if you can work in another job. If it's not an own-occupation policy, you might only see a payout if you can't work in _any_ job. That's a _huge_ difference! If you are in a highly specialized job that requires certain education and experience, you want an own-occupation policy if you can afford it.

Do I Need Disability Insurance?

Yes – if you earn money and want to protect your ability to earn money, **you need long-term disability insurance**.

Price out long-term disability insurance policies.

	Policy #1	Policy #2	Policy #3
Monthly Premium			
Coverage Amount and Details			

Do People Use Short-Term Disability for Parental Leave?

Having a baby is one of the most common causes of short-term disability – which makes sense when most companies offer zero paid parental leave. Some people have short-term disability available through their employers, others get it on their own or qualify through their state. Some use FMLA (Family and Medical Leave Act) for 12 weeks' unpaid leave when they have a baby. FMLA requires companies to keep your job for you while you are out. If you are out on short-term disability, there is no requirement for your employer to hold your job for you. FMLA can be used for paternity leave, but fathers taking leave will not qualify for short-term disability. It's often recommended that moms take short-term disability at the same time as FMLA so they are paid *and* their job is protected.

Long-Term Care Insurance

Long-term care insurance covers the cost of those who are unable to live alone due to chronic illness in old age. The median cost of a nursing home ranges from $93,072 to $105,852 per year.[12] 70% of people 65 and older will require some form of long-term care in their lifetimes, with an average need of three years.[13]

Brian adds that long-term care insurance is something that's gotten more and more complicated. While it's important for many, he recommends making sure you have your other bases covered first. If those things are covered, it's worth exploring. Because of the nature of the insurance industry and the commission people make from selling us products, Brian recommends getting a second opinion from someone who doesn't have a vested interest (or biased interest) from selling you the policy, like a financial planner or fiduciary. You may decide to plan for this without insurance as well.

For some guidance on long-term care insurance pricing, head to the Financial Adulting toolkit for resources.

Revisit Your Insurance When Things Change

Life happens and things change. You start to make more money. You buy a home with a partner. You add a kid to your family. You now have more assets and family to protect. Jennifer points out that because of these changes, we should revisit our insurance needs at least once a year.

Your Financial Adulting Action Items

- ☐ Understand your health insurance options and choose the best plan for you.
- ☐ Budget as best you can for annual medical expenses and insurance costs.
- ☐ Take advantage of an HSA plan (if you qualify) or an FSA (if you have one through work) and/or create and fund a sinking fund for medical expenses.
- ☐ If you have one through work, and have kids or dependents with qualifying expenses, set up a Dependent Care FSA.
- ☐ Get familiar with the high cost of medical expenses and how that disproportionately affects BIPOC and women.

☐ If you own a car or home (or lease a car), make sure you are covered by homeowners or car insurance.

☐ If you rent, make sure you have renters insurance.

☐ If you have valuable property, understand the limits of your homeowners/renters policy and look into valuable property insurance.

☐ If you need additional coverage, look into an umbrella policy.

☐ If someone is depending on your income, get term life insurance.

☐ Understand the disability insurance policies offered to you through work, if available.

☐ If you don't have long-term disability insurance through work, look into getting covered.

☐ If you have all your other insurance boxes checked, look into long-term care insurance for yourself or family members.

☐ Add your new policy payments (for all types of insurance) to your financial plan as well as to your sinking fund amounts.

☐ In general, when it comes to insurance, don't be afraid to ask lots of questions and get a second opinion, if possible. You now know what to look out for, so you'll want to do your research on any policy before you choose.

Whew! You did it. You now know all about the types of insurance you may need, how it all works, and what to look out for. That is *no* small feat! Next up, we're on to another riveting topic – taxes.

CHAPTER 11

Tax Basics and Estate Planning

O
h, taxes. You know we have to talk about them. And yes, I'm with you. I want to hit the snooze button as soon as I hear the word, too. There's a lot to cover here because as financial adults, we want to understand some key tax basics that will help us file our taxes, minimize (very legally) what taxes we pay, and generally reduce our stress level.

What Are Taxes?

Taxes are money we pay to our federal, state, and local governments so that they can run and carry out programs. At the federal level, think Social Security and Medicare, and at the state and local levels think roads and parks.

While it can feel like a bummer to pay taxes, they deserve a reframe. In my conversation with Georgia Lee Hussey, she asked, "What would change if we shifted our language from tax burden to collective or community support? I like taxes. I would really like my future employees to go to good schools, I really like to have a park to walk through on my way to work and bridges that don't fall down."

Our current federal income tax system is on a graduated scale. The more money you earn, the higher your tax bracket (well, kind of – more on this later). State taxes vary by state. Nine states don't have income tax and some cities charge their own additional income tax.

	Single	Married, Filing Jointly	Married, Filing Separately	Head of Household
10%	$0–$10,275	$0–$20,550	$0–$10,275	$0–$14,650
12%	$10,276–$41,775	$20,551–$83,550	$10,276–$41,775	$14,651–$55,900
22%	$41,776–$89,075	$83,551–$178,150	$41,776–$89,075	$55,901–$89,050
24%	$89,076–$170,050	$178,151–$340,100	$89,076–$170,050	$89,051–$170,050
32%	$170,051–$215,950	$340,101–$431,900	$170,051–$215,950	$170,051–$215,950
35%	$215,951–$539,000	$431,901–$647,850	$215,951–$323,925	$215,951–$539,900
37%	Over $539,900	Over $647,850	Over $323,925	Over $539,900

2022 Federal Marginal Tax Rates by Income (this doesn't include state and local taxes)
Source: Data from Internal Revenue Service.

Outside of income tax, we may pay Social Security and Medicare taxes (FICA or self-employment tax), capital gains taxes (on investment gains), estate taxes (on money passed on to you after someone dies), property taxes (annual taxes on real estate you own), and sales tax (or value-added or excise taxes on goods and services you buy).

If you have a salaried job, your employer withholds taxes (income and FICA) to pay the **IRS** (Internal Revenue Service – the queen bee government organization in charge of collecting taxes). Your employer determines how much in taxes to take from your paycheck based on your W-4 form.

Fun fact: Your tax dollars help fund the organization that collects your tax dollars. Very meta.

W-4 – Tell Me More

The W-4 form is something you fill out when you start a new job, but you can update it at any time. If too much is withheld from your paycheck for taxes, you get a tax refund when you file your taxes, and if too little is withheld, you'll owe money when you file. Submit a new form with your employer if you want to make changes (or there's an IRS questionnaire linked in the Financial Adulting toolkit).

In order to fill out the form, you will need to select your filing status. Here's a quick rundown of each option.

- **Single:** Filing solo (nonmarried)
- **Married filing jointly:** Married couple filing their taxes together
- **Married filing separately:** Married couple filing separately (two forms)
- **Head of household:** Nonmarried, pays more than half of household expenses, and has either (1) a qualified dependent living with them for at least half the year (i.e., child, relative) or a parent for whom they pay more than half their living expenses
- **Qualifying widow(er):** Within two years of losing a spouse
- **None of your business.** Just kidding – I wish this were an option

If I'm Married, Should I File Jointly or Separately?

The IRS gives out a lot of perks for filing jointly, so in the majority of cases it makes sense to file your taxes jointly if you're married. This was one of the financial benefits withheld from the LGBTQ+ community before gay marriage was legalized.

Some reasons to potentially file separately? If one spouse has high medical expenses, if one spouse's income would be counted toward the other spouse's income-based repayment on their student loans, or if one spouse doesn't trust the other one. You can prepare your taxes both ways to see which way you will pay the least in taxes.

W-2 – More of an Income and Tax Snapshot

Your W-2 is a summary of what actually happened with your taxes over the past year. It shows how much you earned and how much your company withheld for taxes. It also shows how much of your income went to Social Security, Medicare, and benefits. If you earn a salary, you'll need this form to prepare your taxes.

1099 – for Freelance and Other Income

If you work for yourself, are a contract employee, or work freelance, you'll receive a 1099 form from companies that paid you over $600. This is how the government knows what you were paid. That being said, if you don't receive a 1099, you still have to claim that income and file your taxes. No taxes are withheld when you are paid on a contract basis so it will be up to you to set money aside. As a contractor, you will be responsible for income tax and self-employment tax.

Depending on your income, you may owe quarterly estimates to the IRS on or around April 15th, June 15th, September 15th, and January 15th (pending weekends and holidays).

There are many types of 1099 forms. Many of the tax forms in your investment accounts are also called 1099s but are for interest and dividends. You'll want to pull these as well.

Other Income Info to Have Handy

In addition to your W-2 and/or 1099(s), you'll also want to pull any additional tax documents from your lenders and investment accounts. These will also show IRA contributions, student loan details, and mortgage interest. If you aren't sure what you need from each account, you can usually find a "tax documents" section with each financial institution that will show you what you need. You will also want to include any other income, like your state and local refund from the past year (if applicable), any Social Security income, and rental income.

April 15th Is a Big Day

The deadline for filing tax forms and paying what you owe is April 15th (unless it falls on a weekend or holiday). If you are late, you typically pay a 5% penalty on taxes owed for every month you are late (capped at five months and 25%).

It's also your last chance to contribute to your IRA for the year. If you file an extension, you have until October 15th (six months later) to file your taxes, but your IRA deadline does not get extended and you'll still want to make an estimated tax payment (if you owe one).

Why Is This So Hard?

If this seems like a lot of work, it's because it is. What if I told you there was a way to avoid all this meshugas (pronounced mish-eh-GOSS, Yiddish for nonsense)?

Tax prep companies like TurboTax (owned by Intuit) and H&R Block lobby millions of dollars each year when policy has been proposed to make filing your taxes free and easy.[1] Why?

I'm assuming here, but if filing your taxes was free and easy, you wouldn't need to pay those companies to help you do it. Big *ugh*. Burning rage!

Who would have thought that how we file our taxes could be an act of consumer activism? Some call for a boycott of these companies that cost us an average of 13 hours per year and $200 per person. If you want to join the boycott, file your taxes yourself, use the free versions of any software, or hire an accountant.

Hopefully someday our tax system gets simplified, but for now, here's how you can file your taxes.

How to *Actually* File Your Taxes

1. On Your Own

You can file your taxes for free. If you earn under $72,000, you qualify to use tax prep software for free (freefilealliance.org). If you've never heard about that, it's by design. Tax prep companies don't want you to, and have been charged with hiding these options on their websites.[2]

Fun fact: If you earned under $12,550 as of 2021, you don't have to file your taxes, but if you qualify for a refund, you will still want to.

If you are above the income limit, you can still file your taxes on your own, for free, on the IRS website, using FreeFileFillableForms.com.

When you file your taxes, you're submitting a 1040 form (pronounced ten-forty). These forms can look really overwhelming and confusing. Take time to read things over as many times as you need (I need to do this every year!) and give a google any time you are not clear on something. You'll need a Social Security number and birthday for you, your spouse, and any dependents on your form.

2. Using a Tax Prep Service

You can use a tax prep service to help you file your taxes. Depending on the option you choose, and how complicated your return is, the service can be free or paid. Some options are all digital prompts and others allow you to speak to someone and ask questions.

3. Hiring an Accountant

Hiring an accountant makes sense as your taxes get more complicated. They can be expensive but can also make up their fee many times over in smart tax moves (and avoiding costly mistakes). If you have your own business or side hustle, own a property, or get contacted by the IRS, it might be time to hire one.

Important: Hiring an accountant does not make you less liable for your taxes. You are the one who signs on the bottom line and is responsible for any errors, so regardless of whether you've hired an accountant, you want to understand what's going on in your forms.

Hiring an accountant is an important decision. You want someone who will do a good job and whom you can trust. A great way to find an accountant is through a referral from friends and family. If you are looking for an accountant, Accountants of Color is a nonprofit that has an amazing directory of BIPOC accountants that you can search by location.

Minimize the Taxes You Owe (very legally)

It's important to pay what you owe in taxes, but there's no reason to pay more than is required. Tax credits and deductions are the two ways you can decrease your tax bills (very legally). Every tax "break" is some variation of a credit or deduction.

What Are Tax Credits?

Tax credits are the holy grail of tax benefits because they take money off your tax bill dollar for dollar. If you owe $1,000 in taxes and receive a tax credit for $250, you now owe $750 in taxes. If you've overpaid, you get a return. There are refundable and nonrefundable tax credits. With refundable credits if the credit is larger than the taxes you owe, you can get a refund. If you owe $500 in taxes and qualify for a $700 refundable tax credit, you should receive a $200 refund. A nonrefundable tax credit can only reduce your tax bill to $0, nothing more. If you owe $500 in taxes and qualify for a $700 nonrefundable tax credit, you will owe $0 in taxes. Head to the Financial Adulting toolkit for some common tax credits.

Stay Up to Date on Tax Law Changes

Things can change (and sometimes do, very quickly). The amounts and limits for tax credits and deductions change each year so you want to stay up to date. That doesn't mean you have to set up alerts for IRS.gov press releases. You know I haven't. But checking in every few months or so on the tax headlines can save you money when it comes time to prepare and file your tax return. Plus, you'll be the most popular in your friends group come tax season.

What Are Deductions?

Deductions are still your friends, but they don't have as much of an impact as tax credits. Deductions reduce your taxable income, which is the amount of money you're taxed on. This reduces the amount you're taxed by your tax rate, kind of like a discount, and may also put you in a lower tax bracket.

If my taxable income is $75,000 and I receive a $5,000 deduction, I will be taxed on $70,000 ($75,000 – $5,000) rather than $75,000. If my effective tax rate is 30%, I'll be taxed $21,000 instead of $22,500, so the $5,000 deduction saved me $1,500 in taxes.

Here Are Some Common Deductions

You can take each of the following deductions without itemizing your taxes (more on what itemizing means in the next section). The limits will change year to year, so give them a quick google.

- 401(k) contributions
- Traditional IRA contributions

- HSA/FSA contributions
- 529 contributions
- Student loan interest

Should I Take the Standard Deduction or Itemize?

The next group of tax deductions fall into a different category. You can take the standard deduction (a fixed amount you get based on your filing status) or you can itemize. Most of the time people take the standard deduction.

"Fun" fact: For the standard deduction, you don't have to keep receipts or records.

When you qualify for more than the standard deduction (in 2022 it's $12,950 if you're single; $25,900 if you're married filing jointly), you'll itemize your deduction (so you can pay less in taxes). Itemizing means actually breaking out what you spent on deductions like medical bills or charitable contributions.

Here Are Some Common Itemized Deductions

- Medical or dental expenses
- Mortgage interest
- Charitable donations
- Home office expenses
- State income and property taxes
- Casualty, disaster, and theft losses

Some Bonus Definitions

We've already covered a lot, but there are a couple of other terms you will run into during your tax prep.

AGI (adjusted gross income). Your total income for the year after subtracting out certain adjustments. Income includes wages, dividends, capital gains, business income, retirement distributions, and other income. Adjustments include student loan interest, educator expenses, alimony payments, contributions to a retirement account, and HSA/FSA contributions.

Taxable income. This is your AGI minus your deductions (the standard deduction or your itemized deductions). This is the amount you are taxed on.

Avoiding Some Common Mistakes

Double-Check Your Account Number

When you tell the IRS where to take money from (or pay you), triple-check you've given the correct account information. I've made this mistake!

Look Out for Scams

IRS scams are rampant, and identity fraud is a growing issue. The IRS will never reach out by phone or email (unless you have an ongoing case going with an agent). Do not respond to calls or emails from the IRS or open attachments. The IRS will also not ask for immediate payment or threaten to arrest you over the phone.

If Someone Is Claiming You as a Dependent . . .

You can still file your own taxes if someone else is claiming you as a dependent. Just make sure to check the box on your 1040 that says "Someone can claim you as a dependent." Otherwise, when it comes time to file and someone claims you on their return (like your parents or grandmother), if you filed first, their filing will be rejected.

Set Up a System to Make Taxes Less Stressful

As you're filing your taxes is a great time to set up a system so that the next year is less of a cluster. If you are scrambling to gather documentation for all of your charitable contributions for the year, add a monthly calendar reminder to do that monthly going forward.

Make a list of each of the documents you needed this year. That will be a great starting point for next year (if not exactly what you need). Label a folder or digital folder for the next tax year. As you receive any tax documents, file them away.

If there were deductions you wish you were able to take advantage of this year but couldn't, plan ahead for next year. Can you increase your 401(k) contributions, contribute to your HSA, or max out your IRA?

What will you do now and year-round to make next year's taxes less stressful? Go ahead and add items to your calendar.

1. _____

2. _____

3. _____

4. _____

5. _____

How Our Tax System Perpetuates Wealth Inequality

Now that you know the rules and lingo, let's talk systems. Over time the wealthy have been paying less and less taxes (completely legally, I might add). There's so much data that points to this conclusion but I thought, what better source than a financier and billionaire himself? In 2011, Warren Buffett wrote an op-ed in the *New York Times*,[3] where he shared that his tax rate was 17% while the other employees in his office paid rates ranging from 33 to 41%.

A few important terms: A **progressive tax** (like income tax) takes a larger percentage from high-income groups than low-income groups. The name "progressive" comes from how the taxes work: taxes get progressively higher as you earn more, not a political affiliation (although progressives do tend to prefer this tax method). A **regressive tax** takes a larger percentage from low-income groups than high-income groups.

Sales tax is a regressive tax, as those with a lower income are spending a larger percentage of their income on it.

But even though income tax is a progressive tax, it's become less and less progressive, as you can see from the following chart. The tax rate for the highest earners has gone way down since the mid-1980s, the lowest earners haven't benefited from the same decrease, and those in the middle have fared the worst.

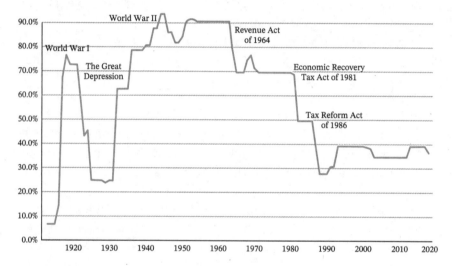

Historical Highest Marginal Income Tax Rates in the United States
Source: Tax Policy Center.

Warren describes the shift in wealth that's been perpetuated by this change in tax policy: "Since 1992, the IRS has compiled data from the returns of the 400 Americans reporting the largest income. In 1992, the top 400 had aggregate taxable income of $16.9 billion and paid federal taxes of 29.2% on that sum. In 2008, the aggregate income of the highest 400 had soared to $90.9 billion – a staggering $227.4 million on average – but the rate paid had fallen to 21.5%."

In 2020 the 400 richest Americans had a true tax rate of 23%. The bottom 50% or least wealthy households paid a true tax rate of 24%. Not so progressive.

Warren points out that many of the mega-rich are "very decent" people who mostly would be happy to pay more in taxes. Congress just has to make them.

Estate Planning – What It Is and How to Do It

Okay, are you ready? Estate planning is one of the most financially adult things you can do. Right? And you might not think it applies to you right off the bat, but it actually is relevant to everyone. Regardless of how much or how little money you have or owe, you have a financial estate. I know, it sounds fancy.

Estate planning is essentially making a plan for what you would like to happen with everything you own and owe when you pass away. There are some specific documents you need to lay all this out.

I interviewed Lori Anne Douglass, an attorney who concentrates in trust and estates and is a founding partner of Douglass Rademacher LLP to help us get this all straight. Lori went into trust and estates because she wanted to practice law in an area where she could help and make a difference for the Black community.

Before we jump in, it's important to note that estate planning is very state-specific. I'm going to take you through some basics, but you'll also want to check in with the specific rules within your state.

First up, you need some disability planning documents:

- **Healthcare proxy.** Appoints someone to make medical decisions when you can't for any reason.
- **Living will.** Shares a person's desires for end-of-life decisions when they are terminally ill, unconscious, or brain-damaged – like a situation where you're on life support, for example.
- **Financial power of attorney** (a.k.a. financial directive). Appoints someone to make financial decisions when you can't make them.

"Fun" fact. The healthcare proxy and living will are also called medical directives, healthcare directives, or advanced directives.

Whom will you choose to be your healthcare proxy and financial power of attorney? You'll need to choose a backup for each. We'll talk about how to actually set these documents up soon.

Healthcare Proxy: _____

Backup Healthcare Proxy: _____

Financial Power of Attorney: _____

Backup Financial Power of Attorney: _____

Next Up Is the Will

Lori says, "Everyone should have a basic estate plan and typically the will is the foundational document." Your **will** is the document that describes your wishes for who inherits your assets, provides a procedure to pay your debts, and also nominates an executor (the name will vary by state) to carry out those wishes after you pass away.

It's also the only document where you can nominate guardians for your children. Guardians are the people who will take care of your children should you (and your partner, if applicable) pass away. As your wealth grows, there are more complex things you can do than a will. I touch on them briefly soon.

In your will, you'll name your **beneficiaries**, or whom you wish to inherit what you leave behind (your estate). If you don't have a will and don't choose beneficiaries, state rules will determine who gets your estate.

"Fun" important fact: Any account or insurance policy where you can list a beneficiary lives outside your will, meaning that when you pass away, the account will go to whoever is listed as the beneficiary (regardless of what your will says). If allowed by the financial institution, you can designate a beneficiary on the account or say "pay on death" or "in trust for" as ways to designate a specific beneficiary. If it's a joint account, it will go to the surviving joint owner before going to the beneficiary. It's important to keep beneficiary designations up to date.

Whom will you name as beneficiaries? Go through each of your accounts and check whether you are able to provide a beneficiary. If you are, make sure who you've selected is up to date.

_____

_____

_____

You will also choose **guardians** and backup guardians – the people who will take care of your children if you pass away. This is a tough scenario to think through and I know in our discussion I cried multiple times. But it's really important.

The physical guardian is the guardian who will live with your child. There can also be a separate guardian of the property or **trustee**, who will take care of the child's money. Guardians are only necessary up until your child or children turn 18.

Then you choose an **executor**. What this role is called varies by state. This is the person you nominate to execute your will after you pass away. Lori points out that most people choose family or friends, and you want to choose someone who will do a good honest job and who typically follows through with things. "If your brother starts projects and doesn't finish them, don't pick him. Don't pick someone with money problems. Don't pick someone whose spouse is over-involved. Pick loving people to be guardians for your children but financially responsible people for the money."

Lori encourages us to talk to our family or friends _before_ we select them for different roles. First of all, some might not want to do it. They might not want to take on this role because it can be a significant time commitment or they might have other reasons for not wanting to take this on. The conversation is also a great way to talk about your wishes and what you would like to happen in the event you die.

"Fun" fact: If you want to take your estate planning to the next level, keep your business private, and have your beneficiaries skip probate, you can set up a **revocable trust**. Important: In order to avoid probate (i.e., going to court), the revocable trust must be fully funded during the lifetime of the grantor. You, who make the revocable trust, are the "grantor" of the trust, and your assets fund the trust. Fully funded means that the assets are no longer in your name but in the name of the trust. Instead of a bank account owned by Ashley Feinstein Gerstley, it's owned by the Ashley Feinstein Gerstley Trust u/a/d (under agreement dated) 11/1/2021. A revocable trust replaces a will. If you forget to include an asset in the revocable trust and it also doesn't have a beneficiary or joint owner, you still go to court, but only for those missed items.

Choose your executor, guardians (if applicable) and trustee (if applicable). Take note if you've had a conversation with them.

	Name	Had Conversation?
Executor		
Backup Executor		
Guardians (if applicable)		
Backup Guardians		
Trustee (if applicable)		
Backup Trustee (if applicable)		

So How Do We Get These Documents Set Up?

Lori says that for the healthcare proxy and living will, we can typically do that ourselves online right now. Go to your state website (you can find a link with more directions in the Financial Adulting toolkit). She encourages anyone who doesn't have them to execute both today.

Setting up the power of attorney can be a bit more involved. Each state is different, but you can usually find your state's form on a local title company website. Make sure it's current, appropriate to your state, and that you execute it properly. Contact an attorney if you have questions before signing it.

Go set up your healthcare proxy, living will, and power of attorney.

_____

_____

_____

There are online services that allow you to set up a will on your own and you're not required to use an attorney. If you go this route, make sure the will complies with the requirements in your state so that it's valid.

Lori does not recommend doing a will (or more complex planning like a trust) on your own (or using DIY services). She says, "If there's anything, from a major mistake to a slight missed detail, you're leaving your estate open to litigation." The cost to set up a will with an attorney will vary by location and someone's expertise but she adds that "the cost of a basic will is nominal," especially when you compare it to what you're going to save your family by having it.

How will you set up your will? Get recommendations or do online research to find an estate planning attorney in your area.

_____

_____

_____

Your Financial Adulting Action Items

- ☐ Update your W-4, if needed.
- ☐ Decide on your filing status (if married, decide whether you will file jointly or separately).
- ☐ Gather the info you need to prepare to file.
- ☐ Choose how you want to file your taxes (on your own, using a tax-prep service, or hiring an accountant).
- ☐ Understand the tax credits and deductions available to you.
- ☐ Set up a system to make next year's taxes less stressful.
- ☐ Understand how a regressive tax system perpetuates wealth inequality.
- ☐ Go through each of your accounts and, if possible, update or add beneficiaries.
- ☐ Understand the estate planning rules in your state.
- ☐ Complete your healthcare proxy, living will, and financial power of attorney.
- ☐ Decide on the key components of your will and create your will (or more complex planning).

In this chapter we covered some major next-level financial adulting and it will pay off each and every year. Do a happy dance – you should be *very* proud! Now we're on to another important topic that we know we should understand but avoid like the sick person who came to work: our credit score. I promise to make it as painless as possible.

CHAPTER 12

Your Credit Score

O ur credit scores tell lenders how risky it is to lend us money (i.e., how likely we are to pay them back). We're assigned a number, typically 300–850 – the higher the better. Many people use their credit score as a proxy for their financial well-being. I wouldn't go that far.

Why Should We Care About Our Credit Score?

Credit, or the ability to take out debt, is an important part of our financial well-being. It allows us to buy a home, purchase a car, start or fund a business, and supports us in the case of the unexpected when our savings aren't enough. When we can and do take out debt, typically, the higher our score, the lower our interest rate. Having a "good" score can save us thousands and tens of thousands of dollars in interest. On the next page I show you an example.

Also, many landlords do a credit check before accepting your application, 29% of employers check your credit score before hiring you, and insurance companies may even price your policy based on your credit.

FICO score	APR	Monthly payment	Total interest paid	Price changes
760–850	2.695%	$1,216	$137,761	If your score changes to 700–759, you could pay an extra $12,752.
700–759	2.917%	$1,251	$150,512	If your score changes to 760–850, you could save an extra $12,752.
680–699	3.094%	$1,280	$160,826	If your score changes to 700–759, you could save an extra $10,314.
660–679	3.308%	$1,315	$173,468	If your score changes to 700–759, you could save an extra $22,955.
640–659	3.738%	$1,387	$199,430	If your score changes to 660–679, you could save an extra $25,962.
620–639	4.284%	$1,482	$233,447	If your score changes to 640–659, you could save an extra $34,017.

How Your Credit Score Affects Your Mortgage Rate

Note: APR rates as of November 5, 2021. Assumes a $300,000 loan principal amount.

Source: Bankrate and FICO.

The Quickest Way to Increase Your Score

There are currently three credit agencies: Equifax, Experian, and TransUnion. Each one of them has a credit report with information on your debt (and payment history), bank accounts, and even your past addresses. You can pull these reports for free, once per year, at annualcreditreport.com. **Important note:** Your credit reports don't include your credit score, but the information in them is used to determine your score, so they're very important.

If you find an error, use their online dispute system to tell them about the error. It can be the quickest way to get your score up! You can find detailed instructions and scripts for handling errors in the Financial Adulting toolkit.

According to the Federal Trade Commission (FTC), one in five people have an error on at least one of their credit reports[1] and sometimes these errors negatively affect your score. I've had clients with loans on their reports that don't belong to them and sometimes those loans have late payments. That's hurting their score!

Pull and read through each credit report to check for errors.

	Equifax	**Experian**	**TransUnion**
Date Credit Report Pulled			
Any Errors?			

Find Out Your Current Score

You might think that there's one universal credit score system that we're all measured by. Nope. That would be too easy! The most common credit score in the United States is the FICO score, and the VantageScore is a close runner-up, but many of the larger lenders also have their own scoring systems.

To get your credit score for free, you can use Credit Karma or Credit Sesame. They also include some background on why your score is what it is and share tips to raise your score. MyFico.com and IdentityIQ offer a similar service for a fee. Many credit card companies and banks now include your credit score on your statements or when you log in.

So what's a good score? Each lender is different, but this gives you an idea:

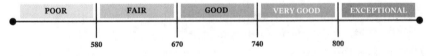

| POOR | FAIR | GOOD | VERY GOOD | EXCEPTIONAL |

580   670   740   800

Source: FICO.

What's your current credit score? Circle where you are on the chart. What's your rating (from poor to excellent)? _____

It doesn't feel great to be labeled "poor" or even "fair" when it comes to your credit rating. Remember, your credit score has nothing to do with your worth as a person and isn't even a great representation of your financial health as a whole. It's a system (a problematic one – see the Financial Adulting toolkit for more!) with a number that we can work to improve. We'll talk more soon about how to improve it!

The Biggest Credit Score Myth

There's a common misconception that checking your credit score will decrease your score. This is not true, but I hear it all the time! **You can check your own credit score as much as you want without impacting your score.**

Where I believe this misconception comes from is that it does decrease your score when a lender or bank makes a **hard inquiry** into your score. They can only legally do this with your permission and it usually happens when you are opening a credit card or taking out a loan. Hard inquiries stay on your credit report for up to two years but typically only impact your score for one year.

When you receive a credit card offer in the mail (meaning you didn't give them permission to inquire into your credit), that's a **soft inquiry**. That won't affect your score.

The Most Damaging Myth

The other common myth that's arguably more financially damaging is that holding a balance on your credit card improves your score. That is *not* the case. This is a very convenient myth for credit card companies because when we keep a balance on our credit cards we pay them interest. Holding a balance on your credit cards can cost you tons of money in interest, especially with credit card interest rates at 20–25%!

We get into the breakdown of how your credit score is actually calculated shortly but know that **holding a balance on your card does not improve your score**. You'll soon find that it can actually *decrease* your score.

The Makeup of Your Credit Score

Because FICO is the most common credit score, let's talk about how they calculate it. Depending on the information available in your credit profile, the importance of these categories can shift. Typically if you don't have a lot of information for them to go on, the categories they do have information for will become more important. How important? No one really knows.

Let me be frank here. This chart gives us guidelines, but this is still an extremely secretive model. I can't close a credit card, spend more on my credit card, or refinance my mortgage and know exactly what will happen to my score. I can make an educated guess, but it's still a guess.

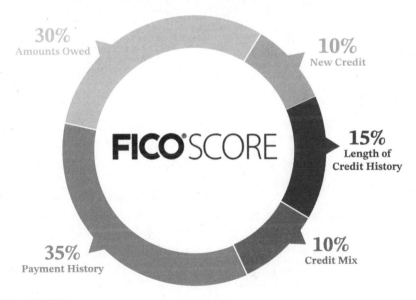

Source: MyFICO.com.

35% Payment History

Making on-time payments is the most important factor. If you have made late payments, the scoring model takes into account the following:

- How late the payment was
- How much the late payment was for
- How recent the payment was
- How many times late payments happened

Making on-time payments doesn't mean you have to pay off your credit card in full each month (although it's ideal if you can!). It just means you are paying the minimum payment by the payment date each month. Nothing is overdue or late.

There is (by law) a 30-day window before your lender can report a late payment. As long as you aren't 30 days late, a late payment will not impact your score.

Do you have any late payments on your credit reports? If so,

- How many? _____
- How late were they?_____
- How much were they for?_____
- How recent were they?_____

30% Amounts Owed

Amounts owed takes into account how much you owe across all types of debt accounts, like credit cards, car loans, student loans, personal loans, and so on. For installment loans like student loans and car loans, FICO looks at how far along you are at paying the loan down (i.e., how much of the loan is left).

A big part of amounts owed is specific to your credit cards, called your **credit utilization**. This is how much of your credit you are using (or utilizing). You can calculate your own credit utilization by adding up your total credit card balances and dividing the total by your total credit card limits. If you have two credit cards, one with a $500 balance and a $1,000 limit and one with a $250 balance and a $500 limit, your credit utilization would be $750 ($500 + $250)/$1,500 ($1,000 + $500), 50%. The lower your credit utilization the better.

Paying off your credit cards in full each month doesn't mean your utilization will be 0%. The calculation is based on your balances at whatever point the credit card company reports it to a credit bureau (like Equifax).

Calculate your credit utilization.

Credit Card Name	Balance	Credit Limit	Credit Utilization
Example: Visa	$500	$1,000	50%
Total			

15% Length of Credit History

Typically, the longer your credit history the better, as you have a longer track record of having credit. This part takes into account the average age of your accounts as well as the age of your oldest account. Because this makes up only 15% of your score, you can have a high credit score even when you are newer to having credit.

What's your oldest account, if you have one? When did you open it? Hint – you can find all this in your credit report, but you'll want to confirm it's true!

_____

_____

10% New Credit

Opening multiple new credit accounts or taking out multiple loans at the same time will typically decrease your credit score. The idea being that new cards increase the risk that you might not pay on time or be able to pay everything back. Opening accounts more slowly is typically favorable for your score and if you need your credit score in the near future, be careful about opening any new accounts at all (because of those hard inquiries).

When was the last time you opened a new card or had a hard inquiry on your credit? How many hard inquiries have there been in the past two years?

_____

_____

10% Types of Credit Used

Having different types of accounts gives the credit-scoring model more information to develop your score. This is a small part of your score and it is not necessary to have multiple types of debt to have a good score.

How many types of debt do you have? This is helpful information to have when we get to the next chapter.

_____

_____

"Fun" fact: To add more complexity where none is needed, FICO updates their model every few years but lenders might still be using a previous version. Of course!

How to Increase Your Credit Score

Building up your credit can take time. You already pulled your free annual credit reports and checked them over for errors. Here are some other credit-building best practices.

Set Up Automatic Payment on Bills and Loans

This prevents late payments. If you are worried about having enough money in your account when bills go through, I am with you. Set up a calendar reminder a few days before or even a week before so you can make sure that enough money is in the account, or you can turn off or change the automatic payment if need be. Some credit card companies send out reminders a few days in advance as well.

Do you have automatic payments set up? If not, make a list of which you'll set up.

1. _____

2. _____

3. _____

4. _____

5. _____

Keep Your Credit Utilization Low

There are a few ways to lower your credit utilization:

- If you have credit card debt, pay down your debt. We make a debt paydown plan in the next chapter.

- If you don't have credit card debt, pay down the balance more often throughout the month (biweekly or weekly) instead of once per month. A credit utilization of 30% or lower is often recommended, but for an "exceptional" credit score, you'll want to keep it below 10%.

- Increase your credit limits. Major warning: If you will spend more money – even slightly more money – with a higher credit limit, this strategy is *not* worth it. If it won't affect your spending, I typically call up my credit card companies every year and ask them to increase the limit as much as possible.

> If you want to decrease your utilization, which strategy will you use? What's your new utilization?
>
> _____
>
> _____

Keep Older Accounts Open

If you are looking to simplify your finances, you aren't earning great rewards, or it's causing you to spend more money, it can make sense to close a credit card. You will hear many people caution against closing your oldest credit card. It will decrease your average age of accounts (but it probably matters less than you think) and affect your credit utilization, *but* if you don't need your credit in the near term, it can be worth doing what makes your life easier and it won't affect your credit for long. If you want to see how much closing your oldest card affects your score, you can find a credit score simulator in the Financial Adulting resources.

If you decide to keep your account open (and are able to not spend on it), you can take it out of your wallet or even put it in your freezer (somewhere out of sight). If you do decide to close the card, scan through your old statements (ideally a full year's worth to catch those annual charges!) to make sure you've moved all bills and automated payments to another account or credit card.

Use a Service to Get Credit for Recurring Payments

We pay a variety of bills on time every month yet historically, these haven't been factored into our credit scores. Not fair! That's why I was so excited to see companies come out with a free service that allows us to build our credit by paying for things like our streaming service subscriptions and utility bills on time. The first two I've seen are Experian Boost and UltraFICO (you can find links to both in the Financial Adulting toolkit) and I bet we'll see more soon.

Open a Credit Card (or Secured Card) If You Don't Have One

If you don't have one already, a great way to build your credit is to open a credit card. That being said, having a credit card comes with another major warning (are you sick of these yet?). Read the next chapter on how credit cards work before you do. And if having a credit card affects your spending (and increases your debt), it's not worth it. If you aren't able to open a credit card given your current credit score, you have a few options. More on these coming up.

If you want to increase your credit score, what steps will you take?

1. _____

2. _____

3. _____

4. _____

5. _____

Some Other Common Credit Score Questions

The following are some other common credit score questions I'm asked all the time.

What About Credit Repair?

Credit repair companies help you remedy errors on your credit report; some of them also monitor and repair your credit from identity theft or fraud. They don't have any magic wand to repair your credit, and they usually charge a fee for their services. All the things credit repair companies do are things you can do yourself. That being said, they are experts at navigating the systems and can save you the time, headache, and confusion it takes to go through the process and increase your chances of success.

Unfortunately, like with most areas of personal finance, there are scams to look out for. If a credit repair company claims they can remove items that are correct from your credit report – like a 60-day late payment – that's a sign they are a scam credit repair company.

What If I Have No Credit (or Low Credit)?

If you have no credit history, you won't have a credit score at all (which is not a zero credit score). How do you improve your credit score if you can't open your own credit card?

1. **Open a secured credit card.** This is exactly like a traditional credit card except you have to put down a cash deposit of typically the same amount as your credit limit ($100 cash deposit means a $100 limit). As you use the card (just like you would a typical credit card), you build your credit and build trust with your bank. Look for one with no (or low) fees and make sure to confirm that this will work to build your credit (i.e., it reports information to the credit agencies). Also ask how long you can expect to use the secured card before moving to an unsecured card.

2. **Become an authorized user on a family member or friend's card.** This requires privilege, as you have to have a family member or friend who has a credit card. It's also important to know that when you become an authorized user, you are now tied to the other person's credit until you are removed from the card. If they pay their bills on time, this will improve your credit. If they don't, this will hurt your credit.

How Does It Work If I'm an Immigrant or International Student?

If you are coming to the United States from another country, you most likely will have no credit history. You can follow these strategies until you are able to open your own credit card. In order to open a secured credit card you will typically need the following:

- Address
- Taxpayer ID (not a Social Security number)
- A job (so they can see that you have income)
- A bank account (to pay your credit card bill)

Many international students stick with debit cards if they are not planning on staying for long or have issues opening a secured card. You can also work with an international bank if they have branches in both the country you're from and the United States.

How Many Credit Cards Should I Have?

There is no perfect number of credit cards to maximize your credit score (that anyone knows of). I personally like to balance maximizing my credit card rewards with keeping my financial life simple. Many families have a joint credit card for joint purchases and then each individual has their own credit card for individual things. Or some have an everyday credit card and then one they use specifically for traveling to maximize travel points. There can also be lesser-known credit card perks like special access to tickets and reservations, concierge service, purchase protection, and travel insurance, among others. Instead of focusing on the number of cards, focus on the criteria in this chapter and know that opening multiple cards in a short time frame can have a negative impact on your score.

Your Financial Adulting Action Items

- ☐ Understand that your credit score isn't a proxy for your financial health.
- ☐ Pull your three free credit reports (annualcreditreport.com) and check them for errors.

☐ If you find errors, go through the process of remedying them.

☐ Find out your current credit score and know what affects your score.

☐ Make a plan and take steps to improve your score if you want to increase it.

☐ Find ways to start or build your credit in a healthy way.

There you have it. The elusive yet important credit score. Next up, we're talking debt: how it all works, the shame that comes with it, and making a plan to pay it down. *Woot!*

CHAPTER 13

All About Debt

N ow we move into the wild world of debt. And believe me, it *is* a wild world. More than 191 million people in the United States have credit cards, and 120 million of those (almost half of all adults) have credit card debt, making credit cards the most common form of debt. BIPOC have disproportionately more credit card debt, and that debt comes with higher interest rates.

I have a love/hate relationship with credit cards. Some use them as a tool to pay for vacations with points. For others, having the ability to use a credit card to bridge the gap when cash isn't available is a lifeline (albeit an expensive one) because there aren't better options available – and nearly one in four people in the United States can't get approved for a credit card.

When we do get a credit card, it doesn't come with a manual or even any directions. And considering they can change the financial trajectory of our lives for the worse (or much worse), that's a big problem. Understanding how credit cards work can help us make informed decisions. You know . . . knowledge is power and all that.

What Are Credit Cards?

A credit card is a **revolving loan** from a bank or other institution. You can use the card to pay for things, pay the balance down, and build up the balance again. It's up to you. And that's why it's called a revolving loan. The loan comes with a plastic card (or other material) that allows you to make purchases. You are given a certain **credit limit**, which is the maximum you are able to borrow (or put on the card) at any given point in time.

How Credit Cards Work

Each month you'll have a **required payment** on your credit card (a.k.a. a **minimum payment**). This is different from your credit card **balance** or the total amount you owe at any given point in time. That bears repeating. Your minimum payment is not the total amount you owe. It's much less.

Each credit card company calculates its minimum payment differently, but it's often 1–3% of your balance. That's why it's not uncommon for your balance to increase over time when you make minimum payments, even if you're not spending on the card. *Woof.* I know.

Then there's the **interest rate** (also called **APR** or **annual percentage rate**), which is the amount we pay to compensate the credit card company for lending us the money. The average credit card interest rate is 14.5%, but for some reason most credit cards I see have interest rates upwards of 20–25%.

The APR is applied to the balance that is not paid off at the end of the month (or cycle). For example, if your balance is $1,000 and you make a $30 minimum payment, you'll pay interest on the remaining $970. For an APR of 20%, that's a 20% interest rate per year, but you are charged interest monthly (20% divided by 12) as part of your monthly bill, which comes to about $16 in interest. If you continue to make payments of $30 per month, it would take you 50 months (over four years) to pay down the credit card and you will have paid $471 in interest or 47.1% more than the original $1,000 balance. To find the exact amount, there is typically a line item on your credit card statement titled "interest charges" or something similar.

If you like to get things on sale (who doesn't?), keeping a balance on your credit card is the opposite. You're paying more for something than it costs. And just like compound interest works wonders for our investments, it works against us with our credit card debt. Most credit card companies compound interest *daily*, meaning the balance used to calculate your interest goes up each day – interest on interest.

Use the calculator in the Financial Adulting toolkit. How much are you
paying in interest on your credit cards?

_____

_____

It's Time to Let Go of the Shame

Before we move on, we need to address the shame many of us feel
about our debt. Sometimes we feel so much shame, we can't even
look at our debt or it can even make us physically ill. But what is debt,
really? Debt is just money you owe for something you bought. I'll say
it again. **Debt is just money you owe for something you bought.**

That's all it is. It doesn't mean anything is wrong with you. It's not
bad. You're not bad.

Take a minute to reflect. What is your debt? Maybe it started with your
expenses while you were going through school, or because your income
didn't cover your expenses during a certain period of your life. Maybe
it's mostly from one specific purchase.

_____

_____

_____

_____

_____

It's also important to remember how much we have working
against us in the first place. If you need a refresher, head back to
Chapter 1. Credit cards add to it because they make it feel like we
have more money available than we do. _And_ if we are spending more
than we'd like, we don't have to deal with it until next month because

we're always paying for last month's expenses. That delay can get our spending all out of whack.

All this is to say, it's no wonder if we're not thriving. Let's give ourselves a break and let go of all that shame. Write yourself a quick love note, specifically about your debt.

Dear Debt,

_____

_____

_____

_____

Lots of Love, _____

We've Got Some Power

If you get charged a late fee, don't be afraid to call your credit card company and ask for it to be removed. If you notice your interest rate is high, you can try reducing that rate as well. Always mention how long you've been a customer and/or how long it's been since your last late payment (if it's been a while). They usually will let you off the hook for the first late payment or two (which can be a $35 fee!). It's easier to negotiate your interest rate down *before* you are carrying a balance.

Take Inventory of Your Credit Cards

The first step to paying down or managing debt is to take inventory. I've done this with hundreds of people and I promise, while it can feel scary to see everything in one place, it's most often a huge weight off their shoulders. Until we know what's going on, we can't do anything about it.

Start with your credit cards. You can take inventory right here or you can download the Excel debt tracker from the Financial Adulting toolkit. You'll want to gather the name of the credit card (so you know which one it is), the balance (how much you owe right now), the interest rate (or APR), the minimum required payment, the payment date (this can help us see if we have a lot of things due at the same time), and the credit card limit.

Do this for each credit card you have. If this feels overwhelming, start with one card. Breaking steps that feel too big into smaller manageable steps sets us up for success.

Take inventory of your credit cards. Leave the "Priority" column blank for now.

Name of Card	Balance	Interest Rate	Minimum Payment	Payment Date	Limit	Priority
Example: Visa	$1,000	20%	$30	1st of the Month	$1,500	
Total						

Make Your Credit Cards Work for You

With this information, you can make a plan to use credit cards (or not) in the way that makes sense for you. Test out the strategies that seem like a good fit and don't be afraid to pass on the ones that don't.

- Pay off your credit card balance each week. This makes your bank account a better reflection of the cash you have available.

- Don't carry a balance, if possible, to save in interest.
- Use sinking funds to smooth out larger irregular expenses (detailed directions in Chapter 5).
- If you travel for work, have a separate credit card for work travel expenses. This is especially important if it takes time to get reimbursed or you get confused about what's work-related. Also, when our credit card balances are relatively high (travel can do that!) our everyday expenses feel small or like less of a big deal, which can cause us to spend more.
- Make sure any credit card fees you pay are worth the perks. You can calculate the value of your credit card perks based on your spending and lifestyle. We have a special calculator to help you do that in the Financial Adulting toolkit.

What strategies will you use or steps will you take to make your credit cards work for you?

1. _____

2. _____

3. _____

On to Student Loans

Before we can make our debt paydown plan, we have to lay out all of our debt, and for many of us, that includes student loans. 70% of people are graduating with some student loans and with college tuition where it is, it's no wonder!

If you think your student loans are complicated, you're right. If you think the systems where you manage your student loans are opaque, you're also right. The good news is, if you already have your student loans, you don't need to know everything about every type; you just want to understand the details of your loans and what that means for your options.

Types of Student Loans

You can break down student loans into two main categories: federal loans (public) and private loans. Federal loans are loans from the government, which sets the interest rate, and there are certain protections in place, including flexible repayment options. Private student loans are provided by banks, credit unions, state agencies, or schools.

Student Loan Repayment Options

One of the most confusing things about student loans, especially federal loans, is the myriad repayment options. Depending on what types of federal loans you have and when you took them out, your options will be different, so not all of these will apply to you. Here are the highlights.

Federal Loan Repayment Options

- **Standard:** Fixed payments (same payment every month) for 10 years. This is typically the fastest method with the least amount of interest paid. It's not a good option if you qualify for Public Service Loan Forgiveness (PSLF) because you'd want to minimize the amount you pay before the loans are forgiven.
- **Graduated:** Still pay the loan over 10 years but payments start smaller and increase over time. You pay a little more interest than the standard but it can be a helpful option if it will become easier to make loan payments as you grow in your career.
- **Extended:** Pay back your loans over a 25-year period. You will pay more interest but the monthly payment will be a lot lower. You have to have $30,000 or more in student loans to be able to do this.
- **Income-based repayment options** (payments are calculated based on income):
  - **REPAYE (Revised Pay As You Earn):** Payments are 10% of your discretionary income and are recalculated every year. If you are married, your spouse's income will be included in this

calculation. Your loans are forgiven after 20 years for an undergrad loan or 25 years for a graduate loan.

- o **Income-Based Repayment (IBR):** Payments are 10 or 15% of monthly discretionary income. Your spouse's income is only included if you file taxes jointly. If you don't want it included, you can file separately. Loans are forgiven after 20–25 years.

- o **Income-Contingent Repayment (ICR):** Monthly payments are the lesser of (1) what you would pay on a repayment plan with a fixed monthly payment over 12 years, adjusted based on your income, or (2) 20% of your discretionary income, divided by 12. Oh, so much math.

- o **Income-Sensitive Repayment Plan:** Pay your loan off in 15 years, but it's based on your annual income.

IMPORTANT "fun" fact about income-based repayment options: In most cases, when your loans are forgiven, the amount forgiven will be counted as taxable income. Say what? If you have $100,000 in loans that are forgiven, that's $100,000 in taxable income coming your way. Using a debt calculator, you can see how big the balance will be at your forgiveness date given your current monthly payments. Then apply your income tax rate to that balance. Set up a sinking fund for that tax bill with the goal of having the money there waiting for you when it comes time to pay it. Otherwise, when your loans are forgiven, you'll switch from having a monthly student loan payment to a monthly payment to the IRS. *Blah.*

> If you chose or plan to choose an income-based repayment method, how much do you need to set aside for taxes and by when?
>
> _____
>
> _____

What About Teacher and Public Service Loan Forgiveness (PSLF)?

If you are a teacher and work for five consecutive years, you can have up to $17,500 in loans forgiven as of 2021. For PSLF, you must work full-time for a qualifying company (i.e., a nonprofit or government organization) and your loans will be forgiven after 120 payments (or 10 years). For teachers and people who qualify for PSLF, there is no tax bill that comes with the forgiveness. It's important to check whether you qualify for PSLF and to know what the requirements are and that you are meeting them. If you are a teacher who stays in your job for four years and then leaves, you will not qualify for forgiveness.

What Is Consolidation? Consolidation is combining all of your federal loans into one payment. Consolidation doesn't change the interest rate. You can lower your monthly payment through consolidation but you will end up paying more over the course of your loans. It's important to know that when you are consolidating your federal loans, any payments you've made toward income-based repayment or forgiveness will be reset. You might see ads for other types of debt consolidation. Outside of federal student loans, this just means refinancing. We talk more about refinancing soon.

Private Loan Repayment Options Repayment options for private loans are much more simple. Typically you'll pay a fixed payment over the course of 10 years. There are longer and shorter options but the time frame is not standardized and completely depends on the lender. You can typically make payments immediately, fully defer payments until after you finish school, or something in between. The sooner you make payments, the less interest you'll pay, but this isn't an option for many since they will not be able to make payments while they are in school.

Some of the Problems with Student Loans

I sat down with Chris Abkarians, co-founder of Juno and Suraiya Ali, head of content at Juno, which is a company that bulk-negotiates student loan refinancing for its members to get really low rates. You know I love that. Chris and Suraiya helped break down the student loan landscape.

Federal Student Loans   Federal loans make up 90% of all student loans. Take it away, Chris.

> *There's absolutely no cap on how much a grad student can borrow from the federal government, which actually makes it a predatory loan in some ways. The same goes for parent PLUS loans. Because there is no cap, the amount of grad and parent lending has ballooned. It doesn't matter if there's no way you could ever pay that amount back, and there is no incentive for schools to rein in their tuition in any way whatsoever.*

Do You Remember the College Scorecard? The Drama Continues . . .   From Chris:

> *The College Scorecard is supposed to provide information about the affordability of a school and even the return on investment. It reports data on the net cost (cost minus scholarships), how much in student debt students who went there took out, among other things. This data was widely used and pulled to thousands of websites. BUT the data doesn't include two really important buckets of financing – it doesn't include any private loans and up until this year, it didn't include parent PLUS loans. Leaving both those things out actually gives you a really incomplete picture.*

Private Student Loans   Private loans make up 10% of all student loans and 89% are undergrad loans. Many undergrads use private loans to fill the gap between federal loan limits and the cost of tuition.

Chris says, "If you were to google 'best student loans' right now, you'd find many websites with very similar top 10 lists. A lot of people would reasonably assume that if the same place is in the top 10 over and over, that it is probably pretty good, but banks don't get listed on the top for offering the best rates, they get listed on the top by paying more to be put there."

On the lists of banks, you'll see very wide interest rate ranges from each lender, which impacts your perception of what's a good deal. Suraiya shares, "If the rate range is 3%–12% and you end up with an 8% offer, that seems really good because you know it could have been as high as 12%. But in reality, with your credit score you should be offered 6% and that difference would save you thousands and thousands of dollars."

Then if you try to ask a financial aid officer to help guide you in the right direction, in most cases, they won't, because there's a regulation that prevents them from making recommendations.

"Fun" fact: Why can't financial aid offices make student loan recommendations? A scandal. Financial aid offices were accepting dinners and other things from private lenders in exchange for recommending them to their students. The regulatory reaction (Chris calls it an overreaction) was to make it so financial aid offices could no longer make recommendations. Chris says it would be great for financial aid offices to work together to get the best deal for their students, but with the regulation they can't do that.

What's the lesson in all this? If you are looking to take out student loans, do your research, expect information to be misleading, and map out what your student loan payments will look like when you graduate (or before) to see if they are workable.

Student Loans Disproportionately Affect the Black Community and Women   Suraiya observes, "If a Black individual gets an MBA

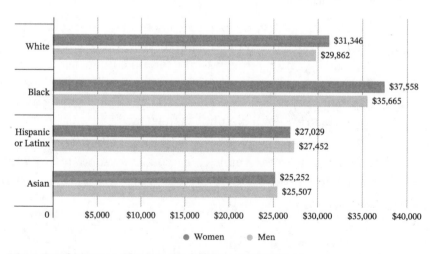

Mean Total Borrowed by Gender and Race/Ethnicity

Note: Analysis excludes those who borrowed no money to finance their educations.

Source: AAUW analysis of U.S. Department of Education, National Center for Education Statistics, "B&B:17 Baccalaureate and Beyond Longitudinal Study."

at the same school as a white individual, and if they're already going to be entering a job market where they're going to be paid less for the same job because they happen to be Black or a person of color, even if they took out the same amount of loans, the amount of time it takes the Black individual to pay those loans off is exponentially higher versus the white individual. And that's only accounting for one type of discrimination – in wages."

With the wealth gap, BIPOC families are sending their kids to college with less family wealth. If your child isn't going to one of the colleges with a huge endowment to provide financial aid, you have to borrow more. Your child hits a cap on the undergrad loans so you either take out a parent PLUS loan or a private loan. For a private loan, your co-signer's credit score impacts your rate or ability to take out the loan in general and credit scores are racially biased (read up about it in the Financial Adulting toolkit). In many cases, parents take out a parent PLUS loan that they aren't able to pay and the burden is on the student to help them pay that off.

Before You Take Out Student Loans . . .

If you plan to take out student loans, Chris and Suraiya share two important pieces of advice.

1. **Reduce the amount you need to borrow.** Try to negotiate the amount the school will pay (so you pay less). If you've already been admitted and if you are politely asking for more financial help, the school is not going to rescind your admission in almost any case. Some financial aid officers have shared that men are far more likely to be the ones to ask for a discount than women.

2. **Rate-shop.** Paying for school looks like a pie chart with many pieces adding up to the total. Once you know how much you truly need to borrow and if private loans are part of that, rate-shop!

Take Inventory of Your Student Loans

Now you can take inventory of your student loans. This will look similar to what you did with your credit cards. With student loans, you'll also want to understand when interest starts accruing (if it hasn't already). That information can help you prioritize which loans to pay off first (which comes later).

Take inventory of your student loans. Leave the "Priority" column blank for now.

Name	Balance	Interest Rate	Monthly Payment	Payment Date	Interest Accruing?	Priority
Example: Student Loan #1	$25,000	9%	$350	15th of the Month	Yes	
Total						

Add Any Other Debt to Your Tracker

If you have other debt outside of credit cards and student loans, like a mortgage, car loan, or personal loan, you'll want to add those to your debt tracker, too.

Take inventory of your other debt. Leave the "Priority" column blank for now.

Name	Balance	Interest Rate	Monthly Payment	Payment Date	Priority
Example: Mortgage	$250,000	3%	$2,000	1st of the Month	
Total					

Make a Plan to Pay Down Your Debt

Whew! You should be really proud. You've taken inventory of your debt, and it's all organized. Now you are ready to make your debt pay-down plan. Here's how to do it.

Prioritize Your Debt; What Comes First?

First you'll want to prioritize which debt you'll plan to pay off first. You'll see a column on your debt tracker where you can rank each piece of debt, starting with #1 (the highest priority) and working your way down the list. How do you decide which comes first? I use one of a combination of three methods.

The snowball method. Pay off the debt with the lowest balance first. This method works really well if you have a card or loan (or a few) with a relatively low balance because it feels amazing to cross it off your list. These wins help us build momentum and I often see people pay down their debt more quickly.

Avalanche method. Pay off the debt with the highest interest rate first. With this method you pay off the most expensive debt first or the debt that technically is costing you the most money. This method works really well if there is a loan or credit card that has a much higher interest rate than the others because paying it off has a big financial impact.

Emotional method. Pay off the debt that has the greatest emotional impact. Sometimes there's a loan that drives us crazy. Maybe you owe your parents money and even though there's no interest you can't wait to pay them back. Or maybe you had a horrible experience with a certain financial institution and you never want to see or hear from them again. If you don't have a loan that elicits a big negative emotional response you can skip this method.

Sometimes our smallest piece of debt also has the highest interest rate. Easy. Sometimes it's really hard to decide which debt comes first. Just go with your gut. I've gone through this exercise with clients and when it's time to put money toward their debt they are moved in a different direction than they had planned. It's okay to change your mind. Just try to understand why you have chosen a certain debt to take priority over the others.

Use one or a combination of the three methods above to prioritize each piece of debt you have, starting with #1 (highest priority) and working your way down. You can relist each piece of debt here with the priority number, or if you use the downloadable tool, add it there.

1.	6.
2.	7.
3.	8.
4.	9.
5.	10.

How Much Do You Want to Put Toward Your Debt?

Ideally, if you are paying down credit card debt, you will want to stop using your credit cards so you can clearly see the progress you're making. If you want to continue to use a credit card, I recommend using a separate one, if possible. That way, you can make sure to pay off your balance each month for new expenses.

The most common mistake I see is the tendency to put too much money toward debt each month and then there's not enough money left for expenses and bills so things end up going back on credit cards. I get it, it feels *so* good to pay down debt – but it then becomes unclear whether you are making progress, because your debt balances are constantly going down and then up again each month. It can start to feel like a futile pay down/build up hamster wheel where you are taking one step forward and two steps back. I don't want that for you.

What are your total minimum monthly payments on all debt? You can find these in your debt tracker or in the previous charts. _____

Plug that amount into your financial plan.

Is there room to increase your payment? If so, how much? If not, do you want to adjust other goals or expenses to make it work?

_____

Your New Best Friend – the Cash Tracker

If you want more clarity on how much you can afford to put toward debt, the cash tracker can be life-changing. It does exactly what the name suggests: it helps you map out or track your cash. Start with the amount that will hit your bank account the next time you receive a paycheck or income. Then, list out all the places that money needs to go (including your bills, debt payments, and everyday expenses) over the next week or two weeks.

Look at your calendar when you map out your expenses. If you have dinner plans, you'll want to allocate some money to pay for dinner. If you are going to a birthday party and plan to bring a gift, you'll want to add that to the list. Map out the next two to three paychecks (or four to six weeks). That way, you can account for paychecks or times of the month where you incur higher expenses (like rent or a mortgage).

After you have your plan, it's just as important to enter in what you actually spent as well as update plans when things change. You'll want to use a debit card or cash for the cash tracker to work. Or if you use a credit card, pay off your credit card expenses frequently. We want the amount in your bank account to reflect the amount of cash you actually have as closely as possible.

Your Debt Paydown Recipe

I like recipes or very specific instructions, so that's what you're getting. For your debt paydown plan:

1. Pay the minimums and monthly payments on each piece of debt, if possible.
2. Any additional amount per month goes toward debt priority #1. You can figure out this amount via your financial plan and cash tracker.

WEEK #1		WEEK #2	
Bank Balance	$500	Bank Balance	$825
Income #1	$2,700	Income #1	$0
Income #2	$0	Income #2	$0
Total Available	**$3,200**	**Total Available**	**$825**
Credit Card #1	$50	Groceries	$150
Credit Card #2	$75	Gift	$35
Rent	$2,000	Utilities	$200
Groceries	$150	Additional Available for Debt Pay Down	$190
Dinner with Friends	$100		
Total Expenses	**$2,375**	**Total Expenses**	**$575**
Ending Bank Balance *	**$825**	**Ending Bank Balance ***	**$250**

*I like to set a minimum balance for my checking account so there's some cushion. In this case, I used $200.

3. Once debt priority #1 is paid off, you will continue to make all the monthly and minimum payments. Any additional money toward debt now goes toward debt priority #2. Don't forget to include the minimum or monthly payment you were paying toward debt priority #1. If that had a minimum payment of $30, that can be an additional $30 that goes to debt priority #2.

4. Go down the list until all debt is paid off.

Write your debt paydown recipe. How much will you put toward debt this month? How much additional can go toward debt priority #1?

1. _____

2. _____

3. _____

What If I Can't Make My Payments?

If you can't make your debt payments, a great place to start is by creating a health and safety budget (Tiffany Aliche taught us how in Chapter 5) and then once you have an idea of what you can put toward your debt, call up your lender(s). They may offer programs where you can pause payments or decrease the payment amount. If you are unable to make payments on your federal student loans, you may qualify for deferment or forbearance (they are pretty similar). If you qualify for **deferment**, you can stop making payments on principal (and interest, if your loan is subsidized). If you don't qualify for deferment, **forbearance** allows you to stop making payments on principal or reduce your monthly payment for up to 12 months. In most cases your loan interest will still accrue and these months won't count toward forgiveness.

During the pandemic in 2020 and 2021, most federal student loans qualified for a student loan payment pause. The interest rate on loans was changed to 0% (for the time) and there were no required payments. Each month still counted toward forgiveness and any payments made went to pay off past interest and then went directly toward principal.

If you are unable to come up with a solution and are not able to make your payments for some time, the late payments will show up on your credit reports and the lender might sell your debt (for a steep discount) to a collections agency. There are very specific ways to handle working with collections. Do some research and even come to the call with a script when you're ready to speak with them.

If your debt situation is extremely unmanageable, there's also bankruptcy, which I mentioned briefly in Chapter 10. This is a huge decision with many repercussions, so it's important to do your research and talk to an attorney before moving forward.

Should I Refinance My Debt?

Refinancing means taking out a new loan (usually at a lower interest rate) to replace some or all of your current debt. The lower interest rate means you'll pay less interest over the course of the loan and it can also lower your monthly payment. You can refinance credit card debt, student loans, and other debt as well. Here's what you need to account for.

Do Your Research without a Hard Inquiry into Your Credit

You'll first do some research to see what's available to you. As you're researching, make sure lenders aren't making hard inquiries into your credit. Hard inquiries typically ding your credit scores for a year and while a few points might not matter, depending on what your score is, that could mean not qualifying for a lower interest rate or could make the difference of your being able to refinance or not.

What terms can you get for refinancing?

	Lender #1	Lender #2	Lender #3
Interest Rate			
Fee to Refinance			
Monthly Payment			
Monthly Interest Paid			
Interest Paid Over Life of Loan			

Run the Numbers

I like to run the numbers on two things: First, how much money I will be saving over the course of the loan with the lower interest rate (you'll find a calculator in the Financial Adulting toolkit). There is usually a fee associated with refinancing – make sure to subtract any refinancing costs from your total savings. If you are saving $100 per month on your loan, and the refinancing costs $300, the cost will break even or start saving you money after three months.

If you went with the best offer, how much would you be saving in interest each month and over the course of the loan? When will the savings break even with the cost to refinance as far as fees?

	Current Loan	Refinanced Loan	Savings (Difference)
Monthly Payment			
Monthly Interest			
Interest Paid Over Life of Loan			

Fee to Refinance	/	Monthly Savings	=	# of Months until Savings Break Even
	/		=	

Make Sure the Payment Is Workable

Sometimes when a loan is refinanced, the interest rate is lower but the monthly payment is higher because the loan will be paid off more quickly (in fewer years). It's important to make sure that the new payment is workable with your income and other spending. You don't want to refinance only to feel strapped and stressed to make your monthly payments each month.

> Is the new payment workable with your financial plan? Go ahead and plug it in and report back.

Understand What Flexibility and Potential Forgiveness You Are Losing

When you refinance a federal student loan, you'll be taking out a private loan. This means you'll lose the flexibility you get with public loans like the variety of payment options and the forbearance and deferment of payments, and you'll lose any progress toward forgiveness. Chris says he thinks about refinancing like insurance. Look at the difference in your payment (or how much money you'll save from refinancing) against that insurance. Is the difference large enough to be worth it? If it's too small, it won't make sense to lose that insurance.

What About 0% Interest Transfers?

This is a strategy where people move their credit card debt to another credit card that has 0% interest (the 0% lasts for a certain number of months). The idea being you pay everything down while the card is at 0% interest and save all that money. Sounds like a no-brainer, right? The thing is, I've seen this backfire many times. Only do this if you have a very solid plan in place where you are clear based on your income and expenses how you will be able to pay off the credit card before the 0% interest rate expires. It takes discipline and planning. And believe me, the interest rate after the 0% expires is usually extra high. In many cases, people end up with a new high-interest credit card and haven't paid down their initial balance. All this is to say, just like with anything, we need to be honest with ourselves. Does this feel like an option that will work for you? If so, great. If not, stay away.

A Warning When Refinancing Credit Cards

Refinancing credit cards sounds like a great deal (as long as the monthly payment is workable) because credit card interest rates are so high. *But* this one can be tricky. Brian Walsh shared, "We see a lot of people use the personal loan (from refinancing) to pay off their credit card debt, but if they keep using the credit cards, then a year from now, they have credit card debt *and* personal loan debt and they're in a worse spot." I've seen this a lot, too. If you refinance, it works well to close your credit cards, or even all but one if you want to keep something open. If you don't close your credit cards, try to spend with cash or a debit card to prevent building up more credit card debt.

Let's Talk About Buying a Car

For those in the market for a car, I'm sorry. For most people, buying or leasing a car is not a fun process. I think the only person I know who truly enjoys it is Justin (my partner) because he loves to negotiate. He spends days negotiating. Here's how to decide whether buying or leasing is best for you:

1. **Know your budget** (including all the extra things that go into maintaining a car). Don't forget insurance, maintenance costs (scheduled and surprise), gas, and parking (especially if you live in a city).

2. **Run the numbers.** List out what each option (lease vs. buy) would cost you over the next 10 or 20 years (including all the extra things, how long you plan to own the car, and the resale value). I've included an example in the Financial Adulting toolkit. Look at these side by side.

   Most financial advice will recommend that you purchase a (used) car. When you run the numbers, buying typically makes the most sense *if* you keep the car after you pay off the car loan. That's the real kicker. Most people don't do this or don't want to do this. But once you pay off your car loan (which can take 5–10 years) and have a car that's payment-free, that's really when buying rather than leasing saves you a lot of money. Be realistic about your plans. Sometimes seeing how much money it would save is enough to get you on board!

3. **Do your research and negotiate.** It's important to know your stuff going into a negotiation. Know what you want and know what's a good price (resources are in the toolkit). Definitely call up multiple places and negotiate. Give each place a chance to beat the other's lowest price. If they do beat it, go back to the other and continue going back and forth. I know this takes work but it's a big purchase you don't make very often. Some places are looking to meet quotas (especially volume dealers) and will even take a loss on a car in order to meet the quota.

Financial Adulting Checklist

- ☐ Let go of the shame around your debt.
- ☐ Understand how credit cards work and create strategies to make them work for you.
- ☐ Calculate how much you are paying in interest each month.
- ☐ Negotiate away late fees, if you have them.
- ☐ Understand the student loan landscape and how they disproportionately impact BIPOC and women.
- ☐ Before you take out student loans, negotiate the bill (a.k.a. tuition) and shop around.
- ☐ Take inventory of your credit cards, student loans, and other debt.
- ☐ Make a plan to pay down your debt and update your financial plan to reflect it.

Okay, that's all I've got for debt. You've made it to the *final* chapter. This is where it all comes together and the magic happens. *And* I'm excited to introduce you to your new money coach!

CHAPTER 14

Become Your Own Money Coach

We've covered so much together. You now understand what it means to be a financial adult and have a plan to show for it. That's worth celebrating. I mean it, go ahead and celebrate. But before you run off into the financial adulting sunset, and look back and wave (and wink), we have to talk about what this all looks like moving forward. This isn't a one-time deal. Being a financial adult is a habit and a lifestyle.

It's a huge accomplishment to know what you know and to have a comprehensive plan, but the real magic is in maintaining that plan. It's in the updates, check-ins, and keeping your motivation.

To keep this all going, you need a financial coach (remember we talked about them in Chapter 8?). And I know the perfect person for the job. *You.*

But What Will You *Actually* Be Doing as a Financial Coach?

You will want to be your own cheerleader. You will make mistakes and get off track. I've been doing this awhile now and it still happens to me all the time. Yes, it's frustrating, but each of these missteps is a learning opportunity.

A money journey is an iterative process and mindset is really important. Come back to forgiveness, kindness, and slow and steady steps and you'll make some major headway toward your money goals.

Now before you get upset about this new role, know that these updates and check-ins don't have to take that long. What I'm talking about takes around two hours per month (but it can be less or more, depending on the complexity of your finances and how many people you're tracking spending for). And I'm going to give you the exact steps and framework so you can do it all yourself.

Enter one of my favorite times of the month, money parties.

Money Parties – The Gist

If you read my first book, *The 30-Day Money Cleanse*, you know about money parties. A money party is time we set aside to deal with our money. Because if we don't create and block off the time, it's not going to happen. Money parties are the most beneficial financial habit we can build. The financial plans you made are wonderful but unless you live and update the plan, you're not going to see the results of your hard work.

Here's everything you need to know to host your own money party.

Get Excited; How Will You Make It Fun?

I call them money *parties* for a reason. How will you make yours fun? Pour your favorite beverage, put on a money party playlist (link in the Financial Adulting toolkit!), light a candle, or get in your comfiest clothes. If you're not sure what will make your money party fun, it's okay to experiment. Try different things to see what feels fun and makes you look forward to your money parties.

How will you make your money party fun?

_____

_____

_____

Up the Ante with Rewards

It might sound silly, but rewarding ourselves really works. Is there something you can give yourself as a reward for completing your money party? It could be as simple as crossing it off your to-do list (so rewarding!) or watching your favorite show guilt-free. Again, don't be afraid to test things out. If something doesn't feel rewarding, try something else. And *always* follow through and give yourself the reward you decide on. If you don't, you'll start to learn it's not coming. This can derail your motivation.

How will you reward yourself when you've had your money party?

_____

_____

_____

Choose a Time and Day

Set aside two hours for your money party. Think about the time and day that will work best. Some like to have them during a leisurely weekend morning. Others prefer to jump in during the afternoon at work or in the evening when they finish work for the day. Don't spend too much time on this decision. If the time you choose doesn't work well, you can always change it.

When will you have your money party?

_____

Now put that time on the calendar. Even better, set up a recurring calendar reminder. How often should you have money parties? I recommend having a money party at least once per month. Some people like to have them weekly. The more frequently you have money parties, the shorter they will be, but you'll have more of them. So it's a personal choice. And again, if the frequency doesn't work, you can always change it.

How often will you have money parties? Set up a recurring calendar invite.

_____

Get Some Accountability – Create Your Dream Team

Accountability works. When we tell someone we're going to do something, there's a 65% likelihood we're going to do it. If we make a plan to check in with them, that goes up to 95%.[1] You can get this accountability from a bestie, family member, colleague, or even your partner. I call these money buddies our dream team.

You don't have to share any money details with them; they are just holding you accountable for having your money party.

Whom will hold you accountable for having your money party?

_____

For the Love of Money: Money Parties

If you have a partner or a (chosen) family you want to include in your money party, great. It's such a good time to get on the same page in terms of goals, spending, and progress. If money tends to be a stressful topic in your relationship, having money parties is a great way to compartmentalize financial conversations by limiting them to this certain time per week or month. If you are bringing in others to your money party, you'll want to include them in the planning so they are excited about the party, rewards, and agenda.

Set Your Money Party Agenda

It's time for the main event. What will you actually cover during your money party? There are some things you'll want to do monthly and others you can do once per quarter (every three months) or once per year.

The good news is, none of this will be new or surprising. You've done each of these things or similar things in the exercises in earlier chapters. Now we're updating, adjusting, and checking in. Head to the Financial Adulting toolkit to get your comprehensive money party checklist.

Monthly: Run Your Numbers

Running your numbers is the most important part of your money party. You know that beautiful financial plan you made? At your money party, you'll enter in what *actually* happened that month in terms of spending, saving, and earning. You can compare that to what you had planned and update your plans going forward accordingly. Maybe you were a bit too optimistic about your takeout spending. Update your future projections to a more realistic goal. Maybe you canceled a subscription that you had in the plan going forward. You can take that out for future months.

You can do this in a spreadsheet or, if you hate spreadsheets, you can do it by hand or using an app. I use a spreadsheet and differentiate between projections (guesstimates/plans) and actuals (what actually happened) by making plans in a blue font and actuals in a black font. This will all happen in the same financial plan template you filled out, starting in Chapter 4.

Some Money Party Pro Tips

- **Keep an account list.** Keeping a list of your accounts and credit cards in the spreadsheet saves a lot of time. You'll want to include any bank accounts and credit cards where you have income or expenses come through. If your money party is for March, log in to the first account and start with the transactions from March 1 (or the earliest date in March). If your first expense of the month is "Trader Joe's for $125," you'd enter 125 into the "groceries" category of your template. Once you've entered in all the transactions for March, you can move on to the next account on the list.

- **Have account usernames and passwords handy (or saved).** Nothing slows us down at a money party like having to reset a bunch of account passwords. If the option's available, you can even bookmark each of the website pages you will need.

- **Have a separate notebook or document open nearby.** As you go through your expenses, you'll inevitably think of things you need or want to do, like cancel a subscription you're not using or call up a vendor. Instead of going off and doing this in the middle of running your numbers, write it down and save it for another time.

- **Set a timer.** If you don't finish what you want in the two hours, it's important to stop anyway. You can schedule more time later in the week. Having a money party is a new skill that we get better at (and quicker at) with time. How long it takes you your first time has nothing to do with how long it will take you in the future. I promise, they will go much faster!

- **Take a guess (for "fun").** Guess what you spent this month. Write it in your notebook. This is for your eyes only.

Is there an app for that? If you use an app or software, you want to make sure you have a perfectly clear picture on your monthly income, spending (and in which categories), goal contributions, and what, if anything, is remaining. It's ideal too if you can have plans for future months and see an entire year total.

What if I don't want to do this? It's ideal to do this exercise every month, but if you know yourself and know you're not going to do it, you can start with a smaller task. Choose a category (or two to three) where you tend to spend the most or you think you might overspend. Tracking that specific category for the month is a great way to build up the habit.

You can also come up with a total spend goal and check in on that total (rather than individual categories). It will take some time to calculate what that total should be (don't forget to include sinking funds!) but as long as you spend within that amount, and are meeting your goals as planned, you know you are hitting your total spending goals.

> Practice running your numbers (for the past month). At your first money party, this might be all you do. And you might not finish. That's okay! It can take time to get the hang of it. You can do this using the spreadsheet in the Financial Adulting toolkit, by hand, or using your preferred app.

Following are some FAQs for running your numbers.

What Do I Do About the Cash I Took Out at an ATM?

Ideally we categorize our cash because it's more informative to know we spent $20 on taxis than that we had $20 in cash. That being said, cash takes more work to track because we have to remember to track it ourselves – there aren't digital records like a bank statement. You can include any unaccounted-for cash in a line item called "cash" in your financial plan.

Should I Include My Credit Card Payments in My Expenses?

Regular credit card debt payments should be included if they are for previous purchases (e.g., you make a $100 monthly credit card debt payment). If you purchased dinner on your credit card for $35 and included that in "dining out," you wouldn't want to also include the payment to your credit card to pay that down because you'd be double-counting the expense. This is another reason it's easier to not use credit cards we're trying to pay off.

What Do I Do About Items I Plan to Return?

If we purchase something using cash or debit, the money has left our accounts even though we expect to get it back. It can be helpful for cash flow purposes to include the purchase. Then, when you get the returned payment, you can take it out of your spending that month. This also holds us accountable for actually returning the things we plan to. If you aren't worried about cash flow, have a buffer in your checking account, or purchase and return the item in the same month, you might decide to just leave it out.

How Should I Handle Expenses My Work Is Going to Reimburse?

It's helpful to track reimbursable work expenses to make sure we get paid what we are owed, but most of us will want to do that in a separate area. Work expenses can throw our budgets out of whack and they aren't expenses that we're going to be paying for, so they don't need to be included in our monthly expenses. I usually recommend having a separate credit card for work expenses to keep this distinct and clear.

Weekly or Monthly – Up the Saving Ante with the Money Game

The Money Game turns saving more money into a game to make the process easier and a lot more fun. Here's how to play.

1. Calculate your Money Game number. Choose some areas of variable spending to include in the game (variable, meaning they change week to week and month to month). These areas can include dining out/takeout, drinks, Lyfts, groceries, shopping, and so on – everything you do on a weekly basis that's variable. Don't include fixed expenses like bills because our rent will be our rent (unless we move). No game in that.

Which variable spending categories will you include in the Money Game?

1. _____

2. _____

3. _____

4. _____

5. _____

How much do you plan to spend in each category? You have this mapped out in your financial plan so you can take it right from there. I like to look at this on a weekly basis. If you have $200 per month planned for dining out, you'll want to convert that into a weekly number ($200 × 12 months = $2,400 per year/52 weeks = $46/week).

Convert numbers as needed and add up the variable spending categories so you have a total spending amount for the week. This is your Money Game number.

Spending Category	Weekly Amount
Example: Dining Out	$46
Total Money Game Number	

2. Choose a goal (or two). Each week, you're going to track your spending in the categories you chose. If you spend under your Money Game number, you win and that amount goes toward your top-priority goal(s). Which goal(s) will it be? Look at your goals list (from Chapter 3). Which goals will have you excited to spend less during the Money Game each week? It's important to decide this ahead of time so you have some major motivation!

Which goal(s) will your Money Game winnings go toward? If you are contributing to multiple goals, how will you split the winnings?

Goal	% of Winnings
Example: Rainy-Day Fund/Vacation	50%/50%

3. Track your spending. To play the game, track those variable spending categories for the week. You can start on any day of the week, but many people like to start on Monday and do their check-in on Sunday nights. You can play the Money Game less frequently and check in on these categories once per month, but I do find that we win more by doing it more frequently because we're more in touch with our spending week to week.

Track your spending for the first week of the Money Game. Calculate your winnings!

Money Game Number	–	Week #1 Spending	=	Money Game Winnings
Example: $250	–	$200	=	$50
	–		=	

4. Transfer your winnings. At the end of the week, you'll total your spending for the week. If you spent less than your Money Game number, you win! If you spent more, try again next week. If you spent $200 during the week and your Money Game number was $250, you won $50. Congrats! That $50 gets to go directly to whatever goal you chose. As soon as you calculate your winnings, transfer the money to that goal immediately. You don't want something else to come up and take your winnings.

If you lose the Money Game, that's okay. We don't win them all. You can carry forward that loss into next week's Money Game. If you spent $300 and your Money Game number is $250, you start the week off with $50 of spending already on the books. If you lose multiple weeks in a row, your estimates might be too optimistic. It's probably time to adjust your spending plan accordingly.

Transfer your Money Game winnings to their respective goal(s). If you lost, add that balance to your spending for next week. Does your Money Game number feel realistic? You want it to be a game you can win!

_____

_____

> ### For the Love of Money: The Money Game with Others
>
> You can also ask a money buddy (partner or friend) to join you in the Money Game. The extra accountability helps and makes it more fun. If it's someone you spend a lot of time with or make decisions with, even better! You can keep your Money Game numbers separate or combine them so that you're going after a spending number together as a family.

Here are some other things you'll want to do at your money parties.

Monthly: Your Financial To-Do List of Things That Come Up

In between money parties, random financial things will inevitably come up. You probably already have a list of things you still want to do just from reading this book. Or maybe you noticed you were charged the wrong amount for a service. Whenever something comes up, add it to the money party agenda. If something urgent comes up, like you see fraud on a card or your account has insufficient funds, deal with that right away.

Are there any things you've been meaning to do or need to accomplish? They can even be exercises from this book that you haven't yet completed. Where will you keep a running list of the items that come up going forward?

_____

_____

_____

_____

_____

Monthly: Revisit Your Contributions to Your Goals

If you want to be saving more for any particular goal, see if you can make that work (or can get closer to making that work) by revisiting your expenses and income. This might be something you expect to do less frequently but it's important to revisit this often because you don't need to make monumental changes to make progress. Can you up the amount by $5? That's great, do it.

> Which goals are you contributing to and how much? By when will you achieve them at this pace? Do you want to increase any contributions?
>
> | Goal | Amount | Timeline | Increase | New Timeline |
> |------|--------|----------|----------|--------------|
> | Example: Rainy-Day Fund | $250 | 12 months | $50 | 10 months |
> | | | | | |
> | | | | | |

Monthly: Use and Adjust Your Sinking Funds

As you use your sinking funds, transfer the money over from your sinking fund accounts to your checking account (to reimburse yourself). Some like to make the transfers in the moment (i.e., right when they make the purchase) and others do it all at the end of the month. This is also a great time to check in on your sinking funds to make sure you are setting aside the right amount of money going forward given how much you plan to spend in each category. You can adjust your automatic transfers accordingly.

Have you done any sinking fund spending? How much? Make sure to transfer those amounts over to your checking account. Are your sinking fund auto-transfers on track with how much you will need to spend in the coming months or even the next 12 months? Make any needed adjustments.

_____

_____

_____

Monthly: Track and Celebrate Your Progress

Track your progress for each goal and decide on some rewards or ways to celebrate as you hit milestones along the way, as well as when you achieve the overall goal. You'll want to update your progress each month and celebrate accordingly. This can be extremely motivating and shows you how far you've come!

Need ideas? When you see a friend, share your recent win so they can celebrate with you (even something as simple as a "cheers" feels festive!). If you'd rather celebrate on your own, you can indulge in a frugal joy or use the money that would have previously gone toward a monthly payment to treat yourself. Think about what would be fun and something you would look forward to.

Goal	Milestones	Milestone Celebrations	Overall Celebration
Example: $3,000	$500	Home Spa Night	Happy Hour Celebration with Friends

If You're Visual, Make a Physical Representation of Your Goals

This can be as beautiful and intricate or as simple as you want. For a simple one, I've included a goal bar chart for you to color in as you make progress. There are others in the Financial Adulting toolkit.

To use this chart, divide your goal by 10, label each box with its respective milestone, and then color them in as you get closer to your goal. For example, if your goal is to save $10,000, you'd label the first box $1,000, the second box $2,000, all the way up to $10,000.

Okay, *whew!* That's what you'll do at your monthly money parties. If this list feels overwhelming, prioritize the following two items each month: (1) run your numbers (including an update of your projections) and (2) go through the financial to-do list of things that come up. Everything else can be done quarterly if need be.

Quarterly and Annual Money Party Checklist

Then there are some things you'll want to do every three months and every year.

Quarterly: Update Your Net Worth Tracker

Your net worth tracker is your moment-in-time snapshot of what you have and where. Quick reminder: your net worth is what you have (your assets) minus what you owe (your debts). You can update this every three months to see the progress you're making. If it's motivating and fun, you are welcome to do it more often. There's space to update it in the spreadsheet version in the Financial Adulting toolkit. If you have debt, you will also update your debt tracker once per quarter to track your progress.

Quarterly: Revisit Your Debt Paydown Plan

If paying down debt is a top-priority goal of yours, you can revisit your debt paydown plan once per quarter. Are you happy with how each piece of debt is prioritized? Do you want to increase or decrease your monthly payments? Because you will have all this information handy and updated, this shouldn't take you long to review. If debt paydown is a lower priority or you are paying off lower-interest debt like a student loan or mortgage, this doesn't need to happen every quarter. You can instead do a quick check-in each year.

Annually: Check in on Long-Term Goals Like Investing and Retirement

The stock market might have grown and the bond market might have shrunk (or vice versa). Getting your portfolio back to your ideal asset allocation is called **rebalancing** and you'll want to rebalance once per year for all your investments (retirement and otherwise). If your retirement portfolio is invested in target-date funds, you don't have to rebalance those accounts because target-date funds do the work for you.

What's the best way to rebalance? The simplest way to rebalance without incurring any taxes is to invest more money in the areas that need it. Let's say you want your portfolio invested 70% in a stock fund and 30% in a bond fund. Your recurring contributions are probably set up to go 70% to the stock fund and 30% to the bond fund. Great, makes sense.

When you check in, you see that your portfolio is now 80% in the stock fund and 20% in the bond fund. To rebalance, you want to beef up the bond fund to get back to that 70/30 split. You can change your recurring contributions to go 100% to the bond fund and 0% to the stock fund until it's back in balance. Check in each month and once the portfolio is back to the 70/30 split, you can go back to your 70% stock fund and 30% bond fund contributions.

When you buy and sell investments in your retirement account, you don't pay capital gains tax, so you can also sell some of the equity (stock) fund and buy more of the bond fund to rebalance in one fell swoop.

Every few years you'll also want to revisit the asset allocation you chose to make sure it's still aligned. If you used a questionnaire to figure out your asset allocation, revisit it. Or if you'd like to try another resource, go to Chapter 8 of the Financial Adulting toolkit.

Annually: Revisit Your Consumer Activism Criteria and Giving Plan, and Conduct a Spending Audit

While you might have a list of action items to accomplish from Chapter 6, you will want to revisit your criteria once per year and conduct another spending audit. From there you can create your consumer activism action items for the next year. You'll also want to relook at companies that you thought met or didn't meet your criteria, as the whole point of consumer activism is getting companies to change their ways! This is also a great time to check in on your giving plan. Do you want to give differently or up your contributions?

We also talked about the wealth gap and what we can do to help close it. Once per year is a great time to check in to reflect on the actions you've taken and what you want to do going forward. If your situation has changed, you might have a privilege you didn't have before that you can now use to help close the gap. This could be a changed position in a company, an improved financial situation, or even more time.

Annually: Reflect and Think Big – Make Your Annual Plan for the Next Year

Once per year we'll want to take a step back to reflect on how things are going and what you want the next year to look like. Just like you put your financial plan together for the current year, you'll want to do that again each and every year. It's a great time to revisit your big goals and decide if you want to change their priority.

You will project out your income and expenses for the next 12 months. To make it "easy," you can even reread this book each year and go through all the exercises. Yep, I said it! This can be a yearly read! That way you have your plan ready to go before the New Year begins.

Other Things to Do Each Year

- ☐ Pull your free credit reports (annualcreditreport.com) and check them for errors. Some people like to pull them all at once and others like to pull one every four months as a way to check in all year long.

- ☐ Map out your medical expenses for the next year and update contributions to your HSA or FSA (if applicable).

- ☐ If something in your life has changed, revisit your insurance. Do you need a new type of insurance? Do you have enough (or too much)?

- ☐ Prepare and file your taxes. If you think of ways to make next year easier, update your system.

- ☐ Are you happy with your current banks and credit cards? Check in and decide whether you'd like to make any switches.

- ☐ If you've had any major life changes, update your will and your beneficiaries.

- ☐ If you contribute to a dependent care FSA, you must reenroll *each year*. Don't miss out on those pretax expenses if you have them!

How to Keep Your Motivation Up

This last chapter shows you the actions to take to maintain, update, and live your plan, which will be the key to your success. You can do it! Financial adulting is a habit and a lifestyle and when things get busy or when we make mistakes it can be hard to keep going. Everything gets a little less shiny over time, but that's where the real magic is.

I asked some of my very brilliant finance friends to give their best pieces of advice for keeping up your motivation. Here's what they said:

Yanely Espinal, YouTuber known as @MissBeHelpful and director of educational outreach at Next Gen Personal Finance: I followed as many relatable financial accounts as I could across all my social media platforms when I first started out on my big goal to pay off $20,000 of credit card debt in my mid-twenties. I built my support network and then I'd tap into it and ask people who used hashtags like #debtfreecommunity or #debtfreejourney what strategies worked for them. The words of encouragement and stories of inspiration alone kept me going! When all else fails, remember that as humans, we're wired for social connection.

Chelsea Fagan, founder and CEO of The Financial Diet, a digital media company about personal finance: Create a plan that involves many small steps that you can celebrate, including pre-planned ways that you are going to celebrate them. Make sure that there are moments along the way where you're really acknowledging and rewarding yourself. There are a lot of studies that show that even just the anticipation of something is often just as fulfilling and rewarding and enjoyable as doing the thing.

Erin Lowry, author of personal finance series Broke Millennial: My absolute favorite strategy for keeping motivated with a financial goal is to nickname my bank accounts. Many banks and credit unions will allow you to change the name of an account from something generic like 15785217 to "South Africa Trip" or "Quit My Job" or "Down Payment." The more specific you can get the better, like "Down Payment June 2025." It's helpful to have a reminder right there for the moments that you're tempted to skim a little bit out of the account for an indulgence today or avoid contributing entirely.

Which of these strategies resonate with you right now? Write one or two down here and incorporate them into your day-to-day. I'll have you check in to see how they've worked (or not) at your monthly money party.

1. _____

2. _____

Financial Adulting Checklist

- ☐ Commit to being your own financial coach.
- ☐ Plan your first money party.
- ☐ Get a money buddy for accountability.
- ☐ Go through the monthly, quarterly, and annual money party checklists or get them from the Financial Adulting toolkit.
- ☐ Test out some strategies to keep your motivation up all year long.
- ☐ Choose how you will celebrate finishing this book and building your Financial Adulting foundation.
- ☐ Continue to use the Financial Adulting toolkit and the book as a reference and resource going forward.
- ☐ Follow @thefiscalfemme and join our community (link in the Financial Adulting toolkit).

Congrats!

You did it! You are now a financial adult. I've said it throughout this book but please celebrate this milestone. You deserve it! Remember, being a financial adult means:

- Taking small, consistent steps that add up to big results
- Facing what's happening with your money
- Feeling confident in your financial plans
- Knowing you will get to have and experience what you want in life (which is the whole point of having money anyway!)
- Understanding the critical context of equity and personal finance
- Recognizing that your privilege can and should be used to help close racial and gender wealth gaps, and/or realizing that you may be starting at a disadvantage due to historic and systemic obstacles

Use this book and the Financial Adulting toolkit to come back to when you have a question or want to make your financial plan for next year.

It's been an honor and pleasure to join you for this part of your money journey.

Notes

Chapter 1 What Is a Financial Adult?

1. Maury Backman, "Most Americans Don't Trust Their Financial Advisors. Should They?" *The Motley Fool* (July 11, 2017), https://www.fool.com/retirement/2017/07/11/most-americans-dont-trust-their-financial-advisors.aspx#:~:text=In%20a%202016%20poll%20by,trust%20them%20%22a%20little.%22.
2. Selena Maranjian, "Surprise – There's a Good Chance Your Broker Is Ripping You Off," *The Motley Fool* (March 9, 2016), https://www.fool.com/investing/general/2016/03/09/surprise-theres-a-good-chance-your-broker-is-rippi.aspx.

Chapter 2 Equity and Personal Finance

1. "CPI Inflation Calculator," U.S. Bureau of Labor Statistics (July 2009–August 2021), https://www.bls.gov/data/inflation_calculator.htm.
2. "Disparities in Wealth by Race and Ethnicity in the 2019 Survey of Consumer Finances," The Federal Reserve (September 28, 2020), https://www.federalreserve.gov/econres/notes/feds-notes/disparities-in-wealth-by-race-and-ethnicity-in-the-2019-survey-of-consumer-finances-accessible-20200928.htm#fig1.
3. Heather McCulloch, "Closing the Women's Wealth Gap" (January 2017), https://womenswealthgap.org/wp-content/uploads/2017/06/Closing-the-Womens-Wealth-Gap-Report-Jan2017.pdf (chart, p. 4). Original source: https://assetfunders.org/wp-content/uploads/Women_Wealth_-Insights_Grantmakers_brief_15.pdf.
4. "Moms Equal Pay Day 2021," Equal Pay Today, http://www.equalpaytoday.org/moms-equal-pay-day-2021.
5. "Disparities in Wealth by Race and Ethnicity."
6. Melany De La Cruz-Viesca, Zhenxiang Chen, Paul M. Ong, Darrick Hamilton, William A. Darity Jr., "The Color of Wealth in Los Angeles," The Federal Reserve Bank of Los Angeles (2016), http://www.aasc.ucla.edu/besol/Color_of_Wealth_Report.pdf (p. 5).
7. Mariko Chang, "Lifting as We Climb: Women of Color, Wealth, and America's Future," Center for Community Economic Development (Spring 2010), https://static1.squarespace.com/static/5c50b84131d4df5265e7392d/t/5c5c7801ec212d4fd499ba39/1549563907681/Lifting_As_We_Climb_InsightCCED_2010.pdf (p. 14).

8. Dedrick Asante-Muhammed, Chuck Collins, Josh Hoxie, and Emanuel Neves, "The Ever-Growing Gap," Institute for Policy Studies (August 2016), https://ips-dc.org/wp-content/uploads/2016/08/The-Ever-Growing-Gap-CFED_IPS-Final-2.pdf.

9. "The Homestead Act of 1862," National Archives (June 2, 2021), https://www.archives.gov/education/lessons/homestead-act#:~:text=President%20Abraham%20Lincoln%20signed%20the,pay%20a%20small%20registration%20fee.

10. Ibid.

11. Ibid.

12. Ian Webster, "Value of $1.25 from 1862 to 2021," CPI Inflation Calculator, https://www.in2013dollars.com/us/inflation/1862?amount=1.25.

13. Keri Leigh Merritt, "Land and the Roots of African-American Poverty," *Aeon* (March 11, 2016), https://aeon.co/ideas/land-and-the-roots-of-african-american-poverty.

14. Mehrsa Baradaran, *The Color of Money: Black Banks and the Racial Wealth Gap* (Cambridge, MA: Belknap Press of Harvard University Press, 2017), p. 30 ($3 million lost in 1874); https://www.in2013dollars.com/us/inflation/1874?amount=3000000.

15. Ibid., p. 108 (entire section).

16. Ibid., p. 109.

17. History.com editors, "Jim Crow Laws," History.com (March 26, 2021), https://www.history.com/topics/early-20th-century-us/jim-crow-laws.

18. "Intersectional Feminism: What It Means and Why It Matters Right Now," UN Women (July 1, 2020), https://www.unwomen.org/en/news/stories/2020/6/explainer-intersectional-feminism-what-it-means-and-why-it-matters.

19. Linda Scott, "Gender Inequality Causes Poverty," *Double X Economy* (March 29 2021), https://www.doublexeconomy.com/post/gender-inequality-causes-poverty.

20. "The Power of Parity: Advancing Women's Equality in the United States," McKinsey Global Institute (April 2016), https://www.mckinsey.com/~/media/mckinsey/featured%20insights/employment%20and%20growth/the%20power%20of%20parity%20advancing%20womens%20equality%20in%20the%20united%20states/mgi-power-of-parity-in-us-full-report-april-2016.ashx#:~:text=Yet%20women%20in%20the%20United,women%20make%20to%20the%20economy, p. 9.

21. "Empowering Girls & Women," Clinton Global Initiative, https://www.un.org/en/ecosoc/phlntrpy/notes/clinton.pdf.

22. "Minimum Wage," Women Employed, https://womenemployed.org/minimum-wage/.

23. Ibid. (for total minimum wage workers); "Characteristics of Minimum Wage Workers, 2020," U.S. Bureau of Labor Statistics (February 2021), https://www.bls.gov/opub/reports/minimum-wage/2020/home.htm.

24. "Deeper in Debt: Women & Student Loans," AAUW (2021), https://www .aauw.org/resources/research/deeper-in-debt/.

25. Ben Steverman and Alexandre Tanzi, "The 50 Richest Americans Are Worth as Much as the Poorest 165 Million," *Bloomberg* (August 10, 2020), https://www.bloomberg.com/news/articles/2020-10-08/top-50-richest-people-in-the-us-are-worth-as-much-as-poorest-165-million.

26. "Report: 1 in 4 Mothers Go Back to Work Less Than 2 Weeks After Giving Birth," Abt Associates (August 20, 2015), https://www.abtassociates.com/ who-we-are/news/in-the-news/report-1-in-4-mothers-go-back-to-work-less-than-2-weeks-after-giving.

27. "Calculating the Hidden Cost of Interrupting a Career for Child Care," Center for American Progress (June 21, 2016), https://www.american progress.org/issues/early-childhood/reports/2016/06/21/139731/ calculating-the-hidden-cost-of-interrupting-a-career-for-child-care/.

28. Linda Houser and Thomas P. Vartanian, "Pay Matters: The Positive Economic Impacts of Paid Family Leave for Families, Businesses and the Public," Rutgers Center for Women and Work (January 2012), https://www .nationalpartnership.org/our-work/resources/economic-justice/other/ pay-matters.pdf.

29. Rosie Colosi, "Paternity Leave Is a Lifesaver for Working Moms ... But Are Dads Taking It?" *CBS News* (July 20, 2019), https://www.nbcnews .com/know-your-value/feature/paternity-leave-life-saver-working-moms-are-dads-taking-it-ncna1036226.

30. Elly Ann-Johansson, "The Effect of Own and Spousal Parental Leave on Earnings," Institute for Labour Market Policy Evaluation (March 22, 2010), https://www.ifau.se/globalassets/pdf/se/2010/wp10-4-The-effect-of-own-and-spousal-parental-leave-on-earnings.pdf (p. 28).

31. Julie Anderson, "Breadwinner Mothers by Race/Ethnicity and State," Institute for Women's Policy Research (September 2016), https://iwpr .org/wp-content/uploads/2020/08/Q054.pdf.

Chapter 3 Your Money Goals

1. "About Financial Abuse," The National Network to End Domestic Violence (NNEDV), https://nnedv.org/content/about-financial-abuse/.

2. Rachel Gurevich, "How Much Does IVF Really Cost?" Very Well Family (March 5, 2020), https://www.verywellfamily.com/how-much-does-ivf-cost-1960212.

3. Holly Hutchison, "Cost," Fertility IQ, https://www.fertilityiq.com/topics/ cost.

Chapter 4 All About Income

1. Robyn Powell, "How to Include Disabled Women in the Fight for Equal Pay," *Bustle* (April 10, 2018), https://www.bustle.com/p/disabled-womens-equal-pay-struggles-often-go-unheard-but-you-can-help-include-them-8730123.
2. Catherine Rampell, "Before That Sex Change, Think About Your Next Paycheck," *New York Times* (September 25, 2008), https://economix.blogs.nytimes.com/2008/09/25/before-that-sex-change-think-about-your-next-paycheck/.
3. Stephen Miller, "Black Workers Still Earn Less than Their White Counterparts," *SHRM* (June 11, 2020), https://www.shrm.org/resourcesandtools/hr-topics/compensation/pages/racial-wage-gaps-persistence-poses-challenge.aspx.
4. Trenton D. Mize, "Sexual Orientation in the Labor Market," *American Sociological Review* (November 15, 2016), https://journals.sagepub.com/doi/pdf/10.1177/0003122416674025.
5. Grace Hauck, "When Will Women Get Equal Pay? Not for Another 257 Years, Report Says," *USA Today* (December 20, 2019), https://www.usatoday.com/story/news/nation/2019/12/20/gender-pay-gap-equal-wages-expected-257-years-report/2699326001/.
6. Patricia Cohen, "Black Women Were Half as Likely to Be Hired for State or Local Jobs Than White Men, a Report Says," *New York Times* (March 18, 2021), https://www.nytimes.com/2021/03/18/business/black-women-hiring-discrimination.html.
7. Alexander W. Watts, "Why Does John Get the STEM Job Rather Than Jennifer?" Stanford University – The Clayman Institute for Gender Research (June 2, 2014), https://gender.stanford.edu/news-publications/gender-news/why-does-john-get-stem-job-rather-jennifer.
8. Sheryl Nance-Nash, "Why Imposter Syndrome Hits Women and Women of Colour Harder," *BBC* (July 27, 2020), https://www.bbc.com/worklife/article/20200724-why-imposter-syndrome-hits-women-and-women-of-colour-harder.
9. Ruchika Tulshyan and Jodi-Ann Burey, "Stop Telling Women They Have Imposter Syndrome," *Harvard Business Review* (February 11, 2021), https://hbr.org/2021/02/stop-telling-women-they-have-imposter-syndrome.

Chapter 5 Your Money Outflows

1. "Multigenerational Households," *Generations United* (2021), gu.org/explore-our-topics/multigenerational-households.

2. Bill de Blasio and Julie Menin, "From Cradle to Cane: The Cost of Being a Female Consumer," NYC Department of Consumer Affairs (December 2015), https://www1.nyc.gov/assets/dca/downloads/pdf/partners/Study-of-Gender-Pricing-in-NYC.pdf.

3. Stephanie Gonzalez Guittar, Liz Grauerholz, Erin N. Kidder, Shameika D. Daye, and Megan McLaughlin, "Beyond the Pink Tax: Gender-Based Pricing and Differentiation of Personal Care Products," *Gender Issues* (May 2021).

4. "Investment Calculator," Calculator.net, https://www.calculator.net/investment-calculator.html?ctype=endamount&ctargetamountv=1000000&cstartingprinciplev=2294&cyearsv=20&cinterestratev=7&ccompound=annually&ccontributeamountv=2294&cadditionat1=end&ciadditionat1=annually&printit=0&x=111&y=24.

Chapter 6 Consumer Activism

1. Maddie Shepherd, "Local Shopping Statistics (2021): Facts on Buying Local," *Fundera* (December 16, 2020), https://www.fundera.com/resources/local-shopping-statistics.

2. "Break Up With Your DAPL-Supporting Bank," *Green America*, https://www.greenamerica.org/break-your-dapl-supporting-bank.

3. Bill Chappell, "2 Cities to Pull More Than $3 Billion from Wells Fargo Over Dakota Access Pipeline," *NPR* (February 8, 2017), https://www.npr.org/sections/thetwo-way/2017/02/08/514133514/two-cities-vote-to-pull-more-than-3-billion-from-wells-fargo-over-dakota-pipelin.

Chapter 7 Work Optional (a.k.a. Retirement)

1. Hal E. Hershfield, Daniel G. Goldstein, William F. Sharpe, Jesse Fox, Leo Yeykelis, Laura L. Carstensen, and Jeremy N. Bailenson, "Increasing Saving Behavior Through Age-Progressed Renderings of the Future Self," *Journal of Marketing Research* XLVIII (November 2011): S23–S37, https://vhil.stanford.edu/mm/2011/hershfield-jmr-saving-behavior.pdf.

2. "National Retirement Risk Index," Center for Retirement Risk at Boston College, https://crr.bc.edu/special-projects/national-retirement-risk-index/ (there is updated data in total but not broken down by race).

3. Alicia H. Munnell, Wenliang Houand, and Geoffrey T. Sanzenbacher, "Trends in Retirement Security by Race/Ethnicity," Center for Retirement

Risk at Boston College (November 2018), https://crr.bc.edu/briefs/trends-in-retirement-security-by-raceethnicity/.

4. Elizabeth Olson, "For Many Women, Adequate Pensions Are Still a Far Reach," *New York Times* (June 3, 2016), https://www.nytimes.com/2016/06/04/your-money/for-many-women-adequate-pensions-are-still-a-far-reach.html.

5. "Disparities in Wealth by Race and Ethnicity in the 2019 Survey of Consumer Finances," The Federal Reserve (September 28, 2020), https://www.federalreserve.gov/econres/notes/feds-notes/disparities-in-wealth-by-race-and-ethnicity-in-the-2019-survey-of-consumer-finances-accessible-20200928.htm#fig5.

6. "SNP – SNP Real Time Price. Currency in USD," *Yahoo! Finance* (September 30, 2007–October 30, 2007), https://finance.yahoo.com/quote/%5EGSPC/history?period1=1191196800&period2=1193788800&interval=1d&filter=history&frequency=1d&includeAdjustedClose=true.

7. "College Cost Calculator," Calculator.net, https://www.calculator.net/college-cost-calculator.html?todaycost=26820&useaverage=26820&costincrease=5&collegelength=4&savingpercent=35&balancenow=0&returnrate=7&interesttaxrate=0&startin=18&x=32&y=14.

Chapter 8 Become an Investor for Good

1. "Survey of Consumer Finances, 1989–2019," The Federal Reserve (September 28, 2020), https://www.federalreserve.gov/econres/scf/dataviz/scf/chart/#series:Stock_Holdings;demographic:all;population:1;units:have.

2. Jean Chatzky, "Why Women Invest 40 Percent Less Than Men (and How We Can Change It)," *NBC News* (September 25, 2018), https://www.nbcnews.com/better/business/why-women-invest-40-percent-less-men-how-we-can-ncna912956 (Survey by Wealth Simple).

3. "Survey of Consumer Finances, 1989–2019," The Federal Reserve (September 28, 2020), https://www.federalreserve.gov/econres/scf/dataviz/scf/chart/#series:Stock_Holdings;demographic:racecl4;population:all;units:have.

4. "Nearly 40 Percent of Americans with Annual Incomes over $100,000 Live Paycheck-to-Paycheck," *PR Newswire* (June 15, 2021), https://www.prnewswire.com/news-releases/nearly-40-percent-of-americans-with-annual-incomes-over-100-000-live-paycheck-to-paycheck-301312281.html.

5. "Disparities in Wealth by Race and Ethnicity in the 2019 Survey of Consumer Finances," The Federal Reserve (September 28, 2020), https://www.federalreserve.gov/econres/notes/feds-notes/disparities-in-wealth-by-race-and-ethnicity-in-the-2019-survey-of-consumer-finances-accessible-20200928.htm#fig1.

6. "Labor Force Statistics from the Current Population Survey," *U.S. Bureau of Labor Statistics* (January 22, 2021), https://www.bls.gov/cps/cpsaat11.htm.
7. "Making More Room for Women in the Financial Planning Profession," CFP Board, https://www.cfp.net/-/media/files/cfp-board/knowledge/reports-and-research/womens-initiative/cfp-board_win_web.pdf?la=en&hash=614591F5084FDE519B27B7A2D3CA3AC6.
8. "Who's the Better Investor: Men or Women?" Fidelity Investments (May 18, 2017), https://www.fidelity.com/about-fidelity/individual-investing/better-investor-men-or-women/.
9. "How to Invest a Lump Sum of Money," Vanguard, https://investor.vanguard.com/investing/online-trading/invest-lump-sum.

Chapter 9 Buying a Home

1. "Disparities in Wealth by Race and Ethnicity in the 2019 Survey of Consumer Finances," The Federal Reserve (September 28, 2020), https://www.federalreserve.gov/econres/notes/feds-notes/disparities-in-wealth-by-race-and-ethnicity-in-the-2019-survey-of-consumer-finances-accessible-20200928.htm#fig4.
2. Stefanos Chen, "The Resilience of New York's Black Homeowners," *New York Times* (August 17, 2021), https://www.nytimes.com/2021/08/17/realestate/new-york-black-homeowners.html.
3. Andre M. Perry, Jonathan Rothwell, and David Harshbarger, "The Devaluation of Assets in Black Neighborhoods," The Brookings Institution (November 27, 2018), https://www.brookings.edu/research/devaluation-of-assets-in-black-neighborhoods/.
4. Ibid.

Chapter 10 Insurance

1. Lorie Konish, "This Is the Real Reason Most Americans File for Bankruptcy," *CNBC* (February 11, 2019), https://www.cnbc.com/2019/02/11/this-is-the-real-reason-most-americans-file-for-bankruptcy.html.
2. Patrick Sisson, "How Health Care Costs Are Linked to Foreclosures," *Curbed* (June 26, 2017), https://archive.curbed.com/2017/6/26/15873206/bankruptcy-obamacare-medical-debt-foreclosures.
3. "The Real Cost of Health Care: Interactive Calculator Estimates Both Direct and Hidden Household Spending," KFF (February 21, 2019), https://www.kff.org/health-costs/press-release/interactive-calculator-estimates-both-direct-and-hidden-household-spending/.

4. Jamila Taylor, "Racism, Inequality, and Health Care for African Americans," The Century Foundation (December 19, 2019), https://tcf.org/content/report/racism-inequality-health-care-african-americans/?agreed=1.

5. Neil Bennett, Jonathan Eggleston, Laryssa Mykyta, and Briana Sullivan, "19% of U.S. Households Could Not Afford to Pay for Medical Care Right Away," United States Census Bureau (April 7, 2021), https://www.census.gov/library/stories/2021/04/who-had-medical-debt-in-united-states.html.

6. Ibid.

7. Edward Berchick, "Most Uninsured Were Working-Age Adults," United States Census Bureau (September 12, 2018), https://www.census.gov/library/stories/2018/09/who-are-the-uninsured.html#:~:text=Over%20half%20of%20all%20people,States%20were%20non%2DHispanic%20white.

8. Bennett, Eggleston, Mykyta, and Sullivan, "19% of U.S. Households," https://www.census.gov/library/stories/2021/04/who-had-medical-debt-in-united-states.html.

9. Loren Adler, Matthew Fiedler, Paul B. Ginsburg, Mark Hall, Benedic Ippolito, and Erin Trish, "Understanding the No Surprises Act," The Brookings Institution (February 4, 2021), https://www.brookings.edu/blog/usc-brookings-schaeffer-on-health-policy/2021/02/04/understanding-the-no-surprises-act/.

10. Alina Comoreanu, "Credit Score & Car Insurance Report," Wallet Hub (December 15, 2020), https://wallethub.com/edu/ci/car-insurance-by-credit-score-report/4343.

11. Amanda Shih, "How Much Does Long-Term Disability Insurance Cost?," Policygenius (July 1, 2021), https://www.policygenius.com/disability-insurance/learn/how-much-does-long-term-disability-insurance-cost/.

12. "Cost of Care Survey," Genworth, https://www.genworth.com/aging-and-you/finances/cost-of-care.html.

13. "How Much Care Will You Need?" LongTermCare.gov (February 18, 2020), https://acl.gov/ltc/basic-needs/how-much-care-will-you-need.

Chapter 11 Tax Basics and Estate Planning

1. Ben Popken, "TurboTax, H&R Block Spend Big Bucks Lobbying for Us to Keep Doing Our Own Taxes," NBC News (March 23, 2017), https://www.nbcnews.com/business/taxes/turbotax-h-r-block-spend-millions-lobbying-us-keep-doing-n736386.

2. Tyler Sonnemaker, "TurboTax and H&R Block Must Make Free Filing Services More Accessible to Taxpayers under New IRS Agreement,"

Business Insider (January 2, 2020), https://www.businessinsider.com/turbotax-hr-block-cannot-hide-free-filing-services-irs-agreement-2020-1.
3. Warren E. Buffett, "Stop Coddling the Super-Rich," *New York Times* (August 14, 2011), https://www.nytimes.com/2011/08/15/opinion/stop-coddling-the-super-rich.html.

Chapter 12 Your Credit Score

1. "In FTC Study, Five Percent of Consumers Had Errors on Their Credit Reports That Could Result in Less Favorable Terms for Loans," Federal Trade Commission (February 11, 2013), https://www.ftc.gov/news-events/press-releases/2013/02/ftc-study-five-percent-consumers-had-errors-their-credit-reports.

Chapter 14 Become Your Own Money Coach

1. Stephen Newland, "The Power of Accountability," AFCPE, https://www.afcpe.org/news-and-publications/the-standard/2018-3/the-power-of-accountability/.

Acknowledgments

I wrote this book during a pandemic and in the same year I had a baby. What's wrong with me? While this is not a choice I would recommend, it forced me to ask for help, build a team, and accomplish things I could not have imagined just a few months earlier.

I couldn't have written this book or survived the process without some very important people. I'm bursting with gratitude for their generosity of wisdom, time, love, and support. I am forever grateful.

Thank you . . .

Leigh Eisenman, my wonderful agent, who understands me, my work, and my vision and champions me every step of the way.

Dr. Akilah Cadet, my brilliant sensitivity editor and teacher. You helped me create a truly inclusive book and I grew so much in my anti-racism journey along the way.

My incredible editors, Jeanenne Ray, Dawn Kilgore, Sally Baker, Chloé Miller-Bess, Linda Brandon, and the rest of the Wiley team for making me look good and carefully crafting this book into the most digestible and succinct version it can be.

With Linda's expert suggestions and hand-holding, we cut down my 130,000 word manuscript to 70,000 words. This was harder for me than writing the book!

Hilary McClellen, my amazing fact checker. Because of her you can be confident everything in my book is factually correct!

Kristen Veit, for your invaluable insight, research, and help running The Fiscal Femme. I'm so grateful to have you on our team!

Kate Sandoval Box, an amazing editor and friend, for showing me the ropes.

To those I interviewed for the book (in alphabetical order): Chris Abkarians, Suraiya Ali, Tiffany Aliche, Lauren Anastasio, Mehrsa Baradaran, Lauren Smith Brody, Lori Douglass, Setareh Ebrahimian, Cinneah El-Amin, Yanely Espinal, Chelsea Fagan, Jennifer Fitzgerald, Fee Gentry, Liz Grauerholz, Emily Green, Tanja Hester, Lauren Hunt, Barbara Huson, Georgia Lee Hussey, Dasha Kennedy, Rachel Sanborn Lawrence, Alex Lieberman, Cleona Lira, Erin Lowry, Kevin Matthews II, Tony Molina, Dan Otter, Kara Peréz, Kiersten Saunders, Julien Saunders, Margaret Scheele, Linda Scott, Elyse Steinhaus, Farnoosh

Torabi, Brian Walsh, and Claire Wasserman. You not only spent time sharing your wisdom and expertise to make the book better, but also helped with fact checking and editing your respective sections, making sure I said everything in the most accurate and helpful way.

A special thank-you to Tiffany Aliche, who at the end of our interview very generously started sharing the marketing strategies and tips that made her book, *Get Good with Money*, a *New York Times* bestseller. I'm blown away by your generosity of spirit and am so grateful for the invaluable advice.

Laura Pennington Briggs, book marketing maven and organizer of organizers. If you're reading this book, you probably have her to thank for its finding its way to you.

Adam Kirschner, my brand manager. You have completely transformed my business and what I've seen is possible. I couldn't have written this book or grown my team without our working together.

Mary Clavieres, Nicole Giordano, and Belma McCaffrey, for the daily inspiration, honest advice, unconditional love, and much-needed laughs along the way. I am so grateful for your friendship and our mastermind (but really sisterhood!).

Leah Gerstley, my sister-in-law, for sharing her time and brilliant perspective.

To those who have and continue to support me and my family at home so I can work during the day. I am so grateful to have you in our lives and I couldn't do any of this without you.

To the many other family and friends who have supported me and helped me along the way – you know who you are. I'm so grateful to have you in my life.

To my Fiscal Femme community, I wrote this book for you. Thank you for the opportunity to join in part of your money journey. Thank you for giving me the opportunity and grace to learn and grow along the way. I promise to keep it going.

Mom, thank you for modeling how to create a career you absolutely love. Thank you for always listening, the pep talks when I wanted to give up, and the late-night goal-setting sessions.

Dad, thank you for showing me what's possible in building a life and business and teaching me to be a "shrewd" business owner. Thank you for talking through my worries with me and for editing my early drafts.

Thank you both for giving me every opportunity. I promise to use that privilege to make this world a more fair place. I love you forever.

My sister and best friend, Ari, for listening to me complain on the hard days, for being my guinea pig when I have an idea, and for making me laugh until my stomach hurts.

My hubby and partner, Justin: Thank you for everything you did to make working on this book possible during a pandemic with a toddler and newborn. I don't even have words. I talk a lot about equal labor in the home and this year I was the unequal partner. You stepped up so I could step into writing this book and (mostly – ha!) never made me feel guilty for it. You also took a lot of the brunt of my book stress – very sorry for that. I don't know how I got so lucky to find you as my life partner.

Eli and Miles, you are everything. So much of this book is about using our privilege to create the world we want to see and that's the world I want to see you both be able to grow up (and grow old) in. Eli, your questions, love of life, and kindness inspire me to be a better person every day. Miles, your joy and curiosity are contagious and inspire me to continue to grow and persevere. I love you both more than anything.

About the Author

Ashley Feinstein Gerstley is a money coach, author, and entrepreneur on a mission to end inequality through financial well-being. She is the founder of The Fiscal Femme, a feminist money platform, and is also the author of *The 30-Day Money Cleanse*.

As a trusted money expert, she has appeared on or been quoted in *The Financial Times*, CNBC, *Forbes*, NBC, *Glamour*, and *The New York Times*.

Ashley has worked in the financial services industry for over 15 years: first as an investment banker, then in corporate finance, and most recently running The Fiscal Femme. She graduated with a bachelor's degree in finance from the Wharton School at the University of Pennsylvania.

Ashley lives in Hoboken, New Jersey, with her husband, two kids, and pup. You can find her on Instagram and Twitter (@TheFiscalFemme) and at TheFiscalFemme.com.

Index